Knowing Christ Crucified

Knowing Christ Crucified

The Witness of African American Religious Experience

M. SHAWN COPELAND

ORBIS BOOKS

Maryknoll, New York 10545

ORBIS ⬤ BOOKS
Maryknoll, New York 10545

Fathers and Brothers
MARYKNOLL

Founded in 1970, Orbis Books endeavors to publish works that enlighten the mind, nourish the spirit, and challenge the conscience. The publishing arm of the Maryknoll Fathers and Brothers, Orbis seeks to explore the global dimensions of the Christian faith and mission, to invite dialogue with diverse cultures and religious traditions, and to serve the cause of reconciliation and peace. The books published reflect the views of their authors and do not represent the official position of the Maryknoll Society. To learn more about Maryknoll and Orbis Books, please visit our website at www.maryknollsociety.org.

Library of Congress Cataloging-in-Publication Data

Names: Copeland, M. Shawn (Mary Shawn), author.
Title: Knowing Christ crucified : the witness of African American religious experience / M. Shawn Copeland.
Description: Maryknoll, NY : Orbis Books, [2018] | Includes bibliographical references and index.
Identifiers: LCCN 2018024385 (print) | LCCN 2018035398 (ebook) | ISBN 9781608337644 (e-book) | ISBN 9781626982987 (print) | ISBN 9781608337644 (ebook)
Subjects: LCSH: African Americans--Religion.
Classification: LCC BR563.N4 (ebook) | LCC BR563.N4 C67 2018 (print) | DDC 277.3/0808996073—dc23
LC record available at https://lccn.loc.gov/2018024385

To the memory
of
Mary Hunt
tailor and midwife
my maternal great-grandmother
who first spoke to me of Jesus crucified

Contents

Acknowledgments

Knowing Christ Crucified comes from my grappling with the meaning of the cross of the Jewish Jesus of Nazareth in relation to the transgenerational and enormous social oppression of African American children, youth, women, and men. This book seeks to honor the faith and hope and love, joy and fortitude and creativity of my ancestors and their mediation of those virtues to the ongoing struggle of black people to live in justice and freedom and to help forge a nation committed authentically to those values.

These pages are the work of reading and wondering, of thinking and writing, of singing and listening, of musing and, sometimes, weeping at the pain and courage of the lived lives of the enslaved peoples as remembered in slave narratives and spirituals. I am immensely grateful to Robert Ellsberg, editor-in-chief of Orbis Books, who greeted this project with enthusiasm, respected it, and nudged it along with generosity and patience. I am thankful to and for superb colleagues and staff in the Theology Department at Boston College. I am grateful to and for cherished friends around the country and around the world for the interest and support of my efforts to do theology: "I thank our good and gracious God every time I think of you, constantly praying with joy in every one of my prayers for all of you" (Philippians 1:3).

Deep gratitude goes to Reverend Dr. Meghan Sweeney, director of Boston College's Pulse Program, for her invitation to teach an elective theology course in the program. The students who participated in the seminar "The Meaning and Way of Jesus" were outstanding in their commitment to prepare thoughtfully and well for our weekly meetings—to probe their beliefs seriously and humbly, to speak their questions forthrightly, to share their faith and pray together each week. This was, for me, a most precious learning and teaching experience.

I owe a debt of gratitude to the core faculty and the staff of Boston College's Interdisciplinary Program in African and African Diaspora Studies for their friendship and support, especially program directors Dr. Cynthia Young, Dr. Rhonda Frederick, and Dr. Martin Summers, and program administrator Mr. Richard Paul. The students who participated in the seminar "Gender and Slavery" were exceptional in their commitment to prepare thoughtfully and well for our weekly meetings—to discuss and debate issues with passion, purpose, and precision, to interrogate white racist supremacy made visible in chattel slavery, Christian hypocrisy, segregation, and structural racism, in misogyny, in cultural imperialism, in economic exploitation, in police brutality, and in mass incarceration. These students taught me so much.

I must express my gratitude to Boston College Presidential Scholar Ms. Sageene Francis for her expert work as my research fellow (2016–2017, 2017–2018). Ms. Francis read this manuscript several times, tracked down citations, and prepared the bibliography. I also express gratitude to Barbara Bzura and Carolyn Caveny for help with proofreading.

The seed of this book lies in the question that at the age of four or five I put to my great-grandmother: "Who is that man hanging on the cross?" I wondered about the picture that hung over her bed. She replied: "Jesus. Jesus who loves you and died for you." Her answer planted a seed that others have watered, nourished, and pruned for growth. My mother, Geraldine Williams, is a woman of unfailing prayer and biblical reflection; I am thankful for her example. Barbara Kaczmarek (the former Sister Mary Bernetta) was my novice mistress during my years as a member of the Felician Sisters; she taught us to take theology seriously and to treasure a relationship with Jesus above all else. Constance FitzGerald, OCD, a perceptive, generous, and wise spiritual director and friend, has helped me to draw closer to the Incarnate Flame of

Love. The prayers, example, and friendship of the Carmelite Nuns, Monastery of the Sacred Heart, Baltimore, Maryland, have been a tremendous gift and an incomparable blessing for me. Where would our world be if not for contemplative lives of prayerful passion for God and continual compassionate prayer for us—for the world!

For more than fifteen years, St. Katharine Drexel Parish, Boston (Roxbury/Dorchester), Massachusetts, has been my church home. We identify ourselves unapologetically as a "Black Catholic Community of believers celebrating and rejoicing in the love of God," even as we are diverse in ethnicity, culture, race, social class, and physical abilities. We are poets and judges, immigrants and a member of the Daughters of the American Revolution, police officers and bus drivers, educators and business executives, community organizers and caterers. We are musicians and researchers, retirees and dancers, social workers and bloggers, nurses and physicians. Ours may be an aging congregation, but infants make their presence known at each Sunday Eucharist. By some standards, we may not be a wealthy parish, but faith and hope and love overflow continually to enrich all our endeavors beyond imagining. Our "church family" knows Christ crucified; we intentionally strive to grow in wisdom and grace, knowledge and courage in order to struggle against injustice—everywhere. And, we at St. Katharine Drexel are so fortunate to have as our pastoral leader Father Oscar J. Pratt II, a fine man, splendid priest, spiritual seeker, gifted homilist, and talented vocalist.

The seed planted, watered, and nurtured has grown into my desire for an authentic way to live—the desire to follow his "way": *"Lord, I want to be a Christian / I want to be more holy / I want to be like Jesus in-a my heart."* On this journey, I could not have a more generous, sensitive, or loving partner than Barbara Bzura.

Traces of the Cross

Social Suffering and Practical-Political Theology

Human existence is so fragile a thing and exposed to such dangers, I cannot love without trembling.
                                        —Simone Weil

You think your pain, and your heartbreak, are unprecedented in the history of the world. But then you read. It was books that taught me, the things that connected me with all the people who were alive—who had ever been alive.   —James Baldwin

I

My Catholic-convert maternal grandmother, Mattie Hunt Billingslea, would often tell the story that, as my parents, Geraldine and John Copeland, were preparing to bring my newborn self home from Detroit's Henry Ford Hospital, she took me in her arms and traced the sign of the cross over me and claimed for me the Catholic education that has shaped my mind, my heart, and my worldview. Of course, I was not and could not have been aware of this event. But I do recall, at the age of four or five, asking my maternal great-grandmother, Mary Hunt, about the picture hanging above her bed. "Who is that man," I asked, "hanging on the cross?" She replied, "Jesus. Jesus who loves you and died for you." That crude representation of the crucified Jesus made an opening in my heart and cast a line of wonder and inquiry that has stretched out from that depiction to the crucifix that hung on the living room wall in our home, to the crucifix that hung above the altar in our small segregated Catholic parish, to the crucifixes that were affixed to the walls of my elementary, secondary, and university classrooms, to depictions of the scourged and tortured Jesus that shaped my religious and aesthetic sensibilities as a young vowed religious, to the crucifix that lies on my desk as I write.

In the summer before beginning seventh grade, I resisted my mother's idea that I attend camp and, instead, registered for two high school courses— elementary French and a survey of modern world history. That history course confronted me with modernity's most recent horror—the attempt to destroy the Jewish people. Genocide was incomprehensible to my not-quite-twelve-year-old mind. But at some moment during that summer, something clicked. I vividly recall standing in our kitchen daydreaming, surely thinking about something quite ordinary, when one of my grandmother's frequent admonitions swam up to consciousness. She would say to me, "Remember, everyone can't like you."[1] On that summer afternoon, my grandmother's words crystallized as a bitter and fragile insight into the meaning and reach of untrammeled power. I formulated this hypothesis: *If those who do not like you should hold power over you, they can kill you.* Genocide mocked the lessons I learned first at home and then at school: that *all* human beings are made in the image and likeness of God, that *all* human beings are invested with great dignity and worth, and that *all* human beings are of enormous value—because they are human.[2] That summer course awakened me to anti-Semitism, to the deadly consequences of xenophobia, to the outright murder of human beings *simply because of their very existence.*

---

1. This may not have been a healthy caution for a shy only child; but, for a black girl-child, who often traveled the city by bus and often alone in *de facto* segregated Detroit, this was a firm yet veiled warning about the dangers of anti-black racism.

2. These statements form what is known as "the Black Christian Principle."

Although I could not have known it at that time, that summer course awakened me to social oppression and social suffering, and that in turn awakened an intuition about (what I now understand to be) the subversive potential of theology in and for the social order. It goes without saying, at the time, that my grasp of the meaning and implications of such an idea were quite inchoate, but for some reason comments made by my then-sixth-grade teacher, Sister Mary Rosalie, CSSF, about theology and the work of theologians left a deep impression. Theology, I imagined, might offer a way to respond to oppression and suffering. Perhaps the work of theology might even foster the conversion of the hearts and minds of those who perpetrate oppression. And so I left behind my previous aspirations for the legal profession and resolved to become a theologian. If I have told this story in other places, I tell it again here because it is, I believe, the truest affirmation of the gift and call of my theological vocation.

The Second Vatican Council called the church to turn again to the fundamental "duty of scrutinizing the signs of the times and interpreting them in the light of the Gospel . . . [in order to] recognize and understand the world in which we live, its explanations, its longings, and its often dramatic characteristics."[3] With its deep commitment to human cultures, the council opened space for the resurgence of the African American Catholic tradition of struggle for human dignity and justice. Providentially, the council coincided with several social and cultural struggles for human rights and freedom that were cresting around the globe and in the United States. At the same time, the vicious intent of white racist supremacy in its manifold and malevolent forms came into focus for me. The 1970s found me reading and studying to better understand the complex, varied, differentiated black[4]

---

3. *Gaudium et Spes*, "The Pastoral Constitution on the Church in the Modern World," #4 (December 7, 1965).

4. Throughout this work I use the terms "black" and "African American" interchangeably to refer to the descendants of the Africans enslaved in the United States. The nomenclature "African American" also may apply to descendants of enslaved Africans in the Americas—Latin America, Brazil, and the Caribbean. Finally, within the geographic and cultural boundary that is the United States,

lifeworld and engaging black and Latin American theologies of liberation, while staffing the National Black Sisters' Conference (NBSC), a national organization of black Catholic vowed women religious.[5] In 1976, I moved to New York to work for the organization and the process that was Theology in the Americas (TIA). Here I came to understand more critically the multifaceted challenge to the struggle for freedom and human liberation around the globe. Here I was inserted deeply and programmatically in the project of black theology, and the Reverend Muhammad Kenyatta (Donald Brooks) and I organized the first national ecumenical consultation on black theology.[6] In TIA's vibrant intellectual setting, through the efforts of exiled Chilean priest Sergio Torres and Filipina Maryknoll Sister Virginia Fabella and my friendship with Sister of Charity Maria Iglesias, I came to know and respect James Hal Cone and Gustavo Gutiérrez, O.P.

---

this appellation has been problematized by contemporary immigration from the continent of Africa and from the Caribbean. Kobina Aidoo popularized this issue in his documentary film *The Neo-African-Americans: Black Immigrant Identities* (2008), but scholars have studied this migration and its impact on U.S. life for some years; for example, see Jean Muteba Rahier and Percy C. Hintzen, *Problematizing Blackness: Self-Ethnographies by Black Immigrants to the United States* (New York and London: Routledge, 2003); Michelle M. Wright, *Becoming Black: Creating Identity in the African Diaspora* (Durham, NC: Duke University Press, 2004); Kwadwo Konadu-Agyemand, Baffour K. Tayki, and John A. Arthur, eds., *The New African Diaspora in North America: Trends, Community Building, and Adaptation* (Lanham, MD: Rowman & Littlefield, 2006); Yoku Shaw-Taylor and Steven A. Tuch, eds., *The Other African Americans: Contemporary African and Caribbean Immigrants* (Lanham, MD: Rowman & Littlefield, 2007).

5. The founding meeting of the National Black Sisters' Conference was held at Carlow College, Pittsburgh, Pennsylvania, in August 1968. The inspiration to organize black vowed women religious came from the leadership of then-Religious Sister of Mercy Martin de Porres Grey (Dr. Patricia Grey). Grey was the only woman in attendance at the meeting of the National Black Catholic Clergy Caucus (NBCC) that met in Detroit, Michigan, ten days after the assassination of the Reverend Dr. Martin Luther King Jr.

6. Gayraud S. Wilmore and James H. Cone, eds., *Black Theology: A Documentary History, 1966–1979* (Maryknoll, NY: Orbis Books, 1979), 9, 253, 254. The first national consultation on black theology was held in Atlanta, Georgia, August 3–7, 1977; see *Black Theology*, 345–49.

Graduate theological study followed, and Boston College proved (and has proved) significant. Here the cognitional and methodological proposals of Jesuit philosopher-theologian Bernard Lonergan and the questions and categories of Johann Baptist Metz equipped me with conceptual tools and categories with which to think rigorously about Christian faith in relation to oppression and the suffering it inflicted on the vast majority of God's human creatures. But, at Boston College, the faith, mind, and life of Frederick Lawrence made all the difference. Fred taught me and so many others to love God, to give our excellence to theology and to our students, to cherish friendship, and, above all, to remember that theology is not a career but a vocation.

Almost from the beginning, my theological project has been and remains the relation of theology's intellectual and spiritual praxis to the violation of human persons and the potential of their flourishing in ecclesial, cultural, and social (i.e., political, economic, technological) contexts—in other words social oppression and the thematization of a practical-political theology in light of the *memoria passionis*.[7] The historical, cultural, social, existential, and religious experience of peoples of African descent in the United States—black experience—has served as the starting point for my theology even as that reflection highlights difference as an integral aesthetic in understanding the *concrete universal who is the human*.[8] Thus, black human experience can be neither so particular, nor so unique, as to evade universal human relevance and relation. At the same time, the exploration, expropriation, and greed that followed in the wake of colonialism and that spawned

---

7. These two *foci* of my theological project share many of the concerns of theologians who foreground the oppression of "the poor" and "crucified peoples" of Latin America. The third prong of my project is the critical interrogation of black experience in the service of formulating Catholic theology in and from an African American perspective.

8. See Bernard Lonergan, *Insight: A Study of Human Understanding* 5th ed., rev. and aug., *Collected Works of Bernard Lonergan*, vol. 3 (Toronto: University of Toronto Press, 1988), 3:668, 674, for the notion of human beings as many by matter but *one in having one nature*.

the cruel commodification and negative racialization of peoples of the African continent have resulted in peculiar forms of oppression and suffering. Still, do not our shared human nature and our common human experience teach us that every human creature, at some point in time, will meet with some measure of suffering and sorrow, pain and loss? Is not the fundamental message of the gospel found in the demands posed by the radical indissolubility of love of God and love of neighbor? To quote Metz, "There is no suffering in the world that does not concern us."[9]

II

Suffering forms an inescapable dimension of the human condition, but its deepest anguish may come from efforts to draw meaning from the pain. Questions about unjust suffering, in particular, recur in religion and theology, but over the past few decades, documentarians, journalists, medical anthropologists, physicians, psychologists, and sociologists have studied social suffering as a topic of formal analytical inquiry. These researchers have uncovered and chronicled

> forms of social experience and lived conditions that determine how suffering takes place and what this does to people. In the study of social suffering, people's pains and miseries are taken as grounds on which to make our social state of being a matter for critical and moral inquiry.[10]

This inquiry exposes the very "character of society"[11] by charting evidence of human suffering caused by societal policies and pro-

9. Johann Baptist Metz, "Under the Spell of Cultural Amnesia: An Example from Europe and Its Consequences," in *Missing God? Cultural Amnesia and Political Theology*, ed. John K. Downey et al. (Münster: LIT Verlag; New Brunswick and London: Transaction Publishers, 2006), 10.

10. Iain Wilkinson and Arthur Kleinman, "The Origins of Social Suffering," in *A Passion for Society: How We Think about Human Suffering*, ed. Iain Wilkinson and Arthur Kleinman (Oakland, CA: University of California Press, 2016), 14. Available at http://www.jstor.org.

11. Ibid.

grams, aggravated by a cultural ecology infused with fear, callousness, and indifference.[12]

These social-scientific and humanistic analyses join the work being done already by theologians and ethicists to counter notions of suffering as individualistic and deserving of a spiritualized response. Rebecca Chopp names this socially produced travail as "massive public suffering," encompassing torture, genocide, extermination, "ethnic cleansing," "disappearance," enslavement, and cultural decimation. Such suffering, Chopp argues,

> cannot be fully explained, understood, or represented . . . [nor can such suffering] be forgotten or ignored in history's interpretation or construction; once progress has shoved the masses of humanity onto life's margins, history is broken, its end forever in question, and its purpose lost in suspension.[13]

Such events of massive public suffering often render its victims powerless or mute, push them to borders of hopelessness or despair. Yet, despite intense and protracted suffering, many of these children, women, and men confound the sheer horror of their pain, claim agency, seize righteous anger, and struggle against the evil so manifest in cruelty and injustice.

Theologians, ethicists, and religio-cultural critics writing from within and about the black lifeworld have argued persuasively that black people in the United States endure social suffering not as unusual occurrences or episodic events but rather as a type of systemic or structural evil. In 1951, more than eighty years after emancipation, the Civil Rights Congress under the leadership of

---

12. For some examples, see Paul Farmer, *Pathologies of Power: Health, Human Rights, and the New War on the Poor* (Berkeley: University of California Press, 2003); Paul Farmer and Gustavo Gutiérrez, *In the Company of the Poor: Conversations with Dr. Paul Farmer and Fr. Gustavo Gutiérrez* (Maryknoll, NY: Orbis Books, 2013); Arthur Kleinman et al., eds., *Social Suffering* (Berkeley: University of California Press, 1997); Veena Das et al., eds., *Remaking a World: Violence, Social Suffering, and Recovery* (Berkeley: University of California Press, 2001).

13. Rebecca S. Chopp, *The Praxis of Suffering: An Interpretation of Liberation and Political Theologies* (Maryknoll, NY: Orbis Books, 1986), 2.

Executive Secretary William L. Patterson appealed to the General Assembly of the United Nations for intervention on behalf of the black people of the United States.[14] A little over twenty years later, William Jones charged that the cultural and social power of government had forced black people to endure maldistributed, negative, enormous, and transgenerational suffering.[15]

The oppression of black youth, women, and men is both a fact of history and a contemporary reality. In April 2018, the Equal Justice Initiative (EJI), under the leadership of Bryan Stevenson, opened the National Memorial for Peace and Justice in Montgomery, Alabama. This museum is the nation's first memorial dedicated to the legacy of black people terrorized by lynching and commemorates more than 4,400 lynchings between 1877 and 1950.[16] This painful legacy of lynching is replicated in the torture and murder of Emmett Till in 1955; in the beating, dragging, and decapitation of James Byrd in 1998. The painful legacy of lynching is kept alive in the deaths of Trayvon Martin, Eric Garner, Renisha McBride, Michael Brown, Tamir Rice, Walter Scott, Freddie Gray, Sandra Bland; of Aiyana Stanley-Jones, Jonathan Ferrell, Miriam Carey, Reika Boyd, Akai Gurley, John Crawford, Ezell Ford, Philando Castile; of Sharonda Coleman-Singleton, DePayne Middleton Doctor, Cynthia Hurd, Susie Jackson, Ethel Lance, Clementa

---

14. Civil Rights Congress, *We Charge Genocide: The Historic Petition to the United Nations for Relief from a Crime of The United States Government Against the Negro People* (New York: Civil Rights Congress, 1951), xi–xiii, 3–10.

15. William R. Jones, *Is God a White Racist? A Preamble to Black Theology* (Boston: Beacon Press, 1973, 1998), 21–22. Social suffering also includes ethnic suffering—a particular people's or group's undergoing oppression. Nancy Pineda-Madrid, in *Suffering and Salvation in Ciudad Juárez* (Minneapolis: Fortress Press, 2011), develops a social-suffering hermeneutic through which to grapple with the social oppression of feminicide, the nearly two decades of rampant and brutal murder of women and young girls in Juárez, Mexico.

16. Equal Justice Initiative, *Lynching in America: Confronting the Legacy of Racial Terror* (https://lynchinginamerica.eji.org/report-landing); see James H. Cone, *The Cross and the Lynching Tree* (Maryknoll, NY: Orbis Books, 2011); Angela D. Sims, *Lynched: The Power of Memory in a Culture of Terror* (Waco, TX: Baylor University Press, 2016).

Pinckney, Tywanza Sanders, Daniel Simmons, and Myra Thompson. The deaths of these youth, women, and men at the hands of police or in police custody stand as the most recent and egregious manifestations of oppression and suffering.

For some years now, my teaching and writing has been stimulated by the work of political philosopher Iris Marion Young. She specifies five forms (or faces, as she names them) of oppression—economic exploitation, marginalization, powerlessness, cultural imperialism, and violence—that play a characteristic function in our liberal/neoliberal society.[17] This has led me to pair the notion of *social oppression* with that of *social suffering*. Social oppression denotes intentional and unintentional, socio-culturally reproduced choices, decisions, and actions that unjustly and selectively inflict harm on human persons. Social suffering clarifies what social oppression exacts from human persons, as individuals and as groups. Young critically expands the notion of oppression by turning a lens on liberal and neoliberal capitalist societies like the United States. By her account, oppression designates "the disadvantage and injustice some people suffer *not* because a tyrannical power coerces them, but because of the everyday practices of a well-intentioned liberal society."[18] This extension of oppression acknowledges the exercise of ruling-group tyranny even as it points to those "systemic constraints" placed on groups or individuals because of "the way things are," because of the mechanisms and operations of social structures or institutions.

The grotesque invisibility of social oppression requires the complicity—intentional and unintentional—of human persons, members of the society in question. As Young explains, their complicity and collusion

> are embedded in unquestioned norms, habits, and symbols, in the assumptions underlying institutional rules and the

---

17. Iris Marion Young, *Justice and the Politics of Difference* (Princeton: Princeton University, 1990), esp. 39–65, 122–55; see also her *Responsibility for Justice* (New York: Oxford University Press, 2011).

18. Ibid., 41.

collective consequences of following those rules. It names "an enclosing structure of forces and barriers which tends to the immobilization and reduction of a group or category of people." In this extended sense oppression refers to the vast and deep injustices that some groups suffer as a consequence of often unconscious assumptions and reactions of well-meaning people in ordinary interactions, media and cultural stereotypes, and structural features of bureaucratic hierarchies and market mechanisms—in short the normal processes of everyday life.[19]

Young further cautions that structural oppression cannot be eradicated through removal or recall or impeachment of those legislators or officials charged with governance, nor can structural oppression be eliminated through passing new laws or amending earlier ones. Rather, these oppressions are structurally reproduced and concealed in major cultural, social, and religious institutions as well as in electoral and legislative procedures and dissenting processes.[20]

Given the asymmetrical dynamics of power relations, the category of social suffering denotes "positional suffering,"[21] that is, the experience of persistent humiliations of invisibility and indifference, of individualizing and relativizing, of distancing and distorting. In this way a person's suffering may be disregarded, demoted, dissed, dismissed. Moreover, the dominant culture's capacity to function simultaneously and "interrelatedly [as] a signifying system"[22] and as a system of material production and reproduction permits the culture and all those who identify with it to "immobilize or diminish" individuals to particular or specified groups, stereotypically reducing them to and with "essentializing arbitrary"

---

19. Young, *Justice and the Politics of Difference*, 41.

20. Ibid.

21. Pierre Bourdieu, "The Space of Points of View," in *The Weight of the World: Social Suffering in Contemporary Society*, ed. Pierre Bourdieu et al. (Stanford, CA: Stanford University Press, 1993, 1999), 4.

22. David Theo Goldberg, *Racist Culture: Philosophy and the Politics of Meaning* (Oxford: Blackwell, 1993), 8.

attributes."[23] In the United States, such essentialization and reduction leaves indigenous peoples, all people of color—irrespective of their societal status; all economically impoverished people—irrespective of their constructed racial designations, including whiteness; all differently abled persons, queer and transgendered persons, Arabs, Muslims, Jews; and all disempowered or powerless social "others" abandoned to societally sanctioned violence and threats of violence.

III

Francis of Assisi is reported to have said that the cross is a book. When we open that book in love and in intelligence, we encounter traces of the crucified Jewish Jesus in human social suffering in our world. We find traces of his cross in the singing of indigenous peoples in the midst of disregard and neglect; in defiant dances of fiesta in the midst of doubt and fear; in painful and painfully true accounts of women and men driven to addiction by abuse, abandonment, and alienation; in the glazed eyes of poor and hungry children, women, and men in nation after nation; in the resigned faces of incarcerated youth, women, and men; in the anguished faces of queer and transgendered people living amidst murderous exclusion; in the grim faces of immigrants and refugees consigned to forgetfulness in detention centers and makeshift camps around the globe.

If the cross is a book, it is one that practical-political theology must read and study. To take oppression as a point of departure for doing theology is to advert to, perhaps even recover and enact, a paradigm

---

23. Young, *Justice and the Politics of Difference*, 46. Socially marginalized persons experience what W. E. B. DuBois called double-consciousness: "It is a peculiar sensation, this double-consciousness, this sense of always looking at one's self through the eyes of others, of measuring one's soul by the tape of a world that looks on in amused contempt and pity. One ever feels his [*sic*] twoness—an American, a Negro; two souls, two thoughts, two unreconciled strivings; two warring ideals in one dark body, whose dogged strength alone keeps it from being torn asunder" (*The Souls of Black Folks* [New York: Fawcett Publications, 1903, 1961], 16–17).

shift in theology.[24] Theology in this paradigm risks encounter and engagement with the dynamic purifying powers of God in history, even, as Edward Schillebeeckx writes, "before we are completely liberated."[25] Thus, the incarnation, the concrete, powerful, paradoxical, even scandalous engagement of God in history, changes forever our perception and reception of one another. The Jewish Jesus of Nazareth forever changes our perception and reception of the human other, of humanity. For humanity is his concern, neither merely, nor incidentally; rather, humanity is his concern comprehensively, fully. It is for the full and complete realization of humanity, for our full and complete realization, that Jesus gave his life. Practical-political theology in this context stands squarely before the cross of the crucified Jewish Jesus, that most mysterious meeting place of grace and freedom. His cross is the concrete example of the cost of self-transcending love. And it is before his cross that the praxis of the Christian community must always be judged. For his cross exposes our pretense to personal innocence, to neutrality. This cross uncovers the poverty as well as the potential of all human efforts and solutions to meet the problem of evil.

The cross of Jesus calls us to conversion, to radical transformation of life for life. For his cross teaches us that conversion of life is not merely something about which we speak; rather, despite whatever consequences, the *living out* and *living out of* that transformation is the subject of our daily struggle. Lived conversion of heart, mind, and action is not what someone else must do, but who we must become. For it is in *our* social dis-order, not someone else's, that social oppression has taken root. It is *our* consciousness, not someone else's, that is permeated with and troubled by disgraces of social sin. The cross of the Jewish Jesus evokes our integrity, calls us to responsibility for one another, calls us to entrust our lives to the dangerous Jesus.

---

24. Edward Schillebeeckx termed this paradigm "theology *after* a Christian history of domination and victors" ("The Role of History in What Is Called the New Paradigm," in *Paradigm Change in Theology: A Symposium for the Future*, ed. Hans Küng and David Tracy [New York: Crossroad, 1989], 317). My italics.

25. Schillebeeckx, "The Role of History," 318.

Theology cannot, *must not,* remain silent or complicit before the suffering of a crucified world and the suffering of God's crucified peoples. When theology comes face to face with the historical reality of social oppression and the enormous suffering inflicted on God's human creatures, it must name explicitly the social, physical, and existential damage—the oppression effected through structural or social, personal or individual sin. Moreover, theology must work out the relation between the murderous crucifixion of Jesus of Nazareth and the murderous crucifixion of countless poor, excluded, and despised children, women, and men. To quote Metz again, "The tradition to which theology is accountable knows a universal responsibility born of the memory of suffering."[26]

IV

The concern of this work is not theodicy—that is, the justification of God in the face of social oppression and the social suffering it causes. As an exercise of practical-political theology, this work affirms (1) that social suffering is not the product of God's will but it arises from that social oppression that results from the abuse of human freedom; (2) that the cross may be apprehended best from within the mystical pattern of experience, which calls for intimate relationship with Jesus; and (3) that discipleship is a *locus* or starting point from which to approach the cross and, in memory of Jesus's death and resurrection, to act in solidarity with all those who suffer social oppression and to join them in the struggle for life and justice.

Three parts comprise this volume: The first, "From the Heart of the Quarter," probes ways in which enslaved peoples responded to Jesus of Nazareth; the second, "Marking and (Re)membering the Body of Christ," considers some challenges to human living in a world shaped and directed by white supremacy; and the third, "Following Jesus Crucified and Risen," presses the meaning of solidarity, freedom, and hope in the concrete. These essays reflect my

---

26. Johann Baptist Metz, *A Passion for God: The Mystical-Political Dimension of Christianity,* trans. J. Matthew Ashley (Mahwah, NJ: Paulist Press, 1997), 134.

efforts to read the book of the cross, to trace the abiding presence of the crucified Jesus among those whom we have crucified in our world, to learn in particular from the witness of African American religious experience, and to grapple with what it might mean "to take up the cross daily and follow Jesus" (Luke 9:23) with all those others crucified in our time. Yet, the effort to understand suffering and oppression cannot be permitted to deplete or drain efforts to eliminate oppression. As Jim Perkinson warns most importantly, "creative appropriation of the conditions of their own suffering exercised by the dominated or exploited is always a sign of warning to those benefitting from such domination/exploitation."[27]

In this sadly gray, grim, and gloomy season around the globe, in our nation, in our culture, we must, as the spiritual counsels, "keep our lamps trimmed and burning, the time is drawing nigh." In this sadly gray, grim, and gloomy season, when casual cruelty, resentment, madness, and hatred defames and demeans, chokes and assaults, shoots and destroys, criminalizes and incarcerates, deports and demonizes children, women, and men simply because of their existence—simply because of their poverty, gender, sexual orientation, race, age, physical or mental abilities, cultural-ethnic identity, or religious practices—we who are followers of the crucified Jewish Jesus must protest the oppression and suffering of each human person and work for their flourishing.

Our theology, as critical interpretation of the role of faith in the social order for the sake of human flourishing, must, in solidarity, take on tasks of memory, witness, and lament. We must take up the cause of all those made abject and oppressed; we must enter into the drama of God's liberation. If we do this, we shall have taken up what James Cone named "the risk of freedom."[28] And that risk places our hopeful hearts before the cross of the crucified Jewish Jesus of Nazareth.

---

27. Jim Perkinson, "The Gift/Curse of 'Second Sight': Is 'Blackness' a Shamanic Category in the Myth of America?" *History of Religions* 41, no. 1 (August 2002): 19–58, at 19.

28. James Cone, *Risk of Faith* (Boston: Beacon Press, 1999), 48.

PART ONE

From the Heart of the Quarter

CHAPTER ONE

Dark Wisdom from the Slaves

Are ye not as children of the Ethiopians unto me,
O children of Israel? saith the Lord.
Have I not brought up Israel out of the land of Egypt?
and the Philistines from Caphtor, and the Syrians
      from Kir?

                      —Amos 9:7

I've heard [the slaves] pray for freedom.
I thought it was foolishness then,
but the old-time folks always felt they was to be free.
It must have been something revealed unto [them].

                —an emancipated man

For the hurt of my people am I hurt;
astonishment hath taken hold on me.
Is there no balm in Gilead; is there no physician there?
why then is not the health of my people recovered?
O that my head were waters, and mine eyes a fountain
      of tear,
That I might weep day and night for the slain of my
      people!

          —after Jeremiah 8:21–22; 9:1

There is a balm in Gilead.

             —Negro Spiritual

> He have been wid us, Jesus / He still wid us, Jesus, /
> He will be wid us, Jesus, / Be wid us to the end.
>
> —Negro Spiritual

The Christianity preached to the enslaved peoples was a peculiar amalgam of texts and admonitions that sanctioned perpetual servitude and bent black bodies and souls to the profit of the slaveholders. In response to a query about sermons commonly preached to enslaved people, Charlie Van Dyke remarked, "All the preacher talked about was for us slaves to obey our masters and not to lie and steal. Nothing about Jesus, was ever said."[1] If nothing, or little, was said about Jesus, how did the enslaved people come to hear of him? We know the story of Jesus of Nazareth—his life, ministry, crucifixion, death, and resurrection—held a significant place in the religious lives of enslaved Africans. So, perhaps, the enslaved people *were listening* very carefully and very closely to learn more about Jesus. Why did he figure so prominently in their religious experience, songs, prayers, and stories? How did he come, as one emancipated person put it, to "hook [them] in the heart?"[2] What wisdom did they gain from their relationship with Jesus?

To probe these questions, we take slave narratives and the Negro or African American spiritual as our guides.[3] The historian John Blassingame states plainly, "If scholars want to know the heart and secret thoughts of slaves, they must study the testimony of the blacks."[4] And, as James Scott suggests, careful study

1. Albert Raboteau, *Slave Religion: The "Invisible Institution" in the Antebellum South* (Oxford: Oxford University Press, 1975), 214.

2. Clifton H. Johnson, ed., *God Struck Me Dead: Voices of Ex-Slaves* (Cleveland, OH: Pilgrim Press, 1969), 19.

3. For one of the major collections, see George P. Rawick, ed., *The American Slave: A Composite Autobiography,* 19 vols. (Westport, CT: Greenwood Publishing Company, 1941, 1972). Begun under the auspices of the Federal Writers' Project of the Works Project Administration (WPA), 1936 to 1938, these interviews augment earlier oral histories begun at Hampton Institute in Virginia, Southern University in Louisiana, and Fisk University in Tennessee.

4. John W. Blassingame, "Using the Testimony of the Ex-Slaves," in *The*

of slave narratives uncovers "hidden transcripts" consisting of those "offstage speeches, gestures, and practices that confirm, contradict, or inflect" the practices and ideology of domination.[5] The words, prayers, musings, and songs of the enslaved people contest the "public transcripts" of the slaveholders. The testimony of the enslaved people presents a critical, even didactic, commentary on chattel slavery and advances a counterdiscourse that recognizes and defends their humanity and spirituality, subjectivity and agency. Here, slave narratives function as what Johann Metz named "dangerous memories, memories that challenge."[6]

Rivaled only by blues and jazz, the Negro or African American spiritual stands as the most widely known of all African American musical genres.[7] I cannot pinpoint the first time I heard a spiritual, but I will forever associate the experience with my grandmother's singing on Sunday mornings—after Mass. The last of eight children born to James and Mary Hunt in Macon, Georgia, my maternal grandmother was born early in the last century. Not long after the First World War, her widowed mother and enterprising brothers moved the family to Detroit, Michigan. Although their family were members of Quinn Chapel African Methodist Episcopal Church, sometime in the 1940s my grandmother became a Catholic and was baptized in Sacred Heart Church, one of the churches in the Archdiocese of Detroit that took the evangelization of black

---

Slave's Narrative, ed. Charles T. Davis and Henry Louis Gates Jr. (New York: Oxford, 1985), 94.

5. James C. Scott, *Domination and the Arts of Resistance* (New Haven: Yale University Press, 1990), 4–5.

6. Johann Baptist Metz, *Faith in History and Society: Toward a Practical Fundamental Theology*, trans. J. Matthew Ashley (New York: Crossroad Publishing Company, 1992, 2007), 105.

7. John Lovell Jr., *Black Song: The Forge and the Flame—The Story of How the Afro-American Spiritual Was Hammered Out* (New York: Macmillan, 1972), 400. Scholarly studies of the spirituals include Howard Thurman, *Deep River and the Negro Spiritual Speaks of Life and Death* (Richmond, IN: Friends United Press, 1975); James H. Cone, *The Spirituals and the Blues: An Interpretation* (Maryknoll, NY: Orbis Books, 1972, 2002); and LeRoi Jones, *Blues People: The Negro Experience in White America and the Music That Developed from It* (New York: William Morrow, 1963).

people as its particular mission. During my childhood, we were members of Holy Ghost Parish, whose small, segregated, and demanding elementary school I attended. Each Sunday, one of the Spiritans (or Holy Ghost Fathers) celebrated the "children's Mass." It was no different than the earlier or later Masses, but during this one the priest would step away from the lectern (pulpit would be far too pretentious a label to describe the outfitting of our basement mission church), stand close to the communion rail, and explain the gospel directly and simply, but not, I think, condescendingly. Although my grandmother already would have attended an earlier Mass, when I returned home I was expected to summarize the gospel and something of the homily. What I remember so well is that very often when I opened the front door, my grandmother's rich alto would be raised in song—a spiritual. Much later, when I heard other black Catholics tell similar stories, I recognized such singing of spirituals as a conserving, healing, even, compensatory religious and psychic practice that affirmed black life before God.

Historians Miles Mark Fisher and Dena J. Epstein trace the spirituals to the early eighteenth century.[8] Certainly the brutal social conditions (natal alienation, legalized perpetual servitude, physical and mental abuse) of their composition were already in place by that time. Reports about the distinctive singing and dancing of the enslaved people gradually drifted northward through travelers' chronicles, newspaper and journal articles, diaries of missionaries and teachers, novels, and the speeches and narratives of fugitive slaves.[9] Anglo-American and European visitors to the antebellum South were struck by the singing and dancing of the enslaved peoples. Many dismissed the songs as "uncouth barbarism, [while] others were stirred by the vigor of the dancing and the weird sadness of the songs."[10] Southerners had commented on

---

8. Miles Mark Fisher, *Negro Slave Songs in the United States* (New York: Citadel Press, 1953); Dena J. Epstein, *Sinful Tunes and Spirituals: Black Folk Music to the Civil War* (Urbana and Chicago: University of Illinois Press, 1977, 1981).

9. Epstein, *Sinful Tunes and Spirituals*, 161–83, 215–37, 241–302.

10. Sterling Brown, "The Spirituals," in *The Book of Negro Folklore*, ed. Langston Hughes and Arna Bontemps (New York: Dodd, Mead, 1958), 279.

the singing and dancing of the enslaved peoples, but most often as evidence of their contentment with enslavement. The white men and women of the South deemed it "bad policy to give slaves credit for any type of cultural achievement."[11]

Because of the prevalence of biblical references and characters, the spirituals are associated with Christianity. We would do well to remember that the Middle Passage did not completely eradicate religious practices, aspects of material culture, beliefs, and cognitive orientations toward reality or life or relationships.[12] While scholars have developed an accurate portrait of significant similarities in customs, mores, and values between and among various cultural-linguistic groups on the African continent, differences remain conspicuous and evocative. No universal "African" religio-cultural heritage existed (or exists).[13] The many and diverse peoples who were captured and sold into slavery thought of themselves as *who* they *were*—Ashanti or Bini or Coromantee or Ewe or Fante or Fon or Fulani or Igbo or Mande or Mende or Yoruba, and so on. The trans-Atlantic slave trade was not, Ashraf Rushdy reminds us, a "dispersal of *one* nation but of *many* peoples."[14] Contact between and among these peoples was not uncommon and occurred through personal or individual and group meetings, festivals, intermarriage, market commerce, climactic events, treaties, and even wars. These activities encouraged the working knowledge of different languages, promoted intergroup etiquette and customs, negotiated practicalities, and generated some shared morals, beliefs, and aesthetic sensibilities.

---

11. Lovell, *Black Song,* 400.

12. Joseph E. Holloway, ed., *Africanisms in American Culture* (Bloomington and Indianapolis, IN: Indiana University Press, 1990), 2–13; Raboteau, *Slave Religion,* 5–7.

13. For some studies, see John S. Mbiti, *African Religions and Philosophies,* 2nd ed. (London: Heinemann, 1989, orig. 1969); Bolaji Idowu, *African Traditional Religions: A Definition* (Maryknoll, NY: Orbis Books, 1975): Charles H. Long, *Significations: Signs, Symbols, and Images in the Interpretation of Religion* (Philadelphia: Fortress Press, 1986).

14. Ashraf H. A. Rushdy, "The Quality of Diaspora," *Diaspora: A Journal of Transnational Studies* 18, no. 3 (Fall 2009): 287–304, at 299. My italics.

Still, diverse and differentiated, complex religio-cultural world-views or sacred cosmologies came into the Americas. The conditions of the Middle Passage and enslavement posed difficulties for religio-cultural integrity. The slave trade forced disruption, fragmentation, even collapse of meanings; it involved loss and conservation, adaptation and rejection, transposition and translation. Certainly, some of these interiorized cosmologies shattered under the weight of water and trauma, and some fared otherwise. Sold into what we know today as Brazil, the Yoruba people were able to preserve their sophisticated religio-cultural cosmology almost intact by concealing the deities within the popular devotions of Portuguese Catholicism.

What survived the Middle Passage and enslavement might be termed "root paradigms."[15] These root paradigms—cognitive and moral orientations, fragments of rite and ritual, cultural memory—emerged from the interstices of loss and pushed upward in recovery and revision, in change and transformation, in improvisation. These coalesced to ground religious consciousness, aesthetic sensibilities, and expressions that differed necessarily from their indigenous antecedents.[16] These root paradigms form the ground or first stratum of a worldview that encounters and critically reenvisions Christian preaching and practice in the traumatizing experience of slavery.

Five sections comprise this chapter. The first probes the encounter between the enslaved African peoples and Christian preaching. The fateful decision of slaveholders, along with ministers, priests, and bishops, to distort the love command of Jesus for the sake of profit and racial privilege brought Christianity to a crossroad. The second section opens a canon of anguish—the suffering of African peoples chained below the decks of sailing ships, handled and sold from auction blocks, forced to labor and endure cruelty and

---

15. Victor Turner, *Dramas, Fields, and Metaphors: Symbolic Action in Human Society* (Ithaca and London: Cornell University Press, 1974), 67, 163.

16. Mechal Sobel, *Trabelin' On: The Slave Journey to an Afro-Baptist Faith* (Westport, CT: Greenwood Press, 1979), 39, also, xxii–xxiv, 3–21.

assault. Their experience rightly may be reckoned as time on the cross.[17] The third considers the suffering of the enslaved people in their efforts to worship in spirit and in truth. The fourth section focuses on the meeting of the enslaved people with Jesus of Nazareth. The fifth teases out the "dark wisdom" they mine from their generative encounter with the *logos* of the cross.

Christianity at a Crossroad

Chattel slavery led Christianity to a crossroad: discipleship or duplicity. That choice was made centuries before the American form of chattel slavery came into existence, but the option for duplicity has made all the difference. Slavery was part of the social and cultural fabric of the ancient world. Indeed, slavery was part of the world in which Jesus of Nazareth lived, healed, preached, suffered, died, and rose; it was part of the fabric of the early Christian community. Jennifer Glancy offers a thought-provoking experiment. She asks us "to ponder how differently Christianity might have developed if early Christian communities had made freeing one's slaves a precondition of baptism."[18] It appears that early on, we followers of Jesus compromised the gospel; rather than fitting our lives into its radical demands, we cheapened the gospel, forced its accommodation to our social and cultural worldviews.

Christian evangelization in colonial North America illustrates the domestication of the gospel to fit the needs of slavery. In 1565, the Spanish established a colony in what we now know as northern Florida and baptized captured and enslaved Africans into the Roman Catholic Church—often with little or no instruction. As Martha Washington Creel points out, not all the clergy commissioned by the Society for the Propagation of the Gospel in Foreign

17. Robert William Fogel and Stanley L. Engerman, *Time on the Cross: The Economics of American Negro Slavery* (New York and London: W. W. Norton, 1974, 1989). In the prologue, the authors contend, "The years of black enslavement and the Civil War in which they terminated were our nation's time on the cross" (4).

18. Jennifer A. Glancy, *Slavery as a Moral Problem in the Early Church and Today* (Minneapolis: Fortress Press, 2011), 25.

Parts (SPG) "used their office prudently or even spiritually. Some-times, those who did found the vestry rallied against them." One SPG clergyman correlated the failure of Christian conversions among the enslaved people to the "wicked and scandalous behavior" of slaveholders.[19] In the eighteenth century, the majority of Anglo-American Protestant slaveholders demonstrated considerable reluctance to expose enslaved people to the Bible or to baptize them. These planters were suspicious that under then-applicable British law Christian baptism would compel manumission. Anglican minister Francis Le Jau, preaching in Goose Creek, South Carolina, under the auspices of the SPG, made enslaved candidates take the following oath prior to being baptized: "You declare in the presence of God and before this congregation that you do not ask for the holy baptism out of design to free yourself from the duty and obedience you owe to your master while you live, but meekly for the good of your soul."[20]

In the French Catholic colony of Louisiana, the Code Noir of 1724 required slaveholders to instruct the enslaved people in Catholic doctrine. On the one hand, like their Protestant counterparts, many Catholic planters displayed a lack of interest and care in meeting this obligation. On the other hand, some Catholic planters did cooperate with missionaries in this effort at evangelization. In 1785, John Carroll, "superior of the American missions, in his report to Rome on the state of the Church in the United States," numbered the Catholic population in Maryland as 15,000, of whom more than 3,000 were enslaved.[21]

Eventually, slaveholders began to maintain that Christian baptism might render the enslaved people less rebellious and more pliable to accept their fate. On some plantations, the enslaved people attended white churches, sitting or standing in designated areas,

---

19. Martha Washington Creel, *"A Peculiar People": Slave Religion and the Community Culture among the Gullahs* (New York and London: New York University Press, 1988), 69.

20. Ibid., 101.

21. Raboteau, *Slave Religion*, 112–13.

even "listening to the same sermons, the same songs, and the same prayers."[22] In some areas of the South, enslaved people attended church along with white slaveholders, but there were no places for them to sit. One enslaved woman, Annie Washington, noted that the black people "sat on the floor of the church or steps and peeped in" from outside.[23]

Some planters allowed white clergy to preach to the enslaved people in the slave quarters, and these men put Christian theology to a dubious purpose. Anglican minister Thomas Bacon published a sermon that exhorted the enslaved people to accept their bondage as part of a natural and divinely ordained social order in which masters were "God's overseers" and slaves were to obey these masters as if they were obeying God.[24] White ministers frequently employed the hermeneutics of sacrifice and servitude in their proslavery arguments. James Furman, a Baptist cleric from South Carolina, declared: "We who own slaves honor God's law in the exercise of our authority."[25] In *A Brief Examination of Scripture Testimony on the Institution of Slavery*, Minister Thornton Stringfellow of Culpeper County, Virginia, argued that slavery derived from Noah's curse of the progeny of Canaan. He contended that the descendants of Canaan were to be servants of servants—at the mercy of their kin. In exegeting the text, Stringfellow stated that the language used showed "the *favor* which God would exercise to the posterity of Shem and Japheth, while they were holding the posterity of Ham in a state of *abject bondage*." He continued: "May it not be said in truth, that God *decreed* this institution before it existed; and has he not connected its *existence*, with prophetic tokens of special favor, to those who should be slave owners or

---

22. John B. Cade, "Out of the Mouths of Ex-Slaves," *Journal of Negro History* 20, no. 3 (July 1935): 327.

23. Ibid., 328.

24. Thomas Bacon, "A Sermon to Maryland Slaves" (1749), in *Religion in American History: A Reader*, ed. Jon Butler and Harry Stout (New York: Oxford University Press, 1998), 77, 83, 86.

25. Donald Mathews, *Religion in the Old South* (Chicago: University of Chicago Press, 1977), 136.

masters? He is the same God now that he was when he gave these views of his moral character to the world."[26] Stringfellow drew a direct line from Noah's curse of the descendants of Ham (Canaan's offspring) to the divinely ordained enslavement of black people in nineteenth-century America. He concluded: "God *decreed slavery*—and shows in that decree, tokens of good-will to the master."[27]

Bishop William Meade advocated a double doctrine of Jesus as the servant of servants and applied this to both slaveholders and slaves. According to Meade, Jesus "chose the form of a servant and became the servant-of-servants, illustrating [the] blessed doctrine [of slavery] by his own meek, patient, suffering life."[28] Since Jesus was "faultless in word and deed toward those in bondage," slaveholders were to imitate him by correct, perfect "Christian" behavior toward those whom they held in slavery. But, since Jesus had been meek and humble, enslaved women and men were to imitate him by accepting their enslavement meekly and humbly, without protest, for their perpetual servitude was ordained by God's divine will.[29]

Frank Roberson, a freed man, paraphrased a typical sermon by white preachers:

> You slaves will go to heaven if you are good, but don't ever think that you will be close to your mistress and master. No! No! there will be a wall between you; but there will be holes in it that will permit you to look out and see your mistress when she passes by. If you want to sit behind this wall, you must do the language of the text "Obey your masters."[30]

---

26. Thornton Stringfellow, *A Brief Examination of Scripture Testimony on the Institution of Slavery, In an Essay, first published in the Religious Herald, and republished by request: with Remarks on a Letter of Elde* GALUSHA, *of New York, to Dr.* R. FULLER, *of South Carolina*, 2. Author's italics. http://docsouth.unc.edu.

27. Ibid.

28. Riggins Earl, *Dark Symbols, Obscure Signs: God, Self, and Community in the Slave Mind* (Maryknoll, NY: Orbis Books, 1993), 33.

29. Ibid.

30. Cade, "Out of the Mouths of Ex-Slaves," 329.

Lucretia Alexander, Wes Beady, and Richard Carruthers corroborated the frequency of such debased injunctions. Carruthers declared:

> When the white preacher come he preach and pick up his Bible and claim he gettin' the text right out of the good Book and he preach. "The Lord say, don't you [slaves] steal chickens from your missus. Don't you steal your master's hogs." That would be all he preach.[31]

And, Beady added, no minister said "nary a word 'bout havin' a soul to save."[32] In order to validate and sacralize racial slavery, these and other clerics anesthetized and coopted the gospel to use it as "an attractive device for slave control."[33]

Time on the Cross

Asked about her suffering under slavery, Delia Garlic replied: "It's bad to belong to folks [that] own you, soul and body, [that] can tie you up to a tree, with [your] face to [the] tree and [your] arms fastened tight around it, who can take a long curlin' whip and cut the blood every lick. Folks a mile away could here dem awful whippings. Dey was a terrible part of livin'."[34]

Slave narratives uncover that such whippings were not uncommon. After the terror of the Middle Passage, the kidnapped youth or adult was sold into the terror of the plantation and its system of chattel slavery, where life became a paradoxical tension of "*death-in-life*."[35] The word "chattel" in its legal denotation refers to a movable article of personal property. Chattel slavery relegated a living human person to an article of personal property to be used or dis-

---

31. Norman R. Yetman, ed., *Voices from Slavery* (New York: Holt, Rinehart and Winston, 1970), 53.

32. Raboteau, *Slave Religion*, 214.

33. Winthrop D. Jordan, *White over Black: American Attitudes toward the Negro, 1550–1812* (Baltimore, MD: Penguin Books, 1969), 191.

34. Yetman, ed., *Voices from Slavery*, 133.

35. Achille Mbembé, "Necropolitics," trans. Libby Meintjes, *Public Culture* 15, no. 1 (Winter 2003): 21.

posed of at the whim of the owner. Chattel slavery abrogated the slave's humanity through discursive and physical (de)formation that taught slaves from childhood to view themselves as property,[36] thus alienating the slave from all that constitutes human being-in-the-world—history, heritage, memory, family and kin, individuality, idiosyncrasies, anxieties, and desires. Chattel slavery achieved such devastation through physical and psychic violence that it sealed slaves in a condition of extreme fear, thus constantly renewing "the shock of slavery"[37] and stifling every valiant hope of freedom. Chattel slavery was an economic racial regime in which only blacks were slaves. Race, as historian Barbara Jeanne Fields puts it, is a "byproduct" of revolutionary era complicity between pro-slaverists and anti-slaverists in "identifying racial incapacity [i.e., *nonwhiteness*] of Afro-Americans as the explanation for enslavement. American racial ideology is as original an invention of the Founders as is the United States itself."[38] The collusion of those who held "liberty to be inalienable," while yet immersed in slaveholding, ended up "holding race to be a self-evident truth."[39]

Enslaved people opposed the violation of their liberty, although not always, not always successfully, and never completely. Eruptions of their defiance should never be romanticized or uncritically appropriated. Some enslaved people resisted through backtalk (or sass), others strategized to disrupt the plantation's rhythms and rituals of work; others ran away; and some feigned madness. Some enslaved people fought back in self-defense; others broke under the weight of physical torture and psychological abuse, but to judge their response as deficient disregards the intricacies of psychic life. The asymmetrical power relation binding master and slave concretizes in the nexus of threat and fear, sale and price, person and

36. Walter Johnson, *Soul by Soul: Life Inside the Antebellum Slave Market* (Cambridge: Harvard University Press, 1999), 20–24.

37. Scott C. Williamson, *The Narrative Life: The Moral and Religious Thought of Frederick Douglass* (Macon, GA: Mercer University Press, 2002), 36.

38. Karen E. Fields and Barbara Jeanne Fields, *Racecraft: The Soul of Inequality in American Life* (London and New York: Verso, 2012, 2014), 121.

39. Ibid.

objectification and reaches its limit in the master's power over life. As Susan Buck-Morss observes, "the slave is the one commodity like no other, as freedom of property and freedom of person are here in direct contradiction."[40] The slave was a legal commodity, an object of property with commercial value, yet the slave was a living human objectified as property, a thing. On this account, it is possible to conclude that the master *may possess* the slave's very life, the master *owns* a human life. Is this not "necropower"?[41] And does it not oppose and dare to depose divine power?

The plantation system, with its outreach for consumption of human flesh through slave traders, the slave market, and slave pens, aimed to reify black humanity. Black children, women, and men could be sold off at whim or need. Katie Rowe recalled how the enslaved people were handled and inspected like so much cattle: "De white men come up and look in de slave's mouth jes lak he was a mule or a hoss."[42] Solomon Northup, a freeborn black man, who was deceived, kidnapped, and sold into slavery, confirmed this practice. Customers calling at the slave pen, Northup recalled, "would feel of our hands and arms and bodies, turn us about, ask us what we could do, make us open our mouths and show our teeth, precisely as a jockey examines a horse."[43] Buyers inspected the bodies of enslaved people for blisters, signs of disease, or scars from whippings that demonstrated a disposition toward rebellion. Joseph Young told one interviewer that

> when a planter owed a debt and was not able to meet it, all of his slaves were called to the yard, placed in a circle and the creditor allowed to select from that number enough slaves to settle the debt. In some instances, the men would be ordered

40. Susan Buck-Morss, *Hegel, Haiti, and Universal History* (Pittsburgh: University of Pittsburgh Press, 2009), 53n90.

41. Mbembé, "Necropolitics," 21, 25.

42. James Mellon, ed., *Bullwhip Days: The Slaves Remember, An Oral History* (New York: Avon Books, 1988), 28.

43. Solomon Northup, *Twelve Years a Slave*, ed. Sue Eakin and Joseph Logsdon (Baton Rouge: Louisiana State University Press, 1968; orig. 1853), 52.

to pull off their shirts, the women to pull off their shirt waists, that prospective buyers might see if they had healthy looking muscles or if their backs were scarred.[44]

And, W. L. Bost insisted that he would remember "the sound of the auctioneer's voice as long as [he] lived."[45]

For the sake of the profits of the plantation, enslaved children, women, and men were reduced to instruments of labor. Both black women and men worked from sunup to sundown, usually six days each week, and sometimes for several hours on Sundays. On some plantations, enslaved people were supervised in the fields by black drivers who, in turn, were under the direction of white overseers. On other estates, they worked the fields under the immediate supervision of white overseers, the plantation owner, or a member of the owner's family.

When it came to heavy labor in the field, there was little gender differentiation. Harriet Robinson said that "women broke in mules, throwed 'em down, and roped 'em. [And] they'd do it better'n [some] men."[46] Ferebe Rogers insisted that she "was a field hand," who had "come up twixt de plow handles. I weren't de fastest one with a hoe, but I didn't turn my back on nobody plowin'."[47] Fannie Moore, who was interviewed at Asheville, North Carolina, said that her mother "work in the field all day and piece and quilt all night."[48] And Sarah Gruder recalled, "I never knowed what it was to rest. I just work all de time from mornin' till late at night. I had to do everythin' dey was to do on de outside. Work in de field, chop wood, hoe corn, till sometimes I feel like my back surely break. I done everythin' [except] split rails."[49]

Richard Carruthers recalled a rough-tempered overseer: "[Tom Hill] used to whip me and the other [slaves] if we don't jump quick

---

44. Cade, "Out of the Mouths of Ex-Slaves," 326.
45. Yetman, ed., *Voices from Slavery*, 36.
46. Ibid., 252.
47. Ibid., 257.
48. Ibid., 227.
49. Ibid., 151.

enough when he holler and [sometimes] he stake us out like you stake out a hide and whip till we bleed. Sometime he take salt and rub on the [slaves] so [we] smart and burn . . . and suffer misery."[50] Both Mary Prince and Mattie Jackson corroborate such treatment. Held in slavery in Bermuda, the West Indies, Prince recounts the death of Hetty, an enslaved woman who had been especially kind to her. One of the cows in Hetty's care pulled away from its tether; this put the master, Captain I— in a rage. Despite her pregnancy, he ordered Hetty to be stripped naked and tied to a tree in the yard; he, then, proceeded to flog her with a whip and cow-skin repeatedly. Prince tells us

> [Hetty's] shrieks were terrible. . . . Poor Hetty was brought to bed before her time, and was delivered after severe labour of a dead child. She appeared to recover after her confinement, so far that she was repeatedly flogged by both master and mistress afterward; but her former strength never returned to her. Ere long her body and limbs swelled to a great size; and she lay on a mat in the kitchen, till the water burst out of her body and she died. . . . I cried very much for her death. The manner of it filled me with horror. I could not bear to think about it; yet it was always present to my mind for many a day.[51]

For five years Prince was held a slave in this household, flogged and mistreated almost daily, until she was sold and shipped away. Mattie Jackson recalls similar brutish behavior by slaveholder Benjamin Lewis, brother to the man who "owned" her: "He used to extend his victim, fastened to a beam, with hands and feet tied, and inflict from fifty to three hundred lashes, laying their flesh entirely open, then bathe their quivering wounds in brine."[52]

---

50. Ibid., 53.
51. "The History of Mary Prince, a West Indian Slave" (1831), in *Six Women's Slave Narratives, The Schomburg Library of Nineteenth-Century Black Women Writers*, gen. ed., Henry Louis Gates Jr. (New York: Oxford Paperbacks/Oxford University Press, 1988), 7.
52. "The Story of Mattie J. Jackson" (1866), in *Six Women's Slave Narratives*, 37.

Black women and men labored literally in the making of the material of the plantation both through production and reproduction. In this way their instrumentalization was nearly total. Slavery thrived on the black woman's body; indeed, her body was that site in which the planter's economic and pornographically erotic desire collided with her sex, sexuality, and reproductive capability. Historian Deborah Gray White observes, "planters made sure that slave women were prolific."[53] This was more than cost-cutting: after the importation of Africans became illegal in 1808, the increase of plantation capital, its laborers or slaves, depended on internal breeding. Biology bound the black woman to capital accumulation. Lizzie Williams, who had been held on a plantation near Selma, Alabama, relayed the fear and resignation that overtook so many enslaved women: "Many de poor [slave] women have chillen for de massa, dat is if de massa mean man. Dey just tell de [slaves] what to do and dey know better dan to fuss."[54]

The following accounts expose the bitter and bleak ordinariness of such abuse and exploitation. One former enslaved woman said: "Ma mama said that a [slave] woman couldn't help herself, [so] she had to do what de marster say."[55] And another gave this plaintive account:

> My sister was given away when she was a girl. She told me and ma that they'd make her go out and lay on a table and two or three white men would have sex with her before they'd let her up. She was just a small girl. She died when she was still in her young days, still a girl.[56]

Harriet Jacobs, writing under the pseudonym Linda Brent, mourned the birth of her daughter with these words: "Slavery is terrible for men; but it is far more terrible for women. Superadded

---

53. Deborah Gray White, *Ar'n't I a Woman? Female Slaves in the Plantation South* (New York: W. W. Norton, 1985), 31.

54. Yetman, ed., *Voices from Slavery*, 317.

55. Dorothy Sterling, ed., *We Are Your Sisters: Black Women in the Nineteenth Century* (New York: W. W. Norton, 1984), 25.

56. Ibid., 25, 26–31.

to the burden common to all, *they* have wrongs, and sufferings, and mortifications peculiarly their own."[57] Sociologist Dorothy Roberts states plainly: "One of the most horrific aspects of slavery's ownership of black bodies was enslaved women's experience of sexual exploitation by white slaveholders, traders, and other men. The institution of slavery created for slaveholders the possibility of unrestrained sexual access and control."[58]

These "dangerous memories" of the maldistributed suffering of black children, women, and men under chattel slavery make demands on our lives. This suffering holds neither pedagogical nor ascetic power; it means to break, not temper, the spirit. It is suffering of a negative quality that all too often ended in the death of enslaved people.

Suffering Even to Pray

If some planters and slaveholders permitted the enslaved people to hold independent, and sometimes, unsupervised worship services, other planters punished slaves for praying and singing. Ellen Butler's master was among the latter and never allowed the slaves to go to church: "Massa never 'lowed us slaves go to church but they have big holes in the fields they gits down in and prays. They done that 'cause the white folks didn't want them to pray. They used to pray for freedom."[59] Another woman reported that on the Scott plantation her husband was beaten often because "[the master] caught him praying." This did not stop her husband from praying: "He just kept on. . . . They didn't have any bible on the Scott plantation she said, for it meant a beating or a killing if you'd be caught with

---

57. Harriet Jacobs [Linda Brent], *Incidents in the Life of a Slave Girl* (New York: Harcourt Brace Jovanovich, 1861, 1983), 79.

58. Dorothy Roberts, "The Paradox of Silence and Display: Sexual Violation of Enslaved Women and Contemporary Contradictions in Black Female Sexuality," in *Beyond Slavery: Overcoming Its Religious and Sexual Legacies*, ed. Bernadette J. Brooten (New York: Palgrave Macmillan, 2010), 43.

59. George P. Rawick, ed., *From Sundown to Sunup: The Making of the Black Community*, vol. 1, *The American Slave: A Composite Autobiography* (Westport, CT: Greenwood Publishing Company, 1941, 1972), 35.

one."[60] The enslaved people prayed anyway. They extended the geographic ground of their religious experience, slipping away at night to thickets and overgrown places. Hannah Lowery remembered that sometimes the people made arbors of small pine trees.

> Some of them didn't have arbors. When they wanted to sing and pray, they would steal off into the woods. During that time, most of the masters were cruel. If they would hear them (slaves) singing, they would get their whips and whip them all the way home. Whipping did not stop them from having meetings. When one place was located they would find another one.[61]

Richard Carruthers's recollection was similar:

> Us [slaves] used to have a prayin' ground down in the hollow and sometime we come out of the field, between eleven and twelve at night, scorchin' and burnin' up with nothin to eat, and we wants to ask the good Lord to have mercy. We puts grease in a snuff pan or bottle and make a lamp. We takes a pine torch, too, and goes down in the hollow to pray. Some gets so joyous they starts to holler loud and we has to stop up they mouth. I see [slaves] get so full of the Lord and so happy they drops unconscious.[62]

In spite of slavery's debasement of Christianity and the ideological distortion of biblical texts, the Bible came to occupy a pivotal place in the religio-cultural life of the enslaved people. "African Americans," biblical scholar Allen Callahan tells us, "are the children of slavery in America. And, the Bible, as no other book, is the book of slavery's children."[63] Biblical characters, stories and events, themes and images gave hope to the struggle of enslaved

60. Henry H. Mitchell, *Black Belief: Folk Beliefs of Blacks in America and West Africa* (New York: Harper & Row, 1975), 100.

61. Cade, "Out of the Mouths of Ex-Slaves," 329.

62. Yetman, ed., *Voices from Slavery*, 53.

63. Allen Dwight Callahan, *The Talking Book: African Americans and the Bible* (New Haven and London: Yale University Press, 2006), xi.

black women and men for emancipation, for freedom, for liberation in this world and triumph in the next. Moreover, they formed a distinctive image of themselves and fashioned "an inner world, a scale of values and fixed points of vantage from which to judge the world around them and themselves."[64]

By law and custom the enslaved people were forbidden to learn to read or write. Their knowledge of the content and message of the Bible came through public readings and sermons. Portions of biblical books or chapters were memorized, repeated, and reshaped. Purged of malicious meanings, these passages became the subject of meditation, reflection, and sermonic interpretation. Biblical scholar Renita Weems has argued that since the enslaved people were not bound intellectually or morally to any *official* written text, translation, or interpretation, they created for themselves an *oral text* of the Bible that displayed affinities with the prophetic and apocalyptic traditions of the Hebrew Scriptures. Since these people were deprived of literacy, Weems states,

> they were, therefore, without allegiance to any official text, translation, or interpretation; hence once they heard biblical passages read and interpreted to them, they in turn were free to remember and repeat in accordance with their own interests and tastes.... [F]or those raised within an aural culture retelling the Bible became one hermeneutical strategy, and resistance to the Bible, or portions of it, would become another.[65]

Slavery exacted a perverse physical, psychological, intellectual, and spiritual toll. Verbally and physically intimidated, the enslaved people were coerced to perform a grotesque pantomime of survival—smiling when they wanted to weep, laughing when they felt anger and rage. For some enslaved people, freedom was

---

64. Johnson, ed., *God Struck Me Dead*, vii.

65. Renita J. Weems, "African American Women and the Bible," in *Stony the Road We Trod: African American Biblical Interpretation*, ed. Cain Hope Felder (Minneapolis: Fortress Press, 1991), 61.

an astonishing prospect, perhaps even an unattainable condition. One freed slave admitted, "I've heard [the slaves] pray for freedom. I thought it was foolishness, then, but the old-time folks always felt they was to be free. It must have been something [re]vealed unto 'em."[66] The enslaved people believed that "the God of history [would act] within American experience, and [act] with the same emancipatory purpose as depicted in the biblical Exodus."[67] Their belief in their divine ordination to freedom is not without biblical evidence.

The unique relationship between God and Israel rests on the covenant and the mighty acts God performed to deliver the people held in the divine heart from slavery in Egypt. Yet, the eighth-century BCE prophet Amos qualified Israel's unique claim to election: "Are ye not as children of the Ethiopians unto me, O children of Israel? saith the Lord. Have I not brought up Israel out of the land of Egypt? and the Philistines from Caphtor, and the Syrians from Kir?" (Amos 9:7). The prophet reminds the people that the Lord God has "brought up" other peoples from danger and oppression, suffering and affliction. With this powerful and pointed rhetorical question, Callahan observes, Amos reminds Israel that their election is not exclusive. The Lord God has acted, may act, and will act on behalf of other peoples—offering to them divine preferential mercy and justice. Amos's question, Callahan ventures, "suggests that God is as close to the Ethiopians as he is to the Israelites. Both the Philistines and the Syrians were Israel's neighbors and ancestral enemies; repeatedly in the past God has given each of them a patrimony. . . . The Exodus is not unique."[68]

Did the enslaved people hear slaveholders and other whites speak of themselves as the "new Israel"? The Protestant planter class and social elites well may have reminisced about the arrival and difficulties of the early colonists and their journey to America. Perhaps

---

66. Mellon, ed., *Bullwhip Days,* 190.

67. Theophus Smith, *Conjuring Culture: Biblical Formations of Black America* (Oxford: Oxford University Press, 1994), 155.

68. Callahan, *The Talking Book,* 108.

those same privileged elites recalled references to John Winthrop's sermon in which he bolstered the courage of the travelers. As these men and women were about to enter into a new land, Winthrop insisted that they also were entering into a covenant with the Lord God. If they would uphold God's laws and commandments, observe faithfully the ordinances and articles that govern their living, then "the Lord will be [their] God and delight to dwell among [them], as His own people, and will command a blessing upon [them] in all [their] ways." Moreover, Winthrop exhorted them to consider themselves as exemplars, "as a city upon a hill." He warned them that should they "deal falsely" with God and "so cause Him to withdraw His present help," they shall "be made a story and by-word through the world"; they shall be shamed and cursed, until they "be consumed out of the good land whither [they] are going."[69] These travelers were to be the "new Israel," assured of a gift from God: a land flowing with milk and honey. Centuries later Thomas Jefferson and Benjamin Franklin would uphold this notion of election and the manifest destiny it guaranteed.[70]

If the enslaved people had heard mention of Winthrop's sermon or the notion that slaveholders and privileged white elites understood themselves as the "new Israel," if they had heard references to Amos's warning regarding election and his identification of God with other peoples, surely they would have recognized their own story and struggle. Certainly, the spiritual "Go Down, Moses" offers evidence that the people made such an identification:

> When Israel was in Egypt's land, Let my people go;
> Oppressed so hard they could not stand, Let my
> people go.
> Go down Moses, way down in Egypt's land;
> Tell old Pharaoh to let my people go.

---

69. John Winthrop, "A Model of Christian Charity," in *The American Puritans: Their Prose and Poetry*, ed. Perry Miller (New York: Columbia University Press, 1956), 83.

70. See Kelly Brown Douglas, *Stand Your Ground: Black Bodies and the Justice of God* (Maryknoll, NY: Orbis Books, 2015), 12–13.

And Alice Sewell testified to the power of that prayer and the divine response: "God planned dem slave prayers to free us like he did de Israelites, and they [the prayers] did."[71] After a profound religious experience, Fannie Moore's mother sang and shouted in joy: "De Lord done tell me I'se saved. Now I know de Lord will show me de way, I ain't gwine to grieve no more. No matter how much you all done beat me and my chillen de Lord will show me de way. And some day we never be slaves."[72] In the midst of slavery's oppression, Moore's mother testified that God could be counted on to lead the enslaved people to freedom. She believed that even from within this brutal situation, God would "grant to them the same future of freedom as the Hebrew slaves were granted in the book of Exodus."[73]

Enslaved women and men defied punishment in order to commune with God. Susan Rhodes remarked, "We had dem spirit-filled meetings at night on de bank of de river, and God met us dere . . . and what a glorious time we did have in de Lord."[74] Alice Sewell told her interviewer that enslaved people in the area where she was held

> prayed for dis day of freedom. We come four and five miles to pray together to God dat if we don't live to see it, to please let our chillen live to see a better day and be free, so dat dey can give honest and fair service to de Lord and all mankind everywhere.[75]

From within the choking circumference of slavery, the people prayed for that which was unseen. We would do well to remember that the vast majority of the children, women, and men enslaved in the Americas died in the bondage in which they lived. To pray for the liberation, the freedom of others, even one's children, is unselfishness at prayer. Such unselfish and persistent prayer signi-

---

71. Yetman, ed., *Voices from Slavery*, 264.
72. Ibid., 228.
73. Smith, *Conjuring Culture*, 60.
74. Mellon, ed., *Bullwhip Days*, 195.
75. Yetman, ed., *Voices from Slavery*, 263.

fies the transcendent dimension of human being and witnesses to an eschatological hope that discredits any facile optimism before God and the condition of enslavement. When Emancipation came, the enslaved people gave God the glory. Mary Reynolds mused: "I sets and 'members the times in the world. . . . I 'members 'bout the days of slavery and I don't 'lieve they ever gwine have slaves no more on this earth. I thank Gawd done took that burden offen his black chillum and I'm aimin' to praise him for it to his face."[76]

Crucified King and Lord

The enslaved people's embrace of the crucified Lord was no act of self-abnegation but an act of signifying resistance. When an interviewer asked, "How did you bear it all, how did you live?" an old emancipated woman replied, "I couldn't 'er done it without Master Jesus. He's held me up. I'd' er died long ago without him."[77] As one of the people remarked, Jesus "hooked [them] in the heart.'[78]

In the composition of the spirituals, John Lovell identifies certain "permeating influences of transformation. . . . The first of these is the love and power of Jesus, and the slave's friendship and alliance with him."[79] In at least three ways, Jesus of Nazareth captured the religious imagination and affections of the enslaved people. First, Jesus identified with and preached the gospel to those who were poor and afflicted, oppressed and dispossessed: *"Did you ever see the like before, King Jesus preaching to the poor. . . ."* The enslaved people understood the similarity of their condition with that of the Bible's outcast and despised. Second, Jesus was a man of word and deed: he does what he says that he will do: *"My Lord's done just what he said, He's heal de sick and rais'd de dead."* The cures and miracles reported by the Gospels witness to Jesus's con-

76. Mellon, ed., *Bullwhip Days*, 23.
77. John W. Blassingame, ed., *Slave Testimony: Two Centuries of Letters, Speeches, Interviews, and Autobiographies* (Baton Rouge and London: Louisiana State University Press, 1977), 541.
78. Johnson, ed., *God Struck Me Dead*, 19.
79. Lovell, *Black Song*, 301.

tinuing transformative power: *"I'll tell you what de Lord done for me / He tuk my feet from de miry clay." "He sat me upon a solid rock / An' gib me David's golden harp."* Finally, because Jesus himself was beaten, tortured, and murdered, the enslaved people believed that he understood them and their suffering like no one else. They believed that he was one with them in their otherness and afflic-tion, that he would help them to negotiate this world with righ-teous anger and dignity. They were motivated not out of despair but out of love and faith when they sang, *"Nobody knows de trouble I've had / Nobody knows but Jesus."*

Caught within the labyrinth of the social oppression of slavery, black people fixed their eyes on Jesus and his cross as they grappled with the absurdity of enslavement. They took Jesus to themselves as one of them; the innocence, agony, and cruelty of his suffering was so very like their own. The enslaved people met Jesus's compassion with compassion, his love with love, his care with care. They knew Jesus as a *friend* with whom they could share their secrets, a *savior* to whom they could entrust their hopes and fears, a *companion* with whom they could walk through life's deep shadows, a *healer* who could make the wounded whole, a *fellow sufferer* who knew in his body the sting of the lash, enduring with them what was their daily portion. Bloodied and nailed to rough wooden planks, he was the One who went all the way with them and for them. Jesus was their "all in all," their joy, their Rose of Sharon. In the paradox and promise of his life and suffering, they found their own. No matter how vicious the oppression to which enslavement consigned them, they sang with confidence:

> He have been wid us, Jesus
> He still be wid us, Jesus,
> He will be wid us, Jesus,
> Be wid us to the end.

King Jesus, Friend of the Enslaved

Lovell states that the Jesus of the spirituals "derives" from the Son of God, the Christ who lived, died, and was resurrected, and is identifiable with the Jesus of basic Christian doctrine. At the same

time, this Jesus walks out of the pages of the Bible and makes himself "available for services of every kind, on earth and in heaven,
in life and death."[80]

From the vantage of the spirituals, Jesus could do anything,
and the enslaved people were not hesitant "to make very unusual
demands of [their] friend Jesus."[81]

> Meet me, Jesus, meet me,
> Meet me in de middle of de air
> So's if my wings should fail me, /
> Meet me with another pair.

or

> Gwine to roll in my Jesus' arms,
> Gwine to roll on my Jesus' breast.

and

> Fix me Jesus, fix me
> Fix me for my long white robe
> Fix me for my starry crown
> Fix me for my journey home
> Fix me for my dying bed.

With confidence the inspired singers of the spirituals cried out

> Didn't my lord deliver Daniel / Didn't my lord
>   deliver Daniel
> Didn't my lord deliver Daniel / And, why not
>   every man?
> The moon run down in a purple stream.
> The sun forbear to shine
> And every star disappear,
> King Jesus shall be mine.
> Didn't my lord deliver Daniel / Didn't my lord
>   deliver Daniel
> Didn't my lord deliver Daniel / And, why not
>   every man?

---

80. Ibid., 301, 302.
81. Ibid., 302.

I set my foot on the Gospel ship,
And the ship it begin to sail
It landed me over on Canaan's shore, /
And I'll never come back anymore

Crucified Lord

We should not be surprised that many spirituals focus on the suffering, the crucifixion, and death of Jesus. The enslaved folk knew in their bodies and minds, hearts and souls what it meant to endure suffering and abuse, and in Jesus's suffering and death they recognized their own. Slave narratives report some especially vicious types of punishment; two of these were called the *buck* and *staking*. In the buck, the slave was bent over or buckled, that is "doubl[ed] in two, until [the man's or woman's] legs were passed over [the] head, where they were kept by a stick passed across the back of [the] neck." While in this position the slave was whipped and the wounds caused by the lash were rubbed with salt and water and pepper.[82]

Staking called for the enslaved man or woman to be forced to lie face down on the ground, with arms and legs extended and tied to stakes; if the slave were a pregnant woman, a hole was dug for her extended belly. Lying in this "x-formation," the person would be flogged. One variation of this punishment required that the enslaved man's or woman's "hands be tied together with a rope, which was then thrown over the limb of a tree or over a beam." The person would be "pulled up till the toes only just reached the ground, feet tied together, and a rail or fence thrust between the legs with a weight on it to keep the body at full stretch."[83]

These types of punishment were not uncommon. It is not too much to assume that the descriptive realism of the spirituals regarding the suffering and death of Jesus draws on the very torture that the enslaved people endured. In the following spiritual of lament, the enslaved folk pour out an empathy for Jesus that

---

82. Yetman, ed., *Voices from Slavery*, 263.
83. Blassingame, ed., *Slave Testimony*, 220.

transcends limitations of time and space. They stood with Jesus in his sufferings, as he stood with them in theirs.

> They nail my Jesus down / They put him on the crown
>   of thorns
> O see my Jesus hangin' high! He look so pale an' bleed
>   so free:
> O don't you think it was a shame / He hung three
>   hours in dreadful pain?

And, there is this spiritual about the crucifixion:

> They crucified my Lord / They nailed him to the tree
> You hear the hammers ring / The blood came trickling
>   down . . .
> Those cruel people! Hammering!

Here is the prayer of another spiritual about the crucifixion and death of Jesus:

> Dey crucified my Lord / An' He never said a mumblin'
>   word.
> Dey crucified my Lord / An' He never said a mumblin'
>   word.
> Not a word—not a word—not a word.
> Dey nailed him to a tree / Dey pierced him in de side
> De blood came twinklin' down / He bowed his head
>   and died
> An' He never said a mumblin' word. / Not a word—
>   not a word—not a word.

Finally, there is this well-known sorrow psalm:

> Were you there when they crucified my Lord?
> Oh! Sometimes it causes me to tremble, tremble,
>   tremble.
> Were you there when they crucified my Lord?
> Were you there when they nailed Him to the tree?
> Were you there when they pierced Him in the side?

Were you there when the sun refused to shine?
Were you there when they laid him in the tomb?

The enslaved people gave great attention and care in this spiritual to represent the suffering that Jesus endured. Lovell writes that the enslaved singer portrays a grave "great wrong [being] committed under the eyes of frightened or uncaring people. For the wrongs of humankind, the finger points to us all. We are all guilty, not so much for what we do, as what we allow to happen. And without a doubt, the slave singer was including [chattel] slavery . . . in the bill of indictment."[84] The repeated inquiry "Were you there?" challenges each person to place him or herself at the scene of crucifixion, to acknowledge her or his collusion with this evil. Lovell's comments are reinforced by the inclusion, in some variants of this spiritual, of verses that confess, "I wuz dere win dey nailed 'im to der cross."[85]

Mrs. Brown, a freed woman living near Nashville, remarked that she first heard the spiritual "I'm Troubled in Mind" from her father when she was a child. After he had been whipped, her father always went and sat upon a certain log near his cabin, and with tears streaming down his face sang the following song:

Oh Jesus, my saviour on thee I'll depend,
When troubles are near me, you'll be my friend.
    If Jesus don't help me, I will surely die.
When laden with trouble and laden with grief,
To Jesus in secret I'll go for relief.
    If Jesus don't help me, I will surely die.
In dark days of bondage to Jesus I prayed,
to help me bear it, and he gave me aid.
    If Jesus don't help me, I will surely die.[86]

We may be tempted to read this refrain as an example of using religion as escape or a soporific: "If Jesus don't help me, I will

---

84. Lovell, *Black Song*, 304.

85. Ibid.

86. *Jubilee Songs as Sung by the Jubilee Singers of Fisk University* (New York: Biglow & Main, 1872), 58.

surely die." Rather, this refrain stands as an affirmation of faith and hope, not doubt or submission; an assertion of confidence, not indecision.

The enslaved people faced their suffering and oppression through nourishing their interior lives in prayer. One person declared that in prayer, "My mind gets fixed on God and I feel a deep love, joy, and desire to be with God."[87] For many of the people, to nourish and expand the *inscape*[88] of their natural desire for God was an act of defiance.

A man known as Praying Jacob was held in bondage in the state of Maryland by a master of exceptional cruelty.

> Jacob's rule was to pray three times a day, at just such an hour of the day; no matter what his work was or where he might be, he would stop and go and pray. His master has been to him and pointed his gun at him, and told him if he did not cease praying he would blow out his brains. Jacob would finish his prayer and then tell his master to shoot in welcome—your loss will be my gain—I have two masters, one on earth and one in heaven—master Jesus in heaven, master Saunders on earth. I have a soul and a body; the body belongs to you, master Saunders, and the soul to Jesus.[89]

"For whosoever will save his life shall lose it; but whosoever shall lose his life for my sake and the gospel's, the same shall save it. For what shall it profit a man, if he shall gain the whole world, and lose his own soul?" (Mark 8:35–36). Praying Jacob disarmed slavery's power over his body through committed Christian discipleship. Death had no power over him; he was a follower of Jesus

---

87. Earl, *Dark Symbols, Obscure Signs*, 23.

88. The term "inscape" comes from the poetic theory of Gerard Manley Hopkins and refers to a person's unique inner nature; see Gerard Manley Hopkins, *The Major Works*, ed. Catherine Phillips (Oxford: Oxford University Press, 1986, 2002), 214, 215.

89. G. W. Offley, *A Narrative of the Life and Labors of Rev. G. W. Offley* (Hartford, Connecticut, 1860), in *Five Black Lives*, ed. Arna Bontemps (Middleton, CT: Wesleyan University Press, 1971), 134–35.

of Nazareth in word and deed. In Jesus, "slavery's children" found a wisdom through which to live so "that they might not perish in the howling wilderness of America."[90]

Dark Wisdom: What the "Old Slaves" Knew

"The old slaves didn't know nothing about books," a freed man remarked, "but they did know God. And knowing [God] they called on him in their trouble and distress, and I can testify that [God] heard them."[91] The knowledge of God the enslaved people possessed came not through intellectual analysis or book learning, although "book learning" was something they desired earnestly for their children. One may speak of the knowledge or the wisdom of the enslaved people as apophatic or dark wisdom, which signifies a wisdom expressed in paradox, a wisdom that countered the wisdom of the world. As one freed man expressed it, "Wisdom in the heart is unlike wisdom in the mind."[92] The enslaved people sought to live by this adage and thus gain a knowledge hidden from the world spawned by the slaveholders. Inasmuch as spirituals mediate the people's negotiation of their cruel situation, of their "otherness," of their blackness, these sacred incantations and chants mediate to us "dark symbols and obscure signs."[93]

In biblical literature, the dark of night signifies the presence of God, for God "dwells in the thick darkness" (1 Kgs 8:12), and "clouds and darkness are round about" the Lord God (Ps 97:2). Moreover, God makes the divine presence manifest in dreams and apparitions: "If there be a prophet among you, I the Lord will make myself known unto him in a vision, and will speak unto him in a dream" (Num 12:6); the child Samuel is called by God in a dream (1 Sam 3:1–10); divine communication comes to Nathan the

---

90. Callahan, *The Talking Book*, xii.

91. Johnson, ed., *God Struck Me Dead*, 70.

92. Ibid., 23.

93. Charles H. Long, "Structural Similarities and Dissimilarities in Black and African Theologies," *Journal of Religious Thought* 32, no. 2 (Fall/Winter 1975): 21; Riggins R. Earl Jr., *Dark Symbols, Obscure Signs: God, Self, and Community in the Slave Mind* (Maryknoll, NY: Orbis Books, 1993).

prophet at night (2 Sam 7:4); and the Lord appears to Joseph, the betrothed husband of Mary of Nazareth, in a dream (Matt 1:20). God is hidden and acts and works in the dark of night to bring the divine intention to fruition.

In these examples, knowledge of God, of God's will and purpose came by hearing, not by sight. Deprived of literacy—reading and writing—the enslaved people too came to knowledge of God, of God's will and purpose, and intimate knowledge of God's Son Jesus through hearing. The enslaved people listened as they stood near the open windows of churches or parlors. They talked and prayed and ruminated among themselves under the boughs of hush arbors, in thickets, or in rude cabins. They prayed silently at day during work in the fields, cried out in hurt at dark midnight. The enslaved people entrusted to memory and heart miracle stories and parables, events and sayings, names and places from the Hebrew Scriptures and Christian Testament. They selected and sifted, worked and shaped this material over and over again. They crafted imagery, fashioned symbols, plumbed meaning, structured musical architecture, and grafted themselves—their yearning and hopes, pain and suffering—into "the aural text." In the opaque enigma of their enslavement, the people prayed and sang and praised the God whom they believed would break the slavery chain at last.

What did the enslaved people know about God? What dark wisdom sprang from their oppression and suffering, their love of and identification with the crucified Jesus?

Here is some of their dark and hidden wisdom: The enslaved people knew themselves as "new creature[s] in Jesus, the workmanship of his hand saved from the foundation of the world." They knew themselves as "chosen vessel[s] before the wind ever blew or before the sun ever shined."[94] They trimmed their lamps and kept them burning on the "main altar of [their] heart[s]" as they waited for the Lord's coming.[95] Yet, even as they waited, they sought him out:

---

94. Johnson, ed., *God Struck Me Dead*, 111.
95. Ibid., 57.

Steal away, steal away, steal away to Jesus!
Steal away, steal away home,
I ain't got long to stay here.

In the dark, enslaved people slipped away to the quiet of thick brush arbors, hollows, or river banks to pray, to sing, to experience God in their misery and obscurity. There, as Susan Rhodes declared, God met them and became their consolation and their joy. There they sang "songs what come a-gushing up from the heart."[96] Like Spanish Carmelite mystic John of the Cross, they too were inflamed with "love's urgent longings"; they too went out into the dazzling dark with "no other light or guide than the [flame] that burned in [their] hearts."[97] The Spirit of the Lord descended, and they experienced an inflow of divine love that gushed up, uniting their hearts in prayer and song and shout that "made heaven ring."[98]

The enslaved people knew in their bruised bodies the power of prayer and openness to the Divine. From the intense and bewildering terror of the dimly lit holds of slave ships during the Middle Passage and the violence of enslavement, these women and men came to apprehend, experience, and surrender to absolute dependence on God. This is their gift of dark wisdom to all who encounter opaque joy wrapped around the "magisterial sorrow" of the spirituals.[99]

Here is some of their dark and hidden wisdom: They knew that no one who consumes human flesh could live. In other words, slavery was death dealing for the slaveholder and the slave trader, for all who lived off of the buying and selling, labor and skill, rape and torture of human beings. They knew the cross as the com-

96. Rawick, *From Sundown to Sunup*, 34.

97. John of the Cross, "The Dark Night," in *The Collected Works of St. John of the Cross*, rev. ed.; trans. Kiernan Kavanaugh, O.C.D. and Otilio Rodriguez, O.C.D. (Washington, DC: Institute of Carmelite Studies, 1991), 358, 359.

98. Rawick, *From Sundown to Sunup*, 40.

99. Matthew Johnson, *The Tragic Vision of African American Religion* (New York: Palgrave Macmillan, 2010), 86.

plete rejection of violence, the very "inversion of force,"[100] of mastery, of dominance. Meditating on stories of Jesus's ministry to the poor and oppressed, the enslaved people loved him as a "Bringer of Life." They understood "the otherness" of Jesus: He, too, was a stranger in a world of death and oppression, meanness and hate. Jesus was for them: "God's Black Slave who had come to put an end to human bondage."[101] Jesus's resurrection meant that death would not be the last word, that slavery would not be the last word. The God who vindicated Jesus would vindicate them. For "God labors on behalf of freedom in the cause of freedom to bring about the fullness of life."[102]

Here is some of their dark and hidden wisdom: The power of God in the cross was the power to live and to love—even when violence does its worst. The enslaved peoples knew that we cannot turn our backs on affliction and loss; the pain of such suffering lasts. Indeed, enslaved women and men wept wrenchingly for the loss of children, parents, husbands and wives—they did not forget. One old freed woman told of her vision and experience of God's love: "I rejoice ever in the love of God. The love of God is beyond understanding. It makes you love *everybody*."[103] So they loved, but never uncritically; they did not allow pain to numb the struggle for freedom.

When the enslaved people sang *"Lord, I want to be a Christian in my heart / Lord, I want to love everybody in my heart,"* they were praying for grace to incarnate a logic radically different from human logic. Human logic is a logic of equivalence, a forensic logic—punishment is exacting and justice is limited to a fairness of sameness, an eye for an eye, hatred for hatred. The enslaved people were seeking the grace of God's logic of "excess, of superabundance."[104] There could be no surrender of human agency

---

100. Paul Ricoeur, *Figuring the Sacred: Religion, Narrative, and Imagination* (Minneapolis, MN: Fortress Press, 1995), 279.

101. Cone, *The Spirituals and the Blues*, 49; Lovell, *Black Song*, 189.

102. Johnson, *The Tragic Vision*, 142.

103. Johnson, ed., *God Struck Me Dead*, 115.

104. Ricoeur, *Figuring the Sacred*, 279.

to hatred or violence. "Beloved, let us love one another; for love is of God; and every one that loveth is born of God, and knoweth God. He that loveth not God knoweth not God; for God is love. . . . Beloved, if God so loved us, we ought to love one another" (1 John 4:7–11).

Here is some of their dark and hidden wisdom: The power of God in the cross is its paradox—the unexpected, unimagined resurrection. God's logic interrupts, reveals, and projects justice, mercy, and love into the bleakest circumstances.

The dark wisdom of the enslaved people shows us that "being human is a *praxis*."[105] This wisdom teaches us what it means to live authentically, with integrity; to live mindfully and thus embody the seed of history, linking past-present-future, the ancestors and those yet to be born. The dark wisdom of the enslaved people teaches us all a love ethic that nurtures proper self-love (a love of blackness, a love that refuses cultural or racial-ethnic or class privilege). The dark wisdom of the enslaved people teaches a love ethic that demands that none of us are to love others uncritically.

The dark wisdom of the enslaved people teaches us that none of us is to be defined by victimization, but, like Jesus, by a commitment in the here and now to the realization of the reign of God. The dark wisdom of the enslaved people teaches us not how to avoid or deny suffering but how to suffer suffering.[106]

---

105. Katherine McKittrick, ed., *Sylvia Wynter: On Being Human as Praxis* (Durham and London: Duke University Press, 2015), 3–4.

106. Paul Ricoeur, "Toward a Hermeneutic of the Idea of Revelation," in *Essays on Biblical Interpretation*, ed. Lewis S. Mudge (Philadelphia: Fortress Press, 1980), 86.

CHAPTER TWO

Meeting and Seeing Jesus in Slaveholding Worlds

For the Son of Man came not to be served but to serve, and to give his life in a ransom for many.

—Mark 10:45

I uz dere win he walk'd in Galilee, Galilee . . .
Oh sometimes my trubbles make me trimble, trimble.
I uz dere win he walk'd in Galilee, Galilee.

—Negro Spiritual

All God's children going to sit together
One of these days, hallelujah.
I'm going sit at the welcome table,
One of these days, hallelujah.

—Negro Spiritual

Betrayed by members of their own communities or by hostile neighbors, captured, chained, then, force-marched to the Atlantic coast, various peoples for whom the African continent was home found themselves first in dark, foul dungeons, then aboard ships bound for an altogether other world. Once the vessels began the infamous Middle Passage, the peoples endured filth, severe beatings, sexual assault, immeasurable psychic trauma, and death.[1] The

---

1. Philip Curtin, *The Atlantic Slave Trade: A Census* (Madison, WI: University of Wisconsin Press, 1969), 275. Statistics suggest that from 15 to 30 percent of the captives died in the Middle Passage. This rate varies in relation to the nation

captive people were described by the whites who saw them as "sad, depressed, in shock," showing "every sign of affliction," despondency, despair, and "torpid insensibility."[2] *En route*, the people would have been compelled to transgress religio-cultural laws and customs that regulated personal modesty, contact between men and women, care of children.

The various African peoples found themselves scattered throughout the Americas:

> From Boston in New England to Montevideo in the Viceroyalty of La Plata, in gold-mining towns in central Brazil; on sugar cane plantations in Jamaica and Cuba; in the coffee-producing hills of Venezuela; on cotton and indigo estates in the southern regions of the USA; and in homes, streets, rivers, fields and even small factories everywhere in between, Africans and their descendants, in generations of bondage, encountered and helped create the new world.[3]

Denied inclusion in the category of "person," the enslaved people had neither legal nor political rights and endured the constant threat of psychological, bodily, and familial violation. The various permutations of enslavement with which they were confronted aimed to control, possess, and dominate, to render them "socially dead"[4] and reduced to property, commodity, and object. Still, the violence of the ontological (metaphysical) remains

---

operating or backing the merchant slave ship. For example, Curtin notes that in the earliest years of the trade, the casualty rate suffered by Africans on Portuguese vessels was about 15 percent, but after "nineteenth-century abolitionist pressure forced the slave-traders to take chances, the casualty rate rose to 25 to 30 per cent" (276).

2. Marcus Rediker, *The Slave Ship: A Human History* (New York: Viking Press, 2007), 17.

3. Rachel Elizabeth Harding, "You Got a Right to the Tree of Life: African American Spirituals and Religions of the Diaspora," *Cross Currents* 57, no. 2 (Summer 2007): 268–69.

4. Orlando Patterson, *Freedom in the Making of Western Culture* (New York: Basic Books, 1991), 5.

unmatched. Cultural critic Frank Wilderson writes: "Africans went into the ships and came out as Blacks. [This] is a human *and* a metaphysical holocaust."[5] In other words, the Middle Passage "destroy[ed] the possibility of ontology because it positions the Black in an infinite and indeterminately horrifying and open vulnerability, an object made available (which is to say fungible) for any subject."[6] And as Frantz Fanon declares, "the black has no ontological resistance in the eyes of the white man"[7]—indeed "in the eyes of Humanity."[8]

Slavery was not uniform in practice but rather, in each geographic area, shaped by necessity, economics, topography, climate, and human temperament. In the United States, slavery was never exclusively southern; slaveholding was practiced in Connecticut, Massachusetts, New York, and New Jersey, and slave shipbuilding thrived in Newport, Rhode Island, just as it did in Liverpool, England.[9] Slaveholders interrupted and controlled any gesture of psychic, interpersonal, cultural, or religious independence. Slaveholders named their human chattel, denied them use of their languages, forbade them to honor their customs or worship their gods. Few permitted stable marriages; toddlers were as likely to be sold as adults, and pregnant women were not exempt from beatings. On some geographically isolated farms or plantations, the enslaved people exerted some control over the affairs of their daily living, although never over their lives and persons. Work days, whether spent in fields or in house settings, were long and enervating. Still, the people shared and shaped, preserved and transmitted practices and attitudes reflective of their African-derived social structures and religio-cultural traditions.

---

5. Frank B. Wilderson III, *Red, White & Black: Cinema and the Structure of U.S. Antagonisms* (Durham and London: Duke University Press, 2010), 36. Kindle edition. Author's italics.

6. Ibid.

7. Frantz Fanon, *Black Skins, White Masks*, trans. Charles Lam Markmann (New York: Grove, 1967), 110.

8. Wilderson, *Red, White & Black*, 36. Kindle edition.

9. Ibid., 50–53.

With confidence and without any resort to sentimentality or exaggeration, we may say that the enslaved people negotiated this ontological and metaphysical assault by audaciously asserting their essential humanness in the face of dehumanizing conditions by choosing transcendence. Transcendence refers to exceeding or rising above ordinary or usual limits. Although tied closely to religious, spiritual, mystical, and aesthetic experiences, the movement of transcendence also may be related to cognitive, physical, and moral experiences. Religious and aesthetic consciousness compose crucial mediations of black individual and communal self-transcendence.

The preaching of salvation in Jesus of Nazareth had a decisive impact on the enslaved peoples, but Christianity did not exhaust black religious faith or religious practices or aesthetic sensibilities. Rather the enslaved people shaped and "fitted" Christian practices, rituals, symbols, myths, and values to their own condition, experiences, expectations, and needs.[10] At the same time, because so very much of the intimate life of the enslaved peoples was hidden from the master and overseer classes, indeed, from nearly all whites, it is not possible to pronounce with certainty the burial of the gods of Africa and the complete disappearance of the traditional religions that honored them. When enslaved Africans moaned,

> I've been 'buked an' I've been scorned,
> Dere is trouble all over dis worl',
> Ain' gwine lay my 'ligion down,
> Ain' gwine lay my 'ligion down,

we can never be completely sure which religion they refused to renounce.

The first section of this chapter considers the spirituals, the "oldest extant religio-cultural form in Black North American life."[11] These songs are simple, yet never simplistic; they possess what Afri-

---

10. Albert Raboteau, *Slave Religion: The "Invisible Institution" in the Antebellum South* (Oxford: Oxford University Press, 1975), 213.

11. Harding, "You Got a Right to the Tree of Life," 268–69.

can American Catholic priest and liturgist Clarence Rivers called "magnitude."[12] Historian Sterling Stuckey cautions against detaching the spirituals from their life setting or religio-cultural context; these psalms form an integral part of the larger and complex matrix of black religious experience and expression.[13] The enslaved people sung themselves a world, a *topos* far from the capricious brutality of slavery, and in that world they met and saw Jesus. The second section examines some aspects of the world in which Jesus of Nazareth lived and carried out his ministry, probes two sayings attributed to him regarding slaves and slavery, and considers the great christological hymn from Philippians. The third section reflects on Jesus as the enslaved people in the United States met him and saw him in the slave quarter. The fourth section sketches the meaning of Jesus for the enslaved people.

Singing a World: Spirituals as "Topos"

Despite massive, protracted suffering and anthropological poverty[14]—dispossessed of personhood, name, kin and culture, land, their very bodies—the enslaved people claimed privileged hermeneutical ground. Prohibited de jure and de facto from learning to read and/or to write, the people gained knowledge of the content, messages, and meanings of the Bible through public readings and sermons. Enslaved people seen or reported to have engaged in reading or writing were penalized and sometimes mutilated by having a finger or hand cut off.[15] Still, they persisted, often with the help of someone who had learned to read surreptitiously or the assistance

---

12. Clarence Joseph Rivers, *The Spirit in Worship* (Cincinnati: Stimuli, 1978), 199.

13. Sterling Stuckey, *Slave Culture: Nationalist Theory and the Foundations of Black America* (New York: Oxford University Press, 1987), 27.

14. The term comes from Engelbert Mveng, "Impoverishment and Liberation: A Theological Approach for Africa and the Third World," in *Paths of African Theology*, ed. Rosino Gibellini (Maryknoll, NY: Orbis Books, 1994), 154–65.

15. See John Lovell Jr., *Black Song: The Forge and the Flame—The Story of How the Afro-American Spiritual Was Hammered Out* (New York: Macmillan, 1972), 257.

of some white person who was willing to breach the laws against black literacy. Yet, whether with or without help, the people took confidence in their own determination and skill; some among them memorized chapters or portions of the Bible. These spoken fragments or passages became the subject of meditation, reflection, discussion, and even sermonic interpretation. Indeed, biblical revelation provided the enslaved people with material for the singular mystical and political mediation of their condition—the spirituals.[16] The Bible, as an "aural text," came under their creative, rhetorical, interpretative, and poetic genius. Thus, the enslaved people developed a tradition of African American interpretation.

The people formed an "aural text," a life-affirming canon. Womanist theologian Delores Williams maintains that the composition of this aural text was a communal process: From among biblical texts preached in sermons or passages read aloud at (white) church services or family prayers, members of the enslaved community listened, evaluated, judged, and selected life-affirming texts. These texts were committed to memory, repeated, and reshaped. Cleansed of vicious meanings, these passages became the subject of meditation, reflection, and sermonic interpretation among the enslaved people. As Renita Weems points out, the people were not tied intellectually or morally to any particular written text or translation or interpretation; the text they developed revealed affinities with the prophetic and apocalyptic traditions of the Hebrew and Christian scriptures. These passages or stories or sayings were handed down from generation to generation, through story and song and moral prescription. These texts were judged as the true word of God in the Bible.

For people dispossessed of land, the Bible as aural/oral text functioned as what historian of religions Charles Long calls a *topos*. In other words, the Bible became for the enslaved people and their descendants "an intimate and familiar place . . . a place that one's ancestors [knew and] humanized . . . a [place of] wisdom for

---

16. James Weldon Johnson, ed., *The Book of American Negro Spirituals* (New York: Viking Press, 1925), 20.

coming generations."[17] They accomplished this by "decod[ing] the textual string with the necessary objectivity and accuracy . . . in an attempt to respond to the otherness, inventiveness, and singularity" of the text.[18] The Bible became a place or *topos*, a symbolic world, a ground on which they might meet and see Jesus.

Poet and literary critic James Weldon Johnson believed that many spirituals were the work of highly gifted individuals. On the other hand, novelist and folklorist Zora Neale Hurston maintained that the spirituals are "Negro religious songs, sung by a group, and a group bent on expression of feelings and not on sound effects."[19] When asked about the composition of their religious songs, some enslaved people replied: "De Lord jes' put hit en our mouf. We is ignorant, and de Lord puts ebry word we says en our mouf."[20] The people knew that slaveholders and whites were committed to preventing them from learning to read and to write. Their frequent, surreptitious, and sometimes successful attempts were met with vicious punishment. To attribute authorship of their songs to divine power dissembles, even as it affirms communion and union with Divine Spirit.

One freed woman from Kentucky insisted that the words of the spirituals were sung to traditional African tunes and familiar songs:

> Us ole head use ter make 'em on de spurn of de moment, after we wressle wid de Spirit and come [through]. But the tunes was brung from Africa by our grandaddies. Dey was jis 'miliar song . . . dey calls 'em spirituals, case de Holy Spirit done

---

17. Charles H. Long, "Structural Similarities and Dissimilarities in Black and African Theologies," *Journal of Religious Thought* 32, no. 2 (Fall/Winter 1975): 12, 13. Of course, the Bible was/is not such a *topos* for *all* black people as womanists Renita Weems and Delores Williams, among others, have noted.

18. Derek Attridge, *The Singularity of Literature* (London and New York: Routledge, 2004), loc. 1639 of 4038, Kindle.

19. Zora Neale Hurston, *The Sanctified Church* (Berkeley, CA: Turtle Island, 1983), 80.

20. M. V. Bales, "Some Negro Folk Songs of Texas," in *Follow de Drinkin' Gou'd,* ed., James Dobie (Austin: Texas Folklore Society, 1928), 85.

revealed 'em to 'em. Some say [Master] Jesus taught 'em, and I's seed 'em start in meetin'. We'd all be at the "prayer house" de Lord's Day and de white preacher he'd splain de word and read whar Ezekiel done say, "Dry bones gwine ter lib again." And, honey, de Lord would come a-shining [through] dem pages and revive dis ole [woman's] heart, and I'd jump up dar and den and holler and shout and sing and pat, and dey would all [catch] de words . . . dey's all take it up and keep at it, and keep a-addin to it and den it would be a spiritual.[21]

When this same query about the making of the spirituals was put to one man, he responded this way:

I'll tell you; it's dis way. My master call me up and order me a short peck of corn and a hundred lash. My friends see it and is sorry for me. When dey come to de praise meeting dat night dey sing about it. Some's very good singers and know how; —dey work it in, work it in, you know; till dey get it right; and dat's de way.[22]

A spiritual takes form in the moaned or sung utterance of an enslaved woman or man in response to or about a given experience that had communal and/or universal application.[23] In and through song, one man's or one woman's experience of sorrow or shout of jubilation became that of a people. And, without a doubt, the spirituals are gifts of the Spirit. In creation and performance, the spirituals are marked by flexibility, spontaneity, and improvisation. The pattern of call–response allowed for the rhythmic weaving or manipulation of time, text, and pitch, while the response or repetitive chorus provided a recognizable and stable foundation for the extemporized lines of the soloist or leader. Moreover, the creation and performance of the spirituals were nourished by the African

---

21. Raboteau, *Slave Religion*, 244–45.

22. James Weldon Johnson and J. Rosamond Johnson, *The Books of American Negro Spirituals* (New York: Da Capo Press, 1969, 1989), 11–12.

23. Mark Fisher, *Negro Slave Songs in the United States* (New York: Citadel Press, 1953), 176.

disposition for aesthetic performance—for *doing* the beautiful—in dance and song.

The spirituals provide access to the "experience[s], expression[s], motivations, intentions, behaviors, styles, and rhythms" of black religio-cultural life.[24] These songs open a window on the religious, social, aesthetic, and psychological worldview of a people. They are best appreciated when we imagine them, not concertized with dissonances "ironed out," but moaned in jagged irregular harmony, falsetto breaking in and keys changing with emotion, and returned to rude wooden-plank cabins or "woods, gullies, ravines, and thickets" (aptly called brush arbors or hush arbors), an overturned iron pot nearby.[25] The songs are inextricably linked to African American adaptations of religious rituals, including funeral and burial ceremonies. Invariably these rites included hand clapping or the stomping of feet, which would have compensated on many plantations for the outlawed drum. The spiritual is linked most intimately to the staid shuffling of the ring-shout. A distinct form of worship, the ring-shout is basically a dancing–singing phenomenon in which the song is danced with the whole body—hands, feet, shoulders, hips. When the spiritual is sounded, the ring-shout begins: The dancers form a circle and move counterclockwise in a ring, first walking slowly, then literally shuffling—the foot just slightly lifted from the floor. Sometimes the people danced silently; most often they sang the chorus of the spiritual as they shuffled; at other times, the dancers themselves sang the song. Frequently, a group of the best singers stood at the side of the room to "base" the others, singing the stanzas of the song and clapping their hands. The dancing and singing would increase in intensity and energy and sometimes went on for hours.[26]

The language employed in the spirituals is intensely poetic and expressive, thick with metaphor, richly ornamented, and poignant.

---

24. Charles H. Long, *Significations: Signs, Symbols, and Images in the Interpretation of Religion* (Philadelphia: Fortress Press, 1986), 7.

25. Hurston, *The Sanctified Church*, 80.

26. Ibid., 70–71.

The vocabulary is filled with vivid simile, creative and effective jux-taposition of images. Rooted in the experience of oppression and suffering, this highly charged symbolic language is most fundamen-tally a language of joy and mysticism in the midst of survival and resistance. Stephen Henderson argues that the language of the spir-ituals is filled with "mascon" images and symbols. With the term "mascon," Henderson notes that "[certain] words and constructions seem to carry an inordinate [connotative] charge of emotional [reli-gious, and spiritual] weight." More precisely, the term denotes "mas-sive concentrations of Black experiential/existential/energy" that powerfully affects the meanings of black speech, song, and poetry.[27]

The language of the spirituals resonates with language that reflects contours of the anamnetic, charismatic, midrashic, and apocalyptic. In anamnetic language or the language of memory, the spirituals venerate and honor the ancestors, the more than twenty million African women and men who disappeared in the Middle Passage, whose bones litter the floor of the Atlantic. Surely, they shall rise on the last day to meet Jesus face to face; the mother or father, wife or husband, brother or sister sold away at whim. In charismatic language, the spirituals sing confidently of the power and gifts of the Spirit to bring life out of death and despair, to bring health and wholeness out of pain, to pour joy into broken hearts. In midrashic language, the spirituals reshape, retell, and conflate characters and stories, parables and pericopes, events and miracles of the Hebrew Bible and Christian Testament. These songs tell the mercy of God anew and testify to the ways in which the enslaved people met Jesus of Nazareth in the slave quarter, at the whipping post, on the auction block, in the hush arbor, in the midnight hour, in flight to freedom. In apocalyptic language, the spirituals weave the stories of women and men who hope and trust in the liberating promises of the merciful reign of God. The spirituals are expect-ant and evocative—healing and creating life for those outcast, oppressed, and marginalized; projecting a new future for God's

---

27. Stephen Henderson, *Understanding the New Black Poetry: Black Speech & Black Music as Poetic References* (New York: William Morrow, 1973), 43.

little ones in Jesus. To borrow a phrase from Walter Benjamin, the spirituals are "shot through with chips of messianic time."[28]

In the spirituals, a distinctive history of salvation takes place before our very eyes, and *we* are included in it. The spirituals dialogue with the scriptures, wrestle with passages and sayings, lay the religio-cultural experiences of the enslaved peoples beside those of the ancient Israelites—and do so with confident expectation that the Lord God of Hosts will deliver, comfort, and console them. In the spirituals, a distinctive history of salvation takes place before our very eyes, and we are included in it. The spirituals dialogue with the scriptures, wrestle with passages and sayings, lay the religio-cultural experiences of the enslaved peoples beside those of the ancient Israelites and do so with confident expectation that the Lord God of Hosts will deliver, comfort, and console them. Two final comments: First, the language of the spirituals is highly self-critical. The singer admits what slaveholders refuse to admit—the enslaved man and woman is a human being who can, may, and does sin against God and neighbor: "It's me, O Lord, standin' in the need of prayer." Second, the language makes unambiguously clear that God will bring about justice, but never are these songs tainted by hatred or revenge.

Jesus in the Slaveholding World of the First Century

"And it came to pass in those days, that Jesus came from Nazareth of Galilee, and was baptized of John in Jordan" (Mark 1:9). After forty days of prayer and fasting in the wilderness, he takes up an itinerant ministry, moving around the villages of Galilee, proclaiming his message and performing it through startling miracles, cures, and exorcisms, and sharing table fellowship with a remarkably diverse socio-cultural group of men and women. He calls disciples, preaches to crowds, engages in public debates, and before too long provokes the indignation of ruling social and cultural elites and religious leaders, and attracts the attention of the Roman authorities.

---

28. Walter Benjamin, "Theses on the Philosophy of History," in *Illuminations: Essays and Reflections* (New York: Harcourt, Brace, Jovanovich, 1968), 263.

An itinerant preacher, Jesus spoke and taught in synagogues, in private homes, in the open countryside. He prayed often, not only in formal worship but also in private. N. T. Wright observes, "Apart from an early period in the wilderness [Jesus] did not fast—which distinguished him and his followers from other pious Jews."[29] He ate and drank and with sinners and "kept company with people normally on or beyond the borders of respectable society—which of course, in his day and culture, meant not merely social respectability but religious uprightness, proper covenant behavior, loyalty to the traditions and hence to the aspirations of Israel."[30]

With acts of healing, with stories, and parables of "welcome and warning," Jesus advanced a distinctive prophetic praxis on behalf of the kingdom of God.[31] This praxis was, at once, historical and eschatological, ethical and moral, political and religious, personal and communal. It narrated and dramatized reversal and transformation, "invert[ed] the usual ways of thinking about power and authority,"[32] and demanded personal conversion and new solidarities. His praxis appropriated and took as its imperative the ancient jubilee traditions of Israel, and, ever so subversively, enacted the result of the human encounter with the compassionate, yet searing sovereignty of God.

In the context of the spirituals, Galilee is the "home country of Jesus and his friends—slaves in the front ranks—and the meeting place of the faithful."[33] In the past few decades, scholars have ascertained that Galilee was a place of mixed race and ethnicity, of startling cultural diversity. Had they known this, the enslaved people would have been reassured: They too were women and men of mixed race and ethnicity, of startling cultural diversity. Scholars also have generated a large corpus of archaeological and historical

---

29. N. T. Wright, *Jesus and the Victory of God*, vol. 2, *Christian Origins and the Question of God* (Minneapolis: Fortress Press, 1996), 149.

30. Ibid.

31. Ibid., 243, 280.

32. Sharon H. Ringe, "Luke's Gospel: 'Good News to the Poor' for the Non-Poor," in *The New Testament: Introducing the Way of Discipleship*, ed. Wes Howard-Brook and Sharon H. Ringe (Maryknoll, NY: Orbis Books, 2002), 13.

33. Lovell, *Black Song*, 258, 260–61.

studies on Galilee that suggest the villagers of lower Galilee were composed of skilled artisans, carpenters, blacksmiths, and stone-masons; laborers and workers, small farmers or sharecroppers, and fishermen.[34] Had they known this, the enslaved people surely would have been reassured, for they too were people of many and diverse skill, talent, and interest. Scholars have shown that the villagers of lower Galilee resisted both Roman military occupation and intimidation and Herod's economic exploitation and expropriation. These Galileans yearned and fought for freedom.[35] Had they known this, the enslaved people would have been encouraged, for they too yearned for and loved freedom.

Jesus did not hesitate to address the "spiritual and psycho-emotional toll that the elitism and arrogance of the priests [and upper classes] imposed upon the beleaguered Galileans."[36] He affirmed these humble people: "Blessed are you who are poor, for yours is the kingdom of God. Blessed are you who are hungry now, for you will be filled. Blessed are you who weep now, for you will laugh" (Luke 6:20). Somehow the enslaved people heard his words, for they sang up a kingdom where they could sit at the welcome table eating and drinking their fill, where they could tell God how they were treated, where they could sit and talk with Jesus. Jesus defended the struggles of poor Galilean peasant folk with words of reassurance.[37] He said: "Many who are first will be last; the last will be first" (Mark 10:31). Somehow the enslaved people heard those words, for they sang, "everybody talkin' about heaven ain't going there."

---

34. Richard Horsley, *Galilee: History, Politics, People* (Valley Forge, PA: Trinity Press International, 1995); idem, *Archaeology, History and Society in Galilee: The Social Context of Jesus and the Rabbis* (Valley Forge, PA: Trinity Press International, 1996).

35. John Dominic Crossan, *God and Empire: Jesus against Rome, Then and Now* (New York: HarperCollins Publishers, 2008); Halvor Moxnes, *Putting Jesus in His Place: A Radical Vision of Household and Kingdom* (Louisville and London: Westminster John Knox, 2003), esp. 142–57.

36. Obery M. Hendricks, *The Politics of Jesus: Rediscovering the True Revolutionary Nature of the Teachings of Jesus and How They Have Been Corrupted* (New York: Doubleday, 2006), 73.

37. Ibid.

That the New Testament has become so familiar to believers is a wondrous and treasured good. At the same time, it is no surprise that we believers overlook and ignore, read without actually grasping or confronting, the slavery and slaveholding that formed the backdrop of the New Testament. While slavery in the Greco-Roman world differed from chattel slavery in the United States, it was no less cruel and inhumane; enslaved persons, Jennifer Glancy writes, lived in bodily vulnerability and in fear.[38]

During his youth in Nazareth, Jesus well may have heard stories of the rebellion in the Galilean town of Sepphoris. Three Roman legions were required to quell the uprising; two thousand men were crucified, and the entire population of Sepphoris was sold into slavery.[39] In Galilee, Jesus may well have encountered enslaved people belonging to the Herodian household; in Judea, he may well have come into contact with enslaved people owned by members of the Roman military.[40] References to slavery, slaveholders, and enslaved persons appear in several of the parables and stories that Jesus tells. In the Gospels of Matthew (8:5–13) and Luke (7:1–10), a centurion appeals to Jesus to heal his slave, and Jesus does so. Glancy compiles a list of historical figures who plausibly *could have been* slaveholders:

> the leader of a synagogue, identified in Mark and Luke as Jairus, who requests healing for his daughter (Matt 19:16–22; Mk 5:21–34; Lk 8:40–55); the rich young man who approaches Jesus to ask about eternal life (Matt 19:16–22; Mk 10:17–22; in Lk 18:18–25, a rich ruler); the Syrophoenician woman (Mk 7:24–30; cf. Matt 15:21–28); and Nicodemus (who first appears in Jn 3:1–10).[41]

A detailed discussion of slaveholding in early Christianity or in the Gospels is beyond the scope of this work. But by reviewing some

---

38. Jennifer A. Glancy, *Slavery as Moral Problem in the Early Church and Today* (Minneapolis: Fortress Press, 2011), 5.

39. Ibid., 9.

40. Ibid., 10.

41. Ibid., 13.

key texts, we can begin to uncover the position of enslaved people in slaveholding antiquity: (1) the parable of the tenants in Mark; (2) a saying of Jesus regarding slavery in Mark; and (3) the great christological hymn included in Paul's letter to the Philippians.

1. In the Markan version of the parable of the tenants (12:1–11), the owner of a vineyard leases it to tenants and goes off to another country. When he sends his slaves to collect the rent, the tenants beat the first slave, insult and beat the second slave in such a way as to highlight his dishonored condition, and kill the third slave. The vineyard owner continues to send other slaves to collect the rent, and tenants subject these slaves to the same treatment. Confident that the tenants will respect and honor his son, the man sends him to the vineyard. The tenants seize the son, kill him, and toss his body outside the vineyard as a sign of dishonor and disrespect. The murder of his son incites the owner of the vineyard; he retaliates and destroys the tenants.

The parable puzzles: "Is this father out of his mind? How could he send his son off to likely death in the midst of these vicious tenants?"[42] We modern readers shudder at the murder of the son and heir, but we may fail to pause sufficiently to take in the abuse and murder of the slaves. The Markan Jesus demonstrates, Glancy argues, an "awareness of the conditions in which slaves lived—in a permanent state of dishonor, which left them vulnerable to bodily abuse."[43] But the "impact" of the parable, she points out, "relies on the contrast between the dishonored bodies of slaves and the honorable body of the son."[44] The people of Galilee quite likely were accustomed to the ubiquitous presence of slaves, but the parable challenges hearers (and us) *to see, to hear, to feel* the beatings, insults, dishonor, and murder from within the skin of slaves.

If the enslaved people in the United States had heard this parable, they would have recalled their own fear and helplessness or that of

42. William C. Placher, *Mark,* Belief: A Theological Commentary on the Bible (Louisville, KY: Westminster John Knox, 2010), 167.

43. Jennifer A. Glancy, *Slavery in Early Christianity* (Minneapolis: Fortress Press, 2006), 104.

44. Ibid., 105.

relatives or friends who may have been sent on an errand outside the grounds of the plantation. If the enslaved people in the United States had heard this parable, they would have recalled how enslaved women felt fear and vulnerability as they moved about the plantation, for slavery put black women's bodies on display and rendered them sexually accessible to slaveholders, overseers, and other white men. The slaveholder's ability to induce feelings of anxiety and vulnerability, fear and insecurity in those enslaved was a strategy of dominance. Black bodies had no defense against the putative legality of slavery. Consider the case of Solomon Northup, a free black man, who was kidnapped and held in bondage for twelve years; or Margaret Garner, whose escape to freedom was thwarted by the Fugitive Slave Acts of 1793 and 1850. These laws rendered all black people subject to enslavement, whether or not they were born into freedom. These laws authorized and enabled local government officials to capture and return enslaved people to slaveholders.

2. A second saying of the Markan Jesus regarding slavery is this: "Whoever wishes to become great among you must be your servant, and whoever wishes to be first among you must be slave of all" (Mark 10:43–44). This saying stands in opposition to systems and practices of slaveholding. Although this instruction, as Glancy comments, does not appear in the Gospel of John, Jesus enacts or performs this saying during the last hours of his life. He takes on the role of the slave charged with foot washing and washes the feet of the disciples: "So, if I, your Lord and Teacher, have washed your feet, you also ought to wash one another's feet. For I have set you an example, that you also should do as I have done to you" (John 13:14–15). Foot washing in the ancient world was among the most loathsome tasks; in a large and/or wealthy household it would have been performed by the least regarded among those enslaved, usually a woman. Jesus, whom his disciples know as rabbi, as teacher, enfleshes what it means to be a slave of all. Moreover, Jesus calls his followers to do as he does, to be of complete and utter service to one another; he upends the world of lords and masters, servants and slaves.

3. The third text comes from Paul's letter to the Philippians, 2:5–8. This famous passage has been and remains the subject of

serious scholarly research and study, and a large number of publications have been and continue to be devoted to its interpretation. Stephen Davis observes that this christological hymn is "an
exegetical and lexical minefield, and there has been controversy
about it from the early church until today."[45] The letter in which
this hymn is included was written to a Christian community in
Philippi in eastern Macedonia about 62 CE. My discussion is limited to what this passage discloses about the social world in which
early Christianity developed and the impact of that social world on
early Christianity.

> Let the same mind be in you that was in Christ Jesus,
> who, though he was in the form of God,
> did not regard equality with God
> as something to be exploited,
> but emptied himself,
> taking the form of a slave,
> being born in human likeness.
> And being found in human form,
> he humbled himself
> and became obedient to the point of death—
> even death on a cross. (Philippians 2:5–8)

Paul frequently employs the terms slavery and slave, liberation
and freedom in his letters. But this usage, Sheila Briggs argues,
confronts us with "the fact that the material reality of the social
relationship [master-slave] has been transformed into a metaphor,
that the cultural, including the religious imagination of the Greco-
Roman world, [was] bounded by the mentality of a slave society."[46]
Thus, the grammar of slavery and its attendant meanings function to illustrate the moral condition of the human person (i.e.,
slaves to sin, but freed in Christ) even as that grammar sidesteps

---

45. Stephen T. Davis, "Is Kenosis Orthodox?," in *Exploring Kenotic Christology: The Self-Emptying God,* ed. C. Stephen Evans (Oxford: Oxford University
Press, 2006), 130.

46. Sheila Briggs, "Can an Enslaved God Liberate? Hermeneutical Reflections
on Philippians 2:6–11," *Semeia* 47 (1989): 143.

slavery as a social institution. In the hymn from Philippians, "Paul tells the story of Jesus himself as a saga of reduction to and release from bondage."[47] By casting Jesus in the role of slave, "the hymn emphasizes his obedience to God, and his death on the cross."[48] The hymn neither critiques nor apologizes for slavery, but rather theologically reduplicates the social reality of enslavement and maps that onto Christian living and spirituality.[49] Glancy writes, "The impact of the hymn depends upon boundary crossing. One possessing a high status (in the form of God) assumes a low status (in the form of a slave). . . . The Christ hymn depends on recognition of the shocking humiliation and definitive vindication of one who originally and ultimately bore a God likeness."[50]

That impact would have been felt by slaveholders, *not* by slaves, by oppressors, *not* the oppressed. For nearly two thousand years, we Christians followed the line carved out by Paul and employed slavery as a spiritual and theological metaphor of a "model of dependence and self-surrender."[51] Over that period, with rare exception, did it occur to us to challenge the existence of slavery, the conditions of "social death" and its "paradox of introducing [the enslaved] as a nonbeing"?[52] Not surprisingly, enslavement cultivates desire for personal, sovereignal, and civic freedom. But when such desire is so spiritualized, the concrete desire for freedom is subverted and gives way to a damaging detachment from the social matrix and the short- and long-term fate of human persons within it.

The New Testament places no direct condemnation of slavery nor any defense of slaveholders in the mouth of Jesus. His actions teach his disciples, then and now, a new way of being in and for the world and for one another. But almost from the beginning, we

---

47. Glancy, *Slavery in Early Christianity*, 100.

48. Ibid., 101.

49. Briggs, "Can an Enslaved God Liberate?," *Semeia* 47 (1989): 143.

50. Glancy, *Slavery in Early Christianity*, 101.

51. David Brion Davis, *The Problem of Slavery in Western Culture* (Ithaca, NY: Cornell University Press, 1966), 90.

52. Orlando Patterson, *Slavery and Social Death: A Comparative Study* (Cambridge, MA: Harvard University Press, 1982), 38.

followers of Jesus compromised the Gospel; rather than fitting our lives into its radical demands, we cheapened the gospel, forced its accommodation to our social and cultural worldviews. As Glancy concludes: "A community that conforms itself to him has no places for masters."[53]

Jesus in the Quarter

In the New Testament, Jesus offers no explicit condemnation of slavery; in the "slave quarter," he actively opposes slavery and oppression. The makers of the spirituals identified Jesus as "the slave's only recognized master."[54] They wanted to be like him:

> Lord, I want to be like Jesus
> In-a my heart . . .

They wanted to imitate "his royal manner, his performance of useful and difficult services, his desire that every [human person] be free (for this he died), his concern for the poor and the troubled."[55] The makers of the spirituals sang,

> My soul is a witness for my Lord,
> My soul is a witness for my Lord.

The enslaved people grasped that Jesus had been humble, but he had not been or felt himself "inferior." A song called "The Gift of God" sums up their case:

> When I was seeking Jesus,
> And thought he couldn't be found,
> The grace of God came in my soul,
> And turned me all around.[56]

Given the brutal conditions of enslavement, the peoples' appeals to divine power are not surprising. Indeed, the story of the deliverance of the people of Israel from Egyptian enslavement "became an archetype which enabled the [enslaved people] to live with

---

53. Glancy, *Slavery as Moral Problem*, 26.
54. Lovell, *Black Song*, 276.
55. Ibid., 189.
56. Ibid., 290.

promise."[57] Over time, the enslaved people came to understand the Christian God as an omnipotent and moral deity, responsible for creation and capable of intervening in history. They responded to formal Christian trinitarian discourse with an experiential distinction, borrowing Christian language to express their own understanding of their religious experience and sensibilities. While praising the "Great Supreme Being, who stood by them in the past days of slavery,"[58] the enslaved people and their descendants found a friend, companion, and fellow sufferer in Jesus. He embodied the "notion of the deity as companion and creator, a deity related more to the human condition than deities of the sky, and the subjection of this deity in the hands of human beings."[59]

Thus, the story of Jesus gripped the imaginations of the enslaved peoples. They took Jesus to themselves: the cruelty of his suffering was like their own. Jesus stands at the center of their *topos*—touching, healing, and accompanying them in life's lonesome journey. They sang: He is "rock in a weary land," a "shelter in a storm," and "a little talk with Jesus makes it right." Jesus was the fellow sufferer whose healing touch soothed the burning ache of their salted wounds; he was the companion who wrapped his arms tightly around bodies drenched in sweat from hard work and blood from whippings. Jesus was the friend who kissed their hands torn and bruised from cutting sugar cane or picking cotton. Jesus consoled mothers whose children were sold away; he stood in seething anger beside men whose wives and daughters were raped; he wept hot tears with children whose parents were humiliated. Jesus was the companion who stood by them in the midst of affliction and restored their dignity. No wonder, the maker of the spiritual sang,

> I want Jesus to walk with me / All along my pilgrim
> journey,

---

57. Long, *Significations*, 179.

58. Esau Jenkins, *Been in the Storm So Long: A Collection of Spirituals, Folk Tales and Children's Games from Johns Island, South Carolina*, Folkways Smithsonian (1966–67; Audio CD January 1990).

59. Long, *Significations*, 184n15.

> Lord, I want Jesus to walk with me.
> In my trials, Lord walk with me / When my heart is
>   almost breaking,
> Lord, I want Jesus to walk with me.

Jesus was the comforter in time of trouble and in the most intimate moments of anguish. So, the spiritual cries

> Give me Jesus, Give me Jesus,
> You may have all this world
> Give me Jesus.

Like the excluded, despised, and impoverished children, women, and men who crowd the pages of the Gospels, the enslaved folk relied on, leaned on Jesus. Like African sacred medicine (*Kongo nkisi*), the very name of Jesus brought relief and delight: "I love Jesus for his name's so sweet / I'm just now from the fountain, His name's so sweet"; "Jesus Christ is first and last, No man works like him"; "Fix me, Jesus, fix me"; "I know the Lord has laid his hands on me." The enslaved people saw themselves, read themselves, inscribed themselves on the pages of the Bible. Jesus was for them! Jesus placed his very body between the despised, excluded, and poor and the powers and principalities of the world. They sensed the "otherness" of Jesus; he, too, was a stranger in a world of death and oppression.

Jesus Means Freedom

Freedom was the preeminent theme of black religion, and the enslaved people prayed ardently for freedom. Alice Sewell recalled that the enslaved people prayed for freedom . . . "pray[ed] together to God that if we don't live to see it, to please let our [children] live to see a better day and be free.[60] Mrs. Sewell offers an astonishing testimony to the transcendent dimension of human being: Enslaved women and men prayed for a different future for their

---

60. Norman R. Yetman, ed., *Voices from Slavery* (New York: Holt, Rinehart and Winston, 1970), 263.

children. The freedom for which enslaved people prayed proved impatient of political or social or spiritual or religious distinctions; rather, the freedom for which the enslaved people longed, struggled, fought, and died was holistic—at once, political *and* social, psychic *and* spiritual, metaphysical *and* ontological, this-worldly *and* other-worldly.[61] The spirituals throw out a lifeline that "strengthens, blesses, and animates being."[62] The people run to Jesus; he *is* freedom; he *is* the tree of life.

The enslaved people understood Jesus Christ as the Bringer of Freedom. Thus, long before the seminal theological studies of Ernst Käsemann or James Cone or Gustavo Gutiérrez, oppressed black people in the United States knew in mind and heart that Jesus *meant* freedom; Jesus *was* freedom.[63] They formulated this christological affirmation on the basis of the critical aural text they created and from qualities of spiritedness, courage, and love for the weak expressed in their folktales and stories.[64] Howard Thurman stated: "It was dangerous to let the slave understand that the life and teachings of Jesus meant freedom for the captive and release for those held in economic, social, and political bondage."[65] A fearless and dangerous Jesus, unlike the "model servant" or "compliant slave" breaks the crippling spell cast by the dominant culture. A fearless and dangerous Jesus will set the Spirit working free in the midst of those yearning to be free. A fearless and dangerous Jesus waits with God's crucified people. He knows them and they know him . . . they know Jesus Christ crucified.

---

61. See Henry Mitchell, *Black Belief* (San Francisco: Harper & Row, 1975), 120.

62. Harding, "You Got a Right to the Tree of Life," 267.

63. Ernst Käsemann, *Jesus Means Freedom* (Philadelphia: Fortress Press, 1977); James H. Cone, *A Black Theology of Liberation* (Maryknoll, NY: Orbis Books, 1990; orig. 1971), Gustavo Gutiérrez, *A Theology of Liberation: History, Politics, and Salvation*, trans. Sister Caridad Inda and John Eagleson (Maryknoll, NY: Orbis Books, 1988; orig. 1973).

64. See Zora Neale Hurston, *Every Tongue Got to Confess: Negro Folk-Tales from the Gulf States* (New York: HarperCollins, 2002).

65. Howard Thurman, *Deep River and the Negro Spiritual Speaks of Life and Death* (Richmond, IN: Friends United Press, 1975), 16.

PART TWO

Marking and (Re)membering the Body of Christ

CHAPTER THREE

Marking the Body of Jesus, the Body of Christ

O Lord, you have searched me and known me.
For it was you who formed my inward parts;
    you knit me together in my mother's womb.
I praise you, for I am fearfully and wonderfully made.
    My frame was not hidden from you,
when I was being made in secret,
intricately woven in the depths of the earth.
Your eyes beheld my unformed substance.
                        —Psalm 139:1, 13–16

In the beginning was the Word, and the Word was with God, and the Word was God. . . . And the Word became flesh and lived among us.
                        —John 1:14

The Word of God assumed humanity that we might become [like] God.
                        —Athanasius

Focus on the body, on flesh, is no novelty in theological anthropology. Christian teaching long has struggled to understand and interpret, then to maintain the truth, that the eternal Word, the *Logos,* became flesh, became the bodily, concrete, marked, historical being, Jesus of Nazareth; that Jesus died, rather than betray his mission, his love for God and for human beings; that his fidelity, integrity, and love were vindicated, and his crucified body was

61

raised glorious from the dead. This teaching promotes the value and significance of the body, which is never to be disregarded or treated with contempt.

Yet, the history of human suffering shows how brutally and easily the value and significance of the body may be undermined. For bodies are marked, made individual, particular, different, and vivid through race, sex and gender, sexuality, and culture. The protean ambiguity of these marks transgresses categories, destabilizes identities, and disrupts relational patterns. These marks delight as much as they unnerve. They impose limitation: some insinuate exclusion, others inclusion. In every instance, the marked body denotes a "boundary" that matters. In a finite and sinful context, some unnerved historical human beings violate in multiple vicious ways the bodies of others. Such violence overlooks just how these bodily marks ground intelligence, discovery, beauty, and joy; enable apprehension and response to sensible experience; and shape culture, society, and religion. Such violence ignores the ways in which culture, society, and religion in turn shape our bodies.

In theology, the body is a contested site—ambiguous and sacred, wounded and creative, malleable and resistant—disclosing and mediating "more." Given the view of Christian faith that when God desires to manifest the divine presence, God does so in human flesh, the body can never be simply one element among others in theological reflection. Yet, any formulation that takes body and body marks seriously risks absolutizing or fetishizing what can be seen (race and sex), constructed (gender), represented (sexuality), expressed (culture), and regulated (social order). Moreover, such attention to concrete, specific, nonetheless accidental, characteristics also risks fragmenting human being. What makes such risk obligatory is that the body of Jesus of Nazareth, the Word made flesh, was subjugated in empire. In memory of his body, in memory of the victims of empire, in the service of life and love, theology must protest any imperial word that dismisses his body and seeks the de-creation of human bodies.

Five sections follow. The first section locates Jesus of Nazareth within empire, the principal social (i.e., political, economic, technological) context for thinking about his body as marked (i.e., raced, sexed, gendered, religiously and socially regulated). The second section sketches the situation of marked bodies ensnared in the contemporary globalized imperial order—queer bodies, in particular. The third section considers the teaching of the Catholic Church on homosexuality. The murder of forty-nine people in a nightclub popular among the LGBTQ (lesbian, gay, bisexual, transgender, queer) community of Orlando, Florida, in the summer of 2016, evoked horror, anger, and profound sorrow. In the days that followed, few Catholic Church leaders spoke out forcefully against homophobia, and, as Jesuit author and editor James Martin pointed out, fewer still used the terms gay or LGBT.[1] The fourth proposes to mark the flesh of Christ as "queer," for Jesus of Nazareth must reign as an option for queer folk. Finally, in order to be worthy of the name of Jesus, the name above every name, the name that gathers in all who have been driven away,[2] the church cannot but open its heart and embrace those bodies that empire abuses, negates, and crucifies. Thus, the fifth section calls for a (re)marking of the flesh of his church.

Jesus in Empire

Jesus of Nazareth was born and died in subjugation to the Roman Empire. His flesh, his body, was and remains marked by race, gender, sex, culture, and religion: he was a practicing Jew in a territory controlled by Roman political, military, and economic forces. His flesh also was and remains marked by sex, gender, and sexuality: he was male and, although we cannot speak about his sexual orientation, tradition assumes his heterosexuality.

Under the reign of Rome, Jesus in his body knew refugee status, occupation and colonization, social regulation and control. His life

---

1. James Martin, *Building a Bridge: How the Catholic Church and the LGBT Community Can Enter into a Relationship of Respect, Compassion, and Sensitivity*, rev. and exp. ed. (New York: HarperOne, 2017), 14.

2. See Wendy Farley, *Gathering Those Driven Away: A Theology of Incarnation* (Louisville, KY: Westminster John Knox Press, 2011).

played out amid breakdowns in "the social relationships and political conditions that prevailed in Jewish Palestine under Roman and Herodian rule": military intimidation, surveillance, and brutality; economic exploitation and taxation; and displacement from ancestral lands.[3] His mission cannot be understood apart from the palpable tension between resistance to empire and desire for *basileia theou*, the reign of God. Note how at the center of his praxis were the bodies of common people, peasants, economic and political refugees, the poor and destitute. They were the subjects of his compassionate care: children, women, and men who were materially impoverished as well as those who were socially and religiously marginalized or were physically disabled (those who were blind, paralyzed, palsied, deaf, lepers); those who had lost land through debt peonage, who were displaced through military occupation or religious corruption; those who were possessed and broken in spirit from ostracism and persecution.

Jesus did not shun or despise these women and men; he put his body where they were. He handled, touched, and embraced their marked bodies. He befriended them, not "to show his compassion in a detached, old-fashioned teaching mode," as Marcella Althaus-Reid observes, but in recognition that they were human beings like anyone else, at times with great troubles.[4] Through exorcisms and healings, women and men, shunned and isolated by demon possession or leprosy, hemorrhage or blindness, were restored to synagogue and family, kin and friends. Those lost to human conversation and interaction, physical and affective intimacy, were found; those abandoned or hidden because of deformity were restored to family life.

Central to this mission was the audacious practice of the welcome table. Jesus ate and drank with sinners: tax collectors, who made the already hardscrabble life of peasants even more so;

---

3. Richard Horsley, *Jesus and Empire: The Kingdom of God and the New World Disorder* (Minneapolis: Fortress Press, 2003), 15.

4. Marcella Althaus-Reid, *Indecent Theology: Theological Perversions in Sex, Gender and Politics* (London: Routledge, 2000), 113.

lepers, whose diseased bodies threatened the bodily boundaries of "others"; women, who were forced to sell their bodies for survival; women who were accused of giving their bodies away in adultery. The parable of the great banquet (Luke 14:21–24; Matt 22:9–10) underscores the challenge this practice posed to social and religious conventions. "The host replaces the absent guests with anyone off the streets. But if one actually brought in *anyone off the street*, one could, in such a situation, have classes, sexes, and ranks all mixed up together. Anyone could be reclining next to anyone else, female next to male, free next to slave, socially high next to socially low, ritually pure next to ritually impure.[5]

Through his table practice Jesus acted out just how unrestricted neighbor love must be, just how much "other" bodies matter. The open table embodied egalitarianism, disrupted domination, and abolished the etiquette of empire. In the design of the reign of God, *all* are welcome. Jesus invites all who would follow him to abandon loyalties of class and station, family and kin, culture and nation in order to form God's people anew and, thus, to contest empire.

That Jesus carried out his passion for the reign of God precisely as a male human being raises another profound challenge to empire. This prophet from Nazareth had a human body; his was a male body; he had the genitals of a male human being.[6] Through his preaching and practices, living and behavior, Jesus performed masculinity in ways that opposed patriarchal expressions of maleness

---

5. John Dominic Crossan, *Jesus: A Revolutionary Biography* (New York: Harper & Row, 1994), 68, author's emphasis.

6. Mark Jordan, in *Telling Truths in Church: Scandal, Flesh, and Christian Speech* (Boston: Beacon, 2003), counsels against using the phrase "sexual orientation" with regard to Jesus. However, Jordan suggests, the phrase may be "very useful to undo the heterosexist presumption that Jesus was, of course, heterosexual. . . . As incarnate God, Jesus violated any number of social expectations" (88–89). While I agree with Jordan, I do not assign any sexual orientation to Jesus (the canonical Gospels give us no clues whatsoever about his sexual desires) and I do not suggest that he was homosexual. The canonical Gospels are silent on the marital state of Jesus and offer no clues as to that of his male disciples except for Simon Peter (Matt 8:14–16) and the marital state of some of the women who traveled with Jesus (Luke 8:3).

through coercive or seductive power, control, and exploitation of "other" bodies, exclusion, and violence. He confronted this system through lived example, intentionally choosing courage over conformity, moral conflict over acquiescence, and boldness over caution. Through his oppositional appropriation of masculinity, Jesus countered many gendered cultural expectations. He overturned patriarchal family structure, releasing family members from the denotation as property of the male head of household. He stretched solidarity far beyond the bonds and ties of blood and marriage, insisting on love of enemies, of the poor, of the excluded, of the despised. He chose women as disciples and taught them as he taught the men, defending them against those who questioned, attacked, or belittled them, and he affirmed their agency over against those narrow and constricting roles set for them by culture, religion, and empire. Jesus's performance of masculinity was *kenotic*: he emptied himself of all that would subvert or stifle authentic human liberation. In these ways, his maleness stood as contradictory signification, undermining kyriarchy and its multiple forms of oppression.

A healthy appropriation of sexuality is crucial to generous, generative, and full living. A fully embodied spirituality calls for the integration of sexual energies and drives, rather than repression or even sublimation. Comfortable in his body, sexuality, and masculinity, Jesus lived out of a "creative interplay of both immanent and transcendent spiritual energies."[7] Understanding eros as these creative energies integrated into a dynamic life force, we can say that Jesus had an eros for others; he gave his body, his very self to and for others, to and for the Other. Jesus lived out of a fully embodied spirituality, an eros. In spite of themselves, the suspicious, the timid, the broken-hearted were attracted to his energy and joy. In spite of themselves, the arrogant, the smug, the self-satisfied were drawn to his authority and knowledge. In spite of themselves, hesitant women and men felt intense hope at sharing his struggle for the reign of God. Children, women, and men were

---

7. Jorge N. Ferrer, "Embodied Spirituality, Now and Then," *Tikkun* 2, no. 1 (May/June 2006): 42.

attracted to his eros, and found themselves lifted up, made whole and new, open to others.

Jesus of Nazareth is the measure or standard for our exercise of erotic power and freedom in the service of the reign of God and against empire. He is the clearest example of what it means to identify with children and women and men who are poor, excluded, and despised; to take their side in the struggle for life—no matter the cost. Through his body marked, made individual, particular, and vivid through race, gender, sexuality, religious practice, and culture, Jesus mediates the gracious gift given and the gracious giving gift. His incarnation, which makes the infinite God present, disrupts every pleasure of hierarchy, economy, cultural domination, racial violence, gender oppression, and abuse of sexual others. Through his body, his flesh and blood, Jesus of Nazareth offers us a new and compelling way of being God's people even as we reside in the new imperial order.

The Body in the New Imperial (Dis)Order

Insofar as race and gender are co-constitutive in today's empire spawned by globalization, they are governed by political and economic displays of power; sexuality in this empire is particularly subjugated through commercial exchange. Red, brown, yellow, poor white, and black female bodies, violated and "occupied" in empire building, poached in the process of globalization, function as exotic and standard commodities for trafficking and sex tourism, pornographic fantasy, and sadomasochistic spectacle. Red, brown, yellow, poor white immigrant, and, especially, black male bodies lynched and castrated in empire building, mechanized in the process of globalization, now are caricatured as "sexually aggressive, violent, animalistic."[8] Empire's greedy consumption and debasement of black flesh robs *all* human persons of healthy,

---

8. Dwight N. Hopkins, "The Construction of the Black Male Body: Eroticism and Religion," in *Loving the Body: Black Religious Studies and the Erotic*, ed. Anthony Pinn and Dwight Hopkins (New York: Palgrave Macmillan, 2006), 186–88, 185.

dignified, and generative sexual expression. For in empire, the primary function of sex no longer entails human communication, embrace, and intimacy (not even procreation), but the heterosexual service of white male privilege. Sex is amusement; its imperial purposes are distraction, entertainment, dissipation.

Thus, to be lesbian, gay, transgender in empire is to expect and to undergo intense opprobrium. Empire entices and intimidates its ordinary subjects, and, perhaps especially, its most wretched subjects to react to gay or lesbian or transgender people with panic, loathing, and violence (malevolent heteronormativity); empire permits its privileged subjects to respond with curiosity, experimentation, and tokenism (benign heteronormativity). In empire, self-disclosure and self-disclosive acts by gay or lesbian or transgender people are penalized by repression, expulsion, and, sometimes, death. Malevolent homophobia took the lives of twenty-two-year-old gay Matthew Shepherd, beaten to death in Laramie, Wyoming, in 1998; of fifteen-year-old Saskia Gunn, a black lesbian stabbed to death in Newark, New Jersey, in 2003; of thirty-one- and thirty-year-old Shani Baraka and Rayshon Holmes, lesbians, murdered in Newark, New Jersey, in 2003; and of eighteen-year-old Angie Zapata, a transgender woman, murdered in Colorado in 2008. The vulnerability and marginality of gay and lesbian people make a claim on the body of Jesus of Nazareth, on the body of Christ.

Catholic Church Teaching

Catholic Church teaching on sex and sexuality manifests considerable ambivalence and discomfort toward the body—lesbian and gay and transgender bodies, in particular. Church teaching signals preference for celibacy and promotes marriage chiefly as a means for procreation. Certainly, church teaching acknowledges the presence of gay and lesbian and transgender persons, accords them equal human dignity with heterosexual (cis-gender or non-trans) persons, and urges pastoral care and compassion in their regard.[9]

---

9. Congregation for the Doctrine of the Faith, *Homosexualitatis problema*, "Letter to All Catholic Bishops on the Pastoral Care of Homosexual Persons"

Yet that teaching does little to contest the use and abuse of gay and lesbian and transgender people in empire. Church teaching distinguishes homosexual orientation from homosexual activity, and deems the latter "intrinsically disordered."[10] Sexual acts between persons of the same sex are deemed contrary to the natural law, and the *Catechism of the Catholic Church* declares that such acts "close the sexual act to the gift of life [and] do not proceed from a genuine affective and sexual complementarity" (#2357). This teaching admonishes gays and lesbians and transgender persons to repress or sacrifice their sexual orientation, to relinquish genital expression, to deny their bodies and their selves. But, if the body is a sacrament, if it is the concrete medium through which persons realize themselves interdependently in the world and in freedom in Christ, then, according to Catholic teaching, in and through (genital) bodily expression, gay and lesbian and transgender persons are compelled to render themselves disordered. For according to Catholic teaching, the condition of homosexuality constitutes a transgression that approximates ontological status. Can the (artificial) distinction between orientation and act (really) be upheld? What are gays and lesbians to do with their bodies, their selves?

Consider the response of *Homosexualitatis problema* to these questions:

> Fundamentally [homosexuals] are called to enact the will of God in their life by joining whatever sufferings and difficulties they experience in virtue of their condition to the sacrifice of the Lord's Cross. That Cross, for the believer, is a fruitful sacrifice since from that death come life and redemption. While any call to carry the Cross or to understand a

---

(January 11, 1986); http://www.ewtn.com (May 12, 2006); *The Catechism of the Catholic Church*, #2358, http://www.vatican.va.

10. Congregation for the Doctrine of the Faith, *Persona Humana*, "Declaration on Certain Questions Concerning Sexual Ethics" (December 29, 1975) #8; see also Congregation for the Doctrine of the Faith, "Considerations Regarding Proposals to Give Legal Recognition to Unions Between Homosexual Persons" (March 28, 2003).

Christian's suffering in this way will predictably be met with bitter ridicule by some, it should be remembered that this is the way to eternal life for "all" who follow Christ.

[The Cross] is easily misunderstood, however, if it is merely seen as a pointless effort at self-denial. The Cross is a denial of self, but in service to the will of God himself who makes life come from death and empowers those who trust in him to practice virtue in place of vice.

To celebrate the Paschal Mystery, it is necessary to let that Mystery become imprinted in the fabric of daily life. To refuse to sacrifice one's own will in obedience to the will of the Lord is effectively to prevent salvation. Just as the Cross was central to the expression of God's redemptive love for us in Jesus, so the conformity of the self-denial of homosexual men and women with the sacrifice of the Lord will constitute for them a source of self-giving which will save them from a way of life which constantly threatens to destroy them.

Christians who are homosexual are called, as all of us are, to a chaste life. As they dedicate their lives to understanding the nature of God's personal call to them, they will be able to celebrate the Sacrament of Penance more faithfully and receive the Lord's grace so freely offered there in order to convert their lives more fully to his Way. (#12)

This is stern counsel: It calls for embrace of the cross, for bodily (sexual) asceticism, self-denial, and imposes strict abstinence. In a carefully argued analysis of the document, Paul Crowley affirms the meaningfulness of the cross not only for gay and lesbian people, but for *all* Christians since the cross is *the* condition of discipleship. Crowley rightly objects to the peculiar application of "crucified living" (enforced abstinence) to the (sexual) fulfillment of gay and lesbian people.[11] With regard to the last sentences quoted above, Crowley points out, "While penance is mentioned here as

---

11. Paul G. Crowley, "Homosexuality and the Counsel of the Cross," *Theological Studies* 65, no. 3 (September 2004): 500–529.

an aid to gay persons in attaining a chaste life, no mention is made of the graces accruing from one's baptism or from the life of the Eucharist."[12]

Regarding the command of abstinence, Xavier Seubert reasons that "to prescribe, in advance, abstinence and celibacy for the homosexual person simply because the person is homosexual is to say that, as it is, homosexual bodily existence stands outside the sacramental transformation to which all creation is called in Christ."[13] The writing of *Homosexualitatis problema* surely was motivated by deep pastoral concern. But it rings with what James Alison describes as a reproachful sanctioning ecclesiastical voice, which commands: "'Love and do not love, be and do not be.'" He concludes: "The voice of God has been presented as a double bind, which is actually far more dangerous than a simple message of hate, since it destabilizes being into annihilation, and thinks that annihilation to be a good thing."[14] Church teaching repels gay and lesbian (anti)bodies to the periphery of the ecclesial body, and may well disclose just how afraid the church may be of the body of Jesus of Nazareth.

Moral theologian Stephen J. Pope calls the magisterium's teaching about homosexual orientation "powerfully stigmatizing and dehumanizing." This teaching, he continues,

> is also at least tacitly, if not explicitly, liable to be used to support exactly the kinds of unjust discrimination that the Church has repeatedly condemned. Describing someone's sexual identity as "gravely disordered" would seem to arouse suspicion, mistrust, and alienation. . . . One can understand why observers conclude that the magisterium's teaching about homosexuality stands in tension with its affirmation that each gay person is created in the *imago Dei*.[15]

---

12. Paul G. Crowley, *Unwanted Wisdom: Suffering, the Cross, and Hope* (New York: Continuum International Publishing Group, 2005), 109.

13. Xavier John Seubert, "'But Do Not Use the Rotted Names': Theological Adequacy and Homosexuality," *Heythrop Journal* 40, no. 1 (January 1999): 74n23.

14. James Alison, *Faith beyond Resentment: Fragments Catholic and Gay* (New York: Crossroad Publishing, 2001), 94.

15. Stephen J. Pope, "The Magisterium's Arguments against 'Same-Sex

Church teaching on homosexuality exposes us to the manipulation of agents of empire, and coaxes our collusion in opposing and punishing gay and lesbian and transgender people who refuse to internalize heteronormativity and who live their lives without self-censorship. This teaching feeds innuendo and panic; it nudges us to discipline the body's phrasing and comportment, the curiosity and play of our children; it disturbs our families and relationships; it rewards our disingenuousness as we praise, then, mock women and men whose talents often enrich our daily lives and weekly worship.[16] Seubert poses a grave critique, one that incriminates the very mystery of the church: the "denial of the homosexual body as this group's basis of spiritual, relational, historical experience is tantamount to impeding access to the reality of Christ in a certain moment of human history."[17] This charge brings the church much too close to betraying the great mystery of love that suffuses it and stirs up continually a longing to realize itself as the marked flesh of Christ.

This situation provokes a most poignant, most indecent question: Can Jesus of Nazareth be an option for gay and lesbian and transgender people? This question discloses the pain, anguish, and anger that many gay and lesbian and transgender people feel as we thwart their desire to follow Jesus of Nazareth, to realize themselves in his image. This question springs from "the deep-seated feeling among many queer people that Jesus Christ is not an option for them, that he, as the embodied representative of God, hates them, and that they have no place in either Christ's church or the Kingdom of God he announced during his earthy ministry."[18]

Marriage': An Ethical Analysis and Critique," *Theological Studies* 65, no. 3 (September 2004): 550.

16. For a critical discussion of black church teaching on homosexuality, see Kelly Brown Douglas, *Sexuality and the Black Church: A Womanist Perspective* (Maryknoll, NY: Orbis Books, 1999).

17. Seubert, "'But Do Not Use the Rotted Names,'" 65.

18. Thomas Bohache, "Embodiment as Incarnation: An Incipient Queer Christology," *Theology and Sexuality* 10, no. 1 (2003): 12.

If Jesus of Nazareth, the Christ of God, cannot be an option for gay, lesbian, transgender people, then he cannot be an option. An adequate response to this concern requires a different christological interpretation, one in which we *all* may recognize, love, and realize our body-selves as his own flesh, as the body of Christ.

Marking the (Queer) Flesh of Christ

The words "queer" and "Christ" form a necessary, if shocking, perhaps even "obscene," conjunction.[19] By inscribing a queer mark on the flesh of Christ, I neither propose nor insinuate that Jesus Christ was gay or homosexual. By definition the word "queer" insinuates whatever may be at odds with whatever is considered normal or conventional or legitimate. "There is nothing in particular," argues David Halperin, "to which [queer] necessarily refers. Queer demarcates not a positivity, but a positionality vis-à-vis the normative—a positionality" that is not restricted to sexual orientation or expression.[20] Rather, as he asserts, queer "describes a horizon of possibility whose precise extent and heterogeneous scope cannot in principle be delimited in advance."[21]

Given his preferential outreach to and action on behalf of children, women, and men enduring the weight of spiritual anxiety, of trauma and self-paralysis, helplessness, economic impoverishment and dispossession, physical disease and debility, Jesus of Nazareth projected a distinctive queer horizon or vision of human life and humane living. This vision contested empire's biopolitical control

---

19. Althaus-Reid, *Indecent Theology*, 111. As a hermeneutical or interpretative lens, queer theory seeks to destabilize social and cultural constructions of gender binaries and identity politics rooted in fixed performative notions of "gay" or "lesbian." Queer theory foregrounds sexuality in order to uncover heretofore unexamined assumptions about sexuality and challenge heterosexist normativity in mainstream feminist analysis. Queer theory charges not only "traditional" theologies regarding these assumptions but also the various theologies of liberation.

20. David Halperin, *Saint Foucault: Towards a Gay Hagiography* (New York: Oxford University Press, 1995), 62.

21. Ibid.

and called for a reordering of the prevailing religio-cultural, societal, political, and economic logics. Jesus's "queer vision" upended empire's ideological relation between power, truth, and desire; his vision affirmed the concrete renewal and living out of covenant practices that supported family life, encouraged cooperation and mutuality, generosity toward those who were impoverished or widowed or orphaned or abandoned.

By inscribing a "queer" mark, I recognize that this mark poses epistemological challenges for theology: Have we turned the (male) body of Christ into a fetish or idol? In an effort to discipline *eros*, have we disregarded "God's proto-erotic desire for us"?[22] Can a Christology incorporate all the dimensions of corporality? These questions target some of the discursive limits of sex, gender, and sexuality in Christianity and disturb cherished symbols. Just as a black Christ heals the anthropological impoverishment of black bodies so too a "queer" Christ heals the anthropological impoverishment of lesbian and gay and transgender bodies. Because Jesus of Nazareth declared himself with and for others—those women and men marked as poor, excluded, and despised—and offered a new "way" and new freedom to all who would hear and follow him, we may be confident that the Christ of our faith is for gay and lesbian and transgender people. Conversely, if the risen Christ cannot identify with gay and lesbian and transgender people, then the gospel announces no good news and the reign of God presents no real alternative to the reign of sin. Only an *ekklesia* that follows Jesus of Nazareth in (re)marking its flesh as "queer" as his own may set a welcome table in the household of God.

Robert Goss takes the experience of homophobic oppression of queer bodies in culture, society, and church as a starting point for a "queer" christological reflection. He grounds this articulation in the "generative matrix" of the *basileia* praxis of Jesus and

---

22. Sarah Coakley, "Living into the Mystery of the Holy Trinity: Trinity, Prayer and Sexuality," *Anglican Theological Review* 80, no. 2 (Spring 1998): 230. Coakley cautions, "No language of eros is safe from possible nefarious application . . ." (231).

in the real suffering of gay and lesbian and transgender people. The immanent and transcendent scope of that praxis allows Goss to detach the radical truth of Jesus Christ from all forms of hegemony and ideology—whether cultural, social, ecclesiastical, biblical, or theological—that might seek to master Infinite God present among us. Further, he constructs a "queer" biblical hermeneutics through which to unmask and discredit any heretical use of the Hebrew and Christian scriptures to justify bigotry and violence against queer people. Goss challenges the abusive use of the cross to justify explicit or implicit oppression and violence against gay, lesbian, and transgender people as well as gay, lesbian, and transgender acquiescence to interiorized oppression.

> The cross symbolizes the political infrastructure of homophobic practice and oppression. It symbolizes the terror of internalized homophobia that has led to the closeted invisibility of gay and lesbian people. It indicates the brutal silencing, the hate crimes, the systemic violence perpetuated against us. The cross now belongs to us. We have been crucified.[23]

Crucifixion was the response of imperial power to Jesus's "*basileia* solidarity with the poor, the outcast, the sinner, the socially dysfunctional, and the sexually oppressed." The death of Jesus "shapes the cross into a symbol of struggle for queer liberation," and Easter becomes the hope and fulfillment of that struggle. "From the perspective of Easter . . . God identifies with the suffering and death of Jesus at the hands of a political system of oppression. For gay and lesbian Christians, Easter becomes the event at which God says no to homophobic violence and sexual oppression. . . . On Easter, God made Jesus queer in his solidarity with us. In other words, Jesus 'came out of the closet' and became the 'queer' Christ. . . . Jesus the Christ is queer by his solidarity with queers."[24]

---

23. Robert Goss, *Jesus Acted Up: A Gay and Lesbian Manifesto* (San Francisco: HarperCollins, 1993), 83.
24. Ibid., 84.

All Christology is interpretation, and, in these passages, Goss articulates an understanding of the cross and resurrection from the perspective of those who endure homophobic or heterosexist oppression. His theological analysis turns on the scandal of the body particular: Jesus of Nazareth in all his marked particularity of race, gender, sex, culture, and religion, teaches us the universal meaning of being human in the world. In Jesus, God critiques any imperial or ecclesiastical practice of body exclusion and control, sorrows at our obstinacy, and calls us all unceasingly to new practices of body inclusion and liberation. In Jesus, God manifests an eros for us *as we are* in our marked particularity of race, gender, sex, sexuality, culture. Note that christological reflection from black, Mexican-American, Asian, African, Latin American, feminist, *mujerista*, womanist perspectives make this same appeal to particularity.

In contrast to christological formulations that avoid or distort sexuality and sexual desire, Goss's work offers an opportunity to honor what Sarah Coakley calls the "profound entanglement of our human sexual desires and our desire for God."[25] A "queer" Christ is not scandalized by human desire but liberates that desire from cloying commonsense satisfaction, misuse, and disrespect. This liberation begins in regard and esteem for the body and comes to proximate fulfillment in authentic love of the body, as authentic love and loving. A "queer" Christ embraces *all* our bodies passionately, revalorizes them as embodied mystery, and reorients sexual desire toward God's desire for us in and through our sexuality. This is not a matter of fitting God into our lives, but of fitting our lives into God. Gay, heterosexual, lesbian, and transgender persons are drawn by God's passionate love for us working in us to bring us into God's love. To live in and live out of this reorientation demands refusal of isolating egoism, of body denial, and of whatever betrays spiritual and bodily integrity. Moreover, living in and out of this reorientation leads us, even if fitfully, toward virtue,

---

25. Coakley, "Living into the Mystery of the Holy Trinity," 224.

helps us to grow lovable and loving, and, in fulfillment, we are gift and gifted with and in love.

In his relationships with women and men, Jesus embodied openness, equality, and mutuality. In his suffering and death on the cross, Jesus showed us the cost of integrity, when we live in freedom, in love, and in solidarity with others. In his resurrection, Jesus became the One in whom "God's erotic power"[26] releases bodily desire from the tomb of fear and loathing, the One who fructifies all loving exchange, the One who, in his risen body, quiets the restless yearning of our hearts.

(Re)Marking the Flesh of the Church

If theological reflection on the body cannot ignore a Christ identified with black, brown, red, yellow, poor white, and queer folk, neither can it ignore reflection on "the flesh of the church."[27] For as Gregory of Nyssa tells us, whoever "sees the Church looks directly at Christ."[28] And as the flesh of the church is the flesh of Christ in every age, the flesh of the church is marked (as was his flesh) by race, sex, gender, sexuality, and culture. These marks differentiate and transgress, they unify and bind, but the flesh of Christ relativizes these marks in the flesh of the church. These marks may count, but the mark of Christ, the baptismal sign of the cross, counts for more, trumps all marks. Still, counting and trumping marks in the body of Christ must give way before *basileia* praxis. These acts of doing justice, empire critique, love, and solidarity mark us as his flesh made vivid leaven in our world.

In a letter to followers of "the way" at Corinth, Paul hands over

---

26. Goss, *Jesus Acted Up*, 169.

27. The phrase comes from Jean-Marie Roger Tillard, *Flesh of the Church, Flesh of Christ: At the Source of the Ecclesiology of Communion* (Collegeville, MN: Pueblo/Liturgical Press, 1992, 2001).

28. Gregory of Nyssa, "On the Making of Man," in *Gregory of Nyssa, Dogmatic Treatises,* ed. Philip Schaff and Henry Wace (Grand Rapids, MI: William B. Eerdmans, 1979), 13.1049B–1052A, cited in Graham Ward, *Cities of God* (London: Routledge, 2000).

the gift he has been given: "For I received from the Lord what I also delivered to you, that the Lord Jesus on the night when he was betrayed took bread, and when he had given thanks, he broke it and said, 'This is my body which is for you.' Do this in remembrance of me" (1 Cor 11:23–24). This is the tradition: the body of the Lord is handed over to us, handled by us as we feed one another. Further on, Paul declares: "You are the body of Christ and individually members of it" (1 Cor 12:27). We are the body raised up by Christ for himself within humanity; through us, the flesh of the crucified and resurrected Jesus is extended through time and space.

In the very act of nourishing our flesh with his flesh, Christ makes us women and men new again, emboldens us to surrender position and privilege and power and wealth, to abolish all claims to racial and cultural superiority, to contradict repressive codes of gender formation and sexual orientation. In Christ, there is neither brown nor black, neither red nor white; in Christ, there is neither Creole nor *mestizo*, neither senator nor worker in the *maquiladoras*. In Christ, there is neither male nor female, neither gay/lesbian nor straight, neither heterosexual nor homosexual (after Gal 3:28). We are all transformed in Christ: *we are his very own flesh.*

If my sister or brother is not at the table, we are not the flesh of Christ. If my sister's mark of sexuality must be obscured, if my brother's mark of race must be disguised, if my sister's mark of culture must be repressed, then we are not the flesh of Christ. For, it is through and in Christ's own flesh that the "other" is my sister, is my brother; indeed, the "other" is me (*yo soy tu otro yo*). Unless our sisters and brothers are beside and with each of us, we are not the flesh of Christ. The sacramental aesthetics of Eucharist, the thankful living manifestation of God's image through particularly marked flesh, demands the vigorous display of difference in race and culture and tongue, gender and sex and sexuality. Again, Gregory of Nyssa: "The establishment of the Church is re-creation of the world. But it is only in the *union of all the particular members* that the beauty of Christ's Body is complete."[29]

---

29. Ibid., emphasis mine.

The body of Jesus the Christ, both before and after his death, radically clarifies the meaning of be-ing embodied in the world. His love and praxis release the power of God's animating image and likeness in our red, brown, yellow, white, black bodies—our queer and heterosexual bodies, our HIV/AIDS infected bodies, our starving bodies, our prostituted bodies, our yearning bodies, our ill and infirm bodies, our young and old and joyous bodies. To stand silent before war and death, incarceration and torture, rape and queer bashing, pain and disease, abuse of power and position is to be complicit with empire's sacrilegious anti-liturgy, which dislodges the table of the bread of life. That desiccated anti-liturgy hands us all over to consumption by the corrupt body of the market.

The only body capable of taking us all in as we are with all our different body marks—certainly, the queer mark—is the body of Christ. This taking us in, this in-corporation is akin to sublation, not erasure, not uniformity: The *basileia* praxis of Jesus draws us up to him. Our humble engagement in his praxis revalues our identities and differences, even as it preserves the integrity and significance of our body marks. At the same time, those very particular body marks are relativized, reoriented, and reappropriated under his sign, the sign of the cross. Thus, in solidarity and in love of others and the Other, we are (re)made and (re)marked as the flesh of Christ, as the flesh of his church.

In sum: Jesus of Nazareth was born of people subjugated by the Roman Empire; an itinerant and charismatic preacher and teacher, his strenuous critique of oppressive structures, whether political or religious or cultural, along with his fearless love of ordinary people provoked those in authority to brand him a criminal. Jesus mediated God's presence among us through a human body marked by race, gender, sex, sexuality, culture, and religion. His radical self-disclosure constitutes the paradigm for all human self-disclosure in contexts of empire and oppression, exclusion and alienation, slavery and death.

The body of Jesus provokes our interrogation of the new imperial deployment and debasement of bodies. The flesh of his church

CHAPTER FOUR

The Dangerous Memory of Chattel Slavery

The wounds of my people wound me too. Is there no
    balm in Gilead?
Who will turn my head into a fountain and my eyes
    into a spring of tears so that
I may weep all day, all night for the wounded out of
    my people?
—after Jeremiah 8:21–23

The being of slavery, its soul and its body, lives and
moves in the chattel principle, the property principle,
the bill of sale principle: the cart-whip, starvation, and
nakedness are its inevitable consequences.
—James W. C. Pennington

We Christian theologians in the United States live and work in a
house haunted by the ghost of chattel slavery. It is true that neither the enslavement of Africans nor antiblack racism is unique
to our country; nearly all the nations of Europe engaged in the
slave trade and benefited from it in social and economic ways. Historical research shows that kidnapped and enslaved Africans were
advertised, bought, and sold in several European countries. Historian David Brion Davis writes: "Negro slaves were bought and
displayed in the courts of Elizabeth and her Stuart successors; they
were publicly advertised for sale through most of the eighteenth
century; and they were bequeathed in wills as late as the 1820s."[1]

---

1. David Brion Davis, *The Problem of Slavery in the Age of Revolution, 1779–
1832* (Ithaca, NY: Cornell University Press, 1975), 472.

Critical research and insights offered by political philosopher Susan Buck-Morss show how sugar production, with its intensification of capital and labor, not only contradicted the understanding and practice of slavery as a private or household matter but transformed it to meet the demands of a new global economy in which "more than twenty percent of the bourgeoisie was dependent upon slave-connected commercial activity.[2]"

Yet, slavery in the United States can be distinguished by the chattel principle. In its legal denotation, the chattel principle referred to a movable article of personal property; slavery reduced human persons to *living property*. Although ratification of the Thirteenth Amendment to the United States' Constitution in December 1865 brought that devastating "regime of racial slavery"[3] to an end, its specter lingers in the continual shape-shifting of white racist supremacy: from the enslavement of Africans and their descendants to lynching's barbarous intimidation, from segregation to institutionalized racism, from intentional deprivation of poor white and minority communities to the world's highest rate of incarceration of black and brown members of those communities, from cultural denigration of the black body to the brutal treatment, even death, of black youth, women, and men at the hands of law enforcement officers or their agents. In the current national dispensation, ordinary (white) citizens feel empowered and justified to monitor, insult, harass, attack, even murder children, women, and men who are black, brown, Jewish, Muslim, immigrants, and refugees.

We, the people of the United States, will our failure of memory. As a modern nation, America was established on ideals of equality and inalienable rights to life, liberty, and the pursuit of happiness. But the founders, as Kelly Brown Douglas shows, almost immediately surrendered to and promoted an "American exceptionalism"

---

2. Susan Buck-Morss, *Hegel, Haiti, and Universal History* (Pittsburgh: University of Pittsburgh Press, 2009), 29.

3. Walter Johnson, *Soul by Soul: Life inside the Antebellum Slave Market* (Cambridge, MA: Harvard University Press, 1999), 81.

that conjoined race (Anglo-Saxon) and religion (Christianity) and proved lethal to the indigenous peoples and the enslaved Africans and their descendants. Indeed, the founders made a religion of race.[4] Excluding colonies in the Caribbean and Brazil, "no other state that professed to be a modern society had internal slavery."[5] Our public memory as a nation suppresses the depth of our entanglement in racial slavery, consigns it to a misbegotten past, and conceals from ourselves its ambiguous confession, the Emancipation Proclamation, and the tragic consequences of our selective memory.[6]

Even if selective memories and sanitized versions of the history of chattel slavery irrupt episodically, the total erasure of slavery is not possible. Chattel slavery may have reduced human beings to living property, but its most vivid reminder are living black bodies which, in that remarkable phrase of historian of religions Charles H. Long, remain "a structural embarrassment." The living black bodies descended from the enslaved Africans prolong their memory and conjure "the black diaspora . . . as a mutually constitutive conjuncture of place and a time, a geography of dislocation, and a history that challenges the limits of historicity."[7] These living black bodies signify the nation's unexamined questions and unresolved anxieties, disturb the nation's aesthetics, and curb the nation's quest for the putative and unreflective postracial. As remainders of the property regime of racial slavery, these living black bodies enflesh the "dangerous memory" of chattel slavery.

How are we to understand history and memory in the shadow

---

4. Kelly Brown Douglas, *Stand Your Ground: Black Bodies and the Justice of God* (Maryknoll, NY: Orbis Books, 2015), 11–26.

5. Derek Heater, *A Brief History of Citizenship* (New York: New York University Press, 2004), 77.

6. The Emancipation Proclamation freed *only* those enslaved in the seceding states of the Confederacy, while those enslaved in Union states remained bound literally and legally by state laws. Hence its ambiguity: "all persons held as slaves within the rebellious areas are, and henceforward shall be free."

7. Sara Kaplan, "Souls at the Crossroads, Africans on the Water: The Politics of Diasporic Melancholia," *Callaloo* 30, no. 2 (Spring 2007): 521.

of the plantation?[8] How might dangerous memories of chattel slavery be important in doing theology today in the United States? What are the tasks of theology in the face of such suffering in history? For the Christian theologian, the suffering and death of the Jewish Jesus of Nazareth rebukes our amnesia, our forgetfulness of enslaved bodies, and our indifference to living black children, women, and men. The memory of his passion and death interrupts our banal resignation to some vague misbegotten past, our smug democratic dispensation, our not-so-benign neglect; it interrupts our affected worship, our pretentious platitudes about justice.

This chapter is organized in three sections: The first uncovers the impact of the plantation and its system of chattel slavery on captive human beings; the second, engages the problem of *forgetting* and *not remembering* in history, particularly the problem of the church and theology forgetting and not remembering chattel slavery; the third, challenges us as Christians, for the sake of the crucified Jewish Jesus, to protect the memory of chattel slavery.

The Plantation: A Site of "Necropower"

The plantation holds a "central place" in the history of chattel slavery in the Americas.[9] The plantation was the *terminus* of the Middle Passage, the stage for the performance of sovereignty as control of mortality, the incubator of "natal alienation." Orlando Patterson argues that this notion

> goes directly to the heart of what is critical in the slave's forced alienation, the loss of ties of birth in both ascending and descending generations. It also has the important nuance of a loss of native status, of deracination. It was the alienation of the slave from all formal legally enforceable ties

---

8. In a fine theological analysis, Beverly Eileen Mitchell indexes the commonalities of black and Jewish social oppression and social suffering in plantations and death camps in *Plantations and Death Camps: Religion, Ideology, and Human Dignity* (Minneapolis: Fortress Press, 2009), esp. 2–36.

9. Paul Gilroy, *Black Atlantic: Modernity and Double Consciousness* (Cambridge, MA: Harvard University Press, 1993), 55.

of "blood," and from any attachment to groups or localities other than those chosen for him by the master. . . .[10]

Natal alienation, then, forms a constituent condition of all slavery and refers to the rupture the enslaved man or woman experiences in all relationships.

From the terror of the Middle Passage, the slave was sold into the terror of the plantation and its system of chattel slavery, where slave life was a peculiar and paradoxical tension of "*death-in-life.*"[11] Patterson isolates three factors that structure power relations within chattel slavery and that stamp it as a "permanent," "violent," and "extreme" form of domination. *First*, chattel slavery is "social and involves the use or threat of violence in the control of one person by another.[12] *Second*, chattel slavery entails "the psychological fact of influence or the capacity to persuade another person to change the way he [and she] perceives his [and her] interests and circumstance."[13] The *third* factor is "the cultural facet of authority."[14] If the cultural refers to those meanings and values that inform a way of life, and if cultural authority regards the ability to mediate and enforce those meanings and values, then slavery debases crucial meanings, values, and institutions in a society—existence and reality, personhood and humanity, life and death, property and possession. The "idiom" of slavery was "power,"[15] power to coerce, to control, to convince. Planters, political, economic, societal, and religious elites colluded to enable race and racism to coalesce as a powerful and abiding ideology through which might became right, obedience became duty.

Enslaved people opposed their violation and assault, although not always, not always successfully, and never completely. Some

---

10. Orlando Patterson, *Slavery and Social Death, A Comparative Study* (Cambridge, MA, and London: Harvard University Press, 1982), 7.

11. Achille Mbembé, "Necropolitics," trans. Libby Meintjes, *Public Culture* 15, no. 1 (Winter 2003): 21.

12. Patterson, *Slavery and Social Death*, 1.

13. Ibid.

14. Ibid., 2.

15. Ibid., 17.

enslaved people resisted through backtalk (or sass); others strategized to disrupt the plantation's rhythms and rituals of work; others ran away; and some, perhaps, feigned madness. Some enslaved
people fought back in self-defense; others broke under the weight
of physical torture and psychological abuse, but to judge their
response as deficient disregards the intricacies of psychic life. The
asymmetrical power relation binding master and slave concretizes
in the nexus of threat and fear, sale and price, person and objectification and reaches its limit in the master's power over life. The
master was sovereign.[16] Buck-Morss observes, "the slave is the one
commodity like no other, as freedom of property and freedom of
person are here in direct contradiction."[17] The slave was a legal
commodity, an object of property with commercial value, yet the
slave was a living object of property—*human*. On this account,
"necropower" accords the master possession or ownership of a
human life.

When interviewed about her suffering under chattel slavery,
one-hundred-year-old Delia Garlic emphatically stated: "Slavery days was hell."[18] Yet, the human spirit would not be denied:
Enslaved people refused to surrender their humanity and resisted
the "soul-killing effects of slavery."[19] They fashioned life anew—
creating families and fictive kin, hush arbors and praise houses,
churches and associations of all kinds. These socio-cultural forms
necessarily were covert and fragile. But above all, the slaves config-
ured and sustained an innermost realm of spiritual consciousness;
the foremost expression of that consciousness is the Negro spiritual. Indeed, the spiritual constitutes a most outstanding example

---

16. Mbembé, "Necropolitics," 21, 25; see Carl Schmitt, *Political Theology:
Four Chapters on the Concept of Sovereignty*, trans. George Schwab (Chicago and
London: University of Chicago Press, 2005; orig. 1922) for a discussion of sover-
eignty and exception.

17. Buck-Morss, *Hegel, Haiti, and Universal History*, 53n90.

18. Norman R. Yetman, ed., *Voices from Slavery* (New York: Holt, Rinehart
and Winston, 1970), 133.

19. Frederick Douglass, *Frederick Douglass: The Narrative and Selected Writings*, ed. Michael Meyer (New York: Modern Library, 1984), 29.

of the *human* capacity to wring transcendent beauty from hellish circumstances. These songs emerged and were nurtured within that religio-cultural "circle"[20] in which historians agree the slaves were able to exercise some measure of autonomy. The spirituals refract a critical reading by the slaves of their profoundly ambiguous, yet crucial, encounter with Christianity, the religion that had been used to justify their enslavement, to shore up an ideology of their inferiority, and to bind them in so perilous a condition and place. Yet, the enslaved people sang for themselves a world.

Forgetting and Not Remembering Chattel Slavery

What does a community or a nation forfeit when it repressively erases memory of the very presence and condition of those whom they have dishonored, when it overlooks and humiliates those groups into silence and invisibility? Remembering *is* terrifying, especially when the perpetrators of wrong are no longer available, when death and decades disrupt the possibility of apology or direct reparations to survivors. How does a nation restore to a subjugated and oppressed people their languages and ceremonies, their lands and cultures, their hopes and dreams? Traumatic wrongs like chattel slavery wield a severe blow to "social life and damage the bonds linking people together and impair the prevailing sense of community."[21] *By forgetting* its past, a community or a nation relinquishes social and moral integrity and risks its cohesion and moral existence.

What might it mean for the church to forget or not to remember chattel slavery? What difference might such forgetting or not remembering make? Perhaps, Joseph Mueller suggests, the church cannot avoid forgetting; indeed, he argues, the "vitality of a self-

---

20. Sterling Stuckey, *Slave Culture: Nationalist Theory and the Foundations of Black America* (New York: Oxford University Press, 1987), 3–97, at 11.

21. Ricardo C. Ainslie, "Trauma, Community, and Contemporary Racial Violence: Reflections on the Architecture of Memory," in *The Ethics of Remembering and the Consequences of Forgetting,* ed. Michael O'Loughlin (Lanham, MD: Rowman & Littlefield, 2014), 313.

correcting Christian tradition nourished by its past so it can face creatively those around it and its own future must forget some of that past."[22] Forgetting may function to make change in the tradition possible, but forgetting something as profoundly detrimental to humanity, to the body of Christ, as chattel slavery can wound the church. If the church should forget its past, it too relinquishes social and moral integrity; moreover, the church risks its unity, mission, and moral authority.

In 1993 Pope John Paul II declared in *Veritatis Splendor* that there are some human acts that by their very nature are "'incapable of being ordered' to God because they radically contradict the good of the person made in [God's] image."[23] Such acts, he continued, "in the Church's moral tradition, have been termed 'intrinsically evil' (*intrinsece malum*)." Slavery is listed as one such act.[24] In fact, the pope stated, always and everywhere has the church taught that slavery is sinful. But John Noonan implies that papal teaching forgot (as have so many of us) that the church had lived with and approved slavery for more than nineteen hundred years.[25]

In a discussion of Noonan's *A Church That Can and Cannot Change*, Avery Dulles took aim at its focus on discontinuities with the tradition and rightly pointed out that although "no father or doctor of the church was an unqualified abolitionist" and that no pope or council ever made a sweeping denunciation of slavery as such, they did urge amelioration of the evils of slavery and condemned the slave trade.[26] Still, Noonan's hypothesis raises the

---

22. Joseph Mueller, "Forgetting as a Principle of Continuity in Tradition," *Theological Studies* 70, no. 4 (December 2009): 770.

23. John Paul II, *Veritatis Splendor* (August 6, 1993), #80. In its condemnation of slavery, the encyclical echoed the teaching of *Gaudium et spes* #27 (December 7, 1965).

24. Ibid.

25. John Noonan Jr., *A Church That Can and Cannot Change: The Development of Catholic Moral Teaching* (Notre Dame, IN: University of Notre Dame Press, 2005), 17–123.

26. Avery Dulles, review of *A Church That Can and Cannot Change*, by John A. Noonan Jr., *First Things* 156 (October 1, 2005): 55–56.

danger of forgetting and not remembering history, the anguish of being forgotten and not remembered in history. In the sketch that follows, the involvement of the regional church in the United States with chattel slavery and with enslaved and emancipated black Catholics makes these difficulties concrete.

During the period of the eighteenth and nineteenth centuries, the church compromised with chattel slavery. Historian Randall Miller writes: "Slavery was the shibboleth of southern civilization. Acceptance in the Old South meant getting right with slavery."[27] Catholic laity and religious orders enslaved, bought, sold, and owned human beings: the Ursulines, Religious of the Sacred Heart, and Capuchins in Louisiana; the Visitation nuns in Washington, DC; the Dominicans, Sisters of Charity, and Sisters of Loretto in Kentucky; the Vincentians in Missouri; the Carmelites, Sulpicians, and Jesuits in Maryland—all were slaveholders.[28]

As a whole, the Catholic hierarchy was reticent to contradict the culture and society that legitimated, sustained, and benefited from chattel slavery. Most southern bishops and priests maintained that slavery, as a legal, economic, and societal institution, was morally legitimate as long as the slaveholder's title of ownership was valid and the slave cared for materially and spiritually.[29] Bishop William Henry Elder of Mississippi sought conscientiously to meet the pastoral needs of the slaves in his diocese over against the objections of slaveholders, even though he deemed blacks inferior to

---

27. Randall M. Miller, "Catholics in a Protestant World: The Old South Example," in Samuel H. Hill, ed., *Varieties of Southern Religious Experience* (Baton Rouge, LA: Louisiana State University Press, 1988), 115, 121; Cyprian Davis, *The History of Black Catholics* (New York: Crossroad Publishing, 1990), 35–41.

28. Jon L. Wakelyn, "Catholic Elites in the Slaveholding South," in Randall M. Miller and Jon L. Wakelyn, eds., *Catholics in the Old South: Essays on Church and Culture* (Macon, GA: Mercer University Press, 1983), 211–39; R. Emmett Curran, "'Splendid Poverty': Jesuit Slaveholding in Maryland, 1805–1838," in *Catholics in the Old South*, 125–46.

29. Francis Maxwell, *Slavery and the Catholic Church* (Westminster, MD: Christian Classics, 1975), 10–12; Davis, *The History of Black Catholics*, 116, 30–49; Joel Panzer, "The Popes and Slavery," *Dunwoodie Review* 18 (1995): 78–109.

whites. Francis Patrick Kenrick, the leading moral theologian of the period and bishop of Philadelphia, validated the institution of slavery by accenting respect for law. He reasoned that "nothing should be attempted against the law, nor anything said or done to free the slaves. . . . But the prudence and the charity of the sacred ministers should appear in their effecting that the slaves, imbued with Christian morals, render service to their masters, venerating God, the supreme Master of all."[30] Archbishop John Hughes of New York maintained that slavery was an evil, but not an absolute evil. Bishops John England of South Carolina, Auguste Martin of Louisiana, and Augustin Verot of Florida held that slavery conformed to Catholic teaching and sacred scripture. And Martin went so far as to pronounce the enslavement of blacks to be "the manifest will of God." When Archbishop Jean-Marie Odin was ordinary of New Orleans, he not only suspended French-born priest Claude Pascal Maistre when he refused to stop preaching publicly against slavery but also put the parish he served, St. Rose of Lima, under interdict.[31] Archbishop John Baptist Purcell of Cincinnati came out against slavery just before the Civil War, and oral evidence suggests Catholics in that city may have aided fugitive slaves.

Certainly, the hierarchy faced a complex pastoral situation— the needs of a growing and culturally and linguistically diverse immigrant population, lay trusteeism, a shortage of clergy and religious, exhausting travel due to geographic distances and poor roads, breakdowns in communication, nativist attacks, and the anti-Catholic sentiments of many abolitionists. Yet, their collusion

---

30. John Peter Marschall, "Francis Patrick Kenrick, 1851–1863: The Baltimore Years" (Ph.D. diss., The Catholic University of America, 1965), 332, cited in Richard R. Duncan, "Catholics and the Church in the Antebellum Upper South," in *Catholics in the Old South*, 76.

31. Cyprian Davis, *Henriette Delille: Servant of Slaves, Witness to the Poor* (New Orleans: Archdiocese of New Orleans / Sisters of the Holy Family, 2004), 73–75; Randall M. Miller, "The Failed Mission: The Catholic Church and Black Catholics in the Old South," 149–70, in *Catholics in the Old South*; Jamie T. Phelps, "The Mission Ecclesiology of John R. Slattery: A Study of an African American Mission of the Catholic Church in the Nineteenth Century" (Ph.D. diss., The Catholic University of America, 1989).

with the socio-economic situation would prove grievous for the enslaved people and for the church. This brief sketch of episcopal responses to chattel slavery intimates that the church either forgot or failed to remember the central teaching of the *imago dei*: that all human beings bear the imprint of the divine image and, therefore, possess equal dignity before God. And, during the antebellum period, the church either forgot or failed to remember its responsibility to offer a prophetic witness to slaveholding society. The Catholic hierarchy, Miller asserts, relegated the question of slavery to the political sphere and "yielded up its social conscience to the status quo and devoted itself to the City of God."[32] The church forgot that some members of the body of Christ had enslaved other members of our body.

The local church of Charleston, South Carolina, quite literally forgot Catholic slaves in a settlement known as the "Catholic Crossroads." This was the site of St. James the Greater Church, established in 1833 by Bishop England for the area's Catholic slaveholding families. When fire destroyed the church in 1856 and war grew imminent, the slaveholding families fled the area, leaving church buildings in disrepair. A small group of black Catholic slaves was left behind.[33] Historian Cyprian Davis writes, "Without priest, church, or sacraments the Catholic faith was kept alive [among them] over a period of forty years through the efforts of Vincent de Paul Davis, former slave and storeowner, who instructed the children."[34] Not until 1897 did a priest from the diocese, Father Daniel Berberich, discover this community of forgotten black Catholics, attend to their sacramental needs, and restore the church building. Being forgotten wounds. We cannot know what these people may have felt or how they may have yearned for the comfort of the sacraments; but if they were forgotten, they did not forget their faith.

---

32. Miller, "Catholics in a Protestant World," *in Varieties of Southern Religious Experience,* 121, 127–28.
33. Davis, *The History of Black Catholics*, 209–10.
34. Ibid.

If before the Civil War the bishops accommodated the custom and culture of slavery, the end of the war provided an occasion to remedy earlier acquiescence. The Second Plenary Council of Baltimore convened in 1866, two years after emancipation. Archbishop Martin J. Spalding placed apostolic work among blacks on the agenda for discussion and action. This had been urged by the cardinal prefect of the Congregation for the Propagation of the Faith, which considered the welfare and evangelization of the newly emancipated slaves to be "of the utmost necessity." The plan called for the creation of a national prefecture to oversee apostolic work on behalf of African Americans. This proposal was met with objections, impatience, outright rejection, and resentment. The pastoral letter issued at the close of the council presented "no coherent policy" and offered little more than an expression of regret at the condition of the freed people.[35]

Perhaps, the council fathers did not consider slavery an issue "belonging to the substance of what the church is and believes."[36] Yet, slavery violated Catholic teaching about the human person. Did the council fathers' indifference to Rome's call for a prefecture constitute a not remembering? There were roughly one million black people in John England's diocese alone, yet his acceptance and defense of slavery had allowed the church to be considered an ally of slavery.[37] Did this not remembering handicap the church's mission of evangelization? Irenically, yet not without sadness, Davis writes:

> The history of the Catholic church's efforts to evangelize the black people of the United States in the period following the Civil War is not a very glorious one. One might note that the ethnic group that [the church] had known longest in this country, aside from the Indians, longer than any of the [many other] . . . immigrant groups in this country, was the

35. Ibid., 116, 118–22.
36. Mueller, "Forgetting as a Principle of Continuity in Tradition," 760.
37. Davis, *The History of Black Catholics*, 48.

group [the church] treated as stepchildren, the last considered and the first to be jettisoned when funds and personnel were scarce.[38]

Did the church choose not to remember this long history? Has such not remembering structured such a pattern of forgetfulness[39] that black membership in the Catholic Church became anomalous rather than customary? Did not such not remembering deprive the church of creativity and insight, of music and stories, of priests and parishioners, of vowed religious women and men? Not remembering and forgetting take a toll, injure, and demoralize. That a vibrant movement of black lay Catholics would emerge less than thirty years after the council might well be attributed to the work of the Holy Spirit.[40]

In 1992, John Paul II apologized for the church's involvement in slavery; this apology took place 126 years after the close of the Second Plenary Council of Baltimore. But, this apology was directed toward the concept of slavery rather than its actual practice. Thus, the most damaging and degrading practices of chattel slavery— buying, selling, mortgaging, inheriting, raping and abusing, torturing and outright killing, and owning human beings—went unacknowledged, uncondemned, and unretracted. Nor did this apology acknowledge, condemn, or retract

the use of slave labor without any measure of just compensation; the denial to slaves of the right to educate their children; the denial to slaves of the full range of conjugal companionship and protection; the denial of any right to personal

---

38. Ibid., 136.

39. Paul Ricoeur, *Memory, History, Forgetting*, trans. Kathleen Blamey and David Pellauer (Chicago and London: University of Chicago Press, 2004), uses the phrase "structure of forgetfulness," 450.

40. Davis, *The History of Black Catholics*, 163–94; see David Spalding, C.F.X., "The Negro Catholic Congresses, 1889–1894," *Catholic Historical Review* 55 (October 1969): 337–57; Congress of Colored Catholics of the United States, *Three Catholic Afro-American Congresses* (Cincinnati: American Catholic Tribune, 1893; reprint ed., New York: Arno Press, 1978).

development; and the complete exclusion of the slave from the political community.[41]

Despite the passage of the Fourteenth Amendment to the Constitution, these very aspects of chattel slavery were extended through "the neoslavery of Jim Crow."[42] For nearly a century African Americans endured disenfranchisement, wanton lynching, racial harassment, the violence of the southern peonage system, and segregation in housing, education, medicine, employment, public transportation, entertainment, and, most tragically, in churches.

With regard to the evil of white racist supremacy, no one demanded more of the church than did Reverend Martin Luther King Jr. "No one observing the history of the church in America," he wrote, "can deny the shameful fact that it has been an accomplice in structuring racism into the architecture of American society. The church, by and large, sanctioned slavery and surrounded it with the halo of moral respectability. It also cast its mantle of sanctity over the system of segregation."[43] King acknowledged the involvement of Christian and Jewish religious groups in the struggle for civil rights. But, he declared, as a whole, the church has been all too negligent. With great indignation he declared:

> [The church] has blessed a status quo that needed to be blasted, and reassured a social order that needed to be reformed. So the church must acknowledge its guilt, its weak and vacillating witness, its all too frequent failure to obey the call to servanthood. Today the judgment of God is upon the church for its failure to be true to its mission. If the church does not recapture its prophetic zeal, it will become an irrelevant social club without moral or spiritual authority.[44]

---

41. Noonan, *A Church That Can and Cannot Change*, 122.

42. Orlando Patterson, *Rituals of Blood: Consequences of Slavery in Two American Centuries* (New York: Basic Books, 1998), xiii.

43. Martin Luther King Jr., *Where Do We Go from Here: Chaos or Community?* (New York: Harper & Row, 1967), 96.

44. Ibid.

True to the moral and spiritual ideals and teachings of Judaism and Christianity, King believed that "every [human person] is heir to a legacy of dignity and worth."[45] These ideals and teaching were "diametrically opposed"[46] to racism; indeed, for Jews and Christians, racism is idolatry and heresy. For racism seeks to replace the One God with an idol of human making and human visage. King asserted: "So long as the Negro or any other member of a minority group is treated as a means to an end, the image of God is abused in [him or her] and consequently and proportionally lost by those who inflict the abuse."[47] Racism damages the person who is abused, brutalized, and assaulted, and racism damages the person who inflicts the abuse, brutality, and assault. "Every human life," he maintained, "is a reflection of divinity, and every act of injustice mars and defaces the image of God in [the human person]."[48] Thus racism stands as both personal sin and social disorder, entailing not only individual prejudice but the exercise of religious, historical, cultural, social (i.e., political, economic, technological) power to keep one race privileged and secure and other races disempowered and vulnerable. Yet, King believed that "racism is a tenacious evil, but it is not immutable."[49] Transformation, change in human persons and change in our social order are possible; hope is possible.

Memory, Mourning, and Hope

Memory, individual or personal as well as common or shared, is an intentional and selective act. It sorts and categorizes, erases and embellishes, conceals and reveals. And, "While memory requires time to become what it is, time also hinders memory."[50] Memory

---

45. Ibid., 97.
46. Ibid., 100.
47. Ibid., 97.
48. Ibid., 99.
49. Ibid., 152.
50. Gerhard Richter, "Acts of Memory and Mourning: Derrida and the Fictions of Anteriority," in *Memory, History, Theories, and Debates*, ed. Susannah Radstone and Bill Schwarz (New York: Fordham University Press, 2010), 150.

may fade, may be filtered or altered or manipulated. Forgetting is the opposite of memory. Forgetting includes both unintentional failures to notice something or someone and intentional acts of erasure or deletion of what once was known.[51] Perhaps unintentional forgetting holds some practical utility, preventing us from an overload of minutiae or distractions that could prove detrimental to well-being. On the other hand, forgetting as an intentional and active "strategy of avoidance, evasion, [or] flight entails the same sort of responsibility as that imputed to acts of negligence, omission, imprudence, [and] lack of foresight."[52]

What might it mean for members of the regional Catholic Church of the United States to open themselves to the dangerous memory of chattel slavery? What might it mean for the members of that regional church to retrieve their own sad history of forgetting and not remembering? What, if anything, from the period of our bleak compromise with slavery, should the church *not* forget? How might the church as sacrament and institution, with its ever-capacious memory, powers of sanctification, and practical attachment to the dead, authentically remember the millions of captured, enslaved black children, women, and men who died over the course of more than three hundred years of slavery? How should the U.S. regional church mourn or lament? How should this regional church hope?

These questions carry historical and eschatological, political and moral import. Their motive springs from commitment to discern and cooperate with the work of the Spirit in history, "to preserve the dangerous memory of the messianic God."[53] Moreover, these questions situate a broken body at the center of Christian reality: "This is my body, which is given for you. . . . This is my

---

51. Miroslav Volf, *The End of Memory* (Grand Rapids, MI/Cambridge, UK: William B. Eerdmans Publishing Company, 2006), 145.

52. Paul Ricoeur, *Memory, History, Forgetting*, trans. Kathleen Blamey and David Pellauer (Chicago and London: University of Chicago Press, 2004), 449.

53. Johann Baptist Metz, "Theology in the Struggle for History and Society," in *The Future of Liberation Theology: Essays in Honor of Gustavo Gutiérrez*, ed. Marc H. Ellis and Otto Maduro (Maryknoll, NY: Orbis Books, 1989), 167.

blood . . . which is shed for you." This Jewish body had been per-
ceived as a threat to the status quo and so was dispensed with by
violence. Those questions also locate a broken body at the center
of American reality. "The being of slavery, its soul and its body,
lives and moves in the chattel principle."[54] This black body was
grasped as an object of property and so used and abused and dispensed with by violence. Yet, the memory of the Jewish Jesus and
the memory of the black (chattel) body coalesce as memories of a
past that is not over, that must be encountered and confronted in
the here and now even as they open onto hope and future life.

Chattel slavery exposed an impoverished and naïve biblicism
that reduced the church—Christianity—to a mere shell of prin-
ciples and ideals that obfuscated the moral and ethical implications of slavery for master and slave alike. The plantation was the
Golgotha of black experience in the United States—often geographically isolated, fairly self-sufficient, equipped with the tools
of corporal punishment and restraint. By law and by custom, the
plantation's chattel system allowed the slaveholder and his/her
agents absolute control over the body and life of the slave. There
can be no redress for chattel slavery; no amount of financial res-
titution can compensate or amend or restore the human futures
lost. Restorative justice may be found only in taking up the ethical responsibility of memory and the "ethical impossibility of
forgetting."[55]

The Christian practice of memory professes to be radically different. We Christians oblige ourselves to remember. We mark
ourselves with a sign that neither can be erased nor easily forgotten. The cross of the crucified Jew traced on our bodies at baptism initiates us into a new life, into a community constituted by
memory, into intimate and irrevocable relatedness to all creatures.
Moreover, the memory of the suffering Jewish Jesus opens the

---

54. James W. C. Pennington, *The Fugitive Blacksmith; or, Events in the History
of James W. C. Pennington, Pastor of a Presbyterian Church, New York, Formerly
a Slave in the State of Maryland, United States* (London: Charles Gilpin, 1849).

55. Kaplan, "Souls at the Crossroads," 522.

church over and over again to other crucified victims in the past and in the present. The Christian practice of memory nourishes and eases thirst, interrogates and revises perspectives, habits, and daily life. Memory and love require that the church act and live *in* history in imitation of the gracious and healing presence of Jesus of Nazareth, who loved human beings and loved being human to the end—and loves still. To fulfill that ethical obligation as church, we—who member it—must refuse to turn away from and must look directly at the dreadful history of chattel slavery. We must assume responsibility for the memory of chattel slavery, protecting that memory from trivialization, outright rejection or denial, and voyeurism; moreover, theology calls the church to lament.

To trivialize chattel slavery is to fix it in the past as if the past is really past and, thus, bears no relation to the present or to the future. Our preoccupation with the present distorts our moral relation to both chattel slavery and the present. On this particular point, historian Michel-Rolph Trouillot comments:

> The denunciation of slavery in a presentist mode is easy. Slavery was bad, most of us would agree. But presentism is by definition anachronistic. To condemn slavery alone is the easy way out. . . . What needs to be denounced here to restore authenticity is much less slavery than the racist present within which representations of slavery are produced.[56]

Authentic memory of chattel slavery entails acknowledgment of and relation to the complex present reality within which we remember it, and, as authentic, that memory obliges solidarity. Moreover, authenticity "is not a type or degree of knowledge, but a relationship to what is known."[57] Necessarily, then, the obligation of solidarity requires knowledge of chattel slavery, but that knowledge dissolves as mere artifact or archive if it is not in relation to the present. Hence, past and present compenetrate each other,

---

56. Michel-Rolph Trouillot, *Silencing the Past: Power and the Production of History* (Boston: Beacon Press, 1995), 148.

57. Ibid.

for the past is never a fixed reality. In 1838, the Jesuit Province of Maryland sold 272 black Catholics they had held in slavery in order to meet the debts of Georgetown University. If this action has claimed attention beginning in 2015, it is because of the contemporary Georgetown community's engagement in remembering, in truth-telling, and in reconciliation.[58]

Attentiveness to the interplay of past and present lays the groundwork for theology's serious and critical understanding of the history of chattel slavery and of the U.S. regional church's gradual, fitful move away from support of its amelioration toward its abolition. This will include grappling with early Christianity's compromise with slavery, with the history of biblical interpretation of slavery as well as the complex (and disturbing) use of slavery as a metaphor for Christian discipleship.[59] Such critical understanding generates concrete solidarity in memory of chattel slavery—opposition to the effect of slavery on the descendants of the Africans as well as opposition to slavery in the present day.[60] Finally, we must protect the memory of chattel slavery from being mobilized for political or personal goals—whether outside or inside the church. If such volatile memory is processed as cultic, rather than loving remembrance of the dead,[61] then the dead will not be safe.[62]

We must protect the memory of chattel slavery from outright rejection or denial. We must "protect the remembering and

---

58. Report of the Working Group on Slavery, Memory, and Reconciliation to the President of Georgetown University, Washington, DC, 2016. http://slavery.georgetown.edu/report/.

59. See Jennifer A. Glancy, *Slavery in Early Christianity* (Minneapolis: Fortress Press, 2006); and Dale B. Martin, *Slavery as Salvation: The Metaphor of Slavery in Pauline Christianity* (New Haven: Yale University Press, 1990).

60. See Bernadette J. Brooten, with Jacqueline L. Hazelton, eds., *Beyond Slavery: Overcoming Its Religious and Sexual Legacies* (New York: Palgrave Macmillan, 2010).

61. Jan Assmann, *Religion and Cultural Memory*, trans. Rodney Livingstone (Stanford, CA: Stanford University Press, 2006; orig. 2000), 7.

62. Walter Benjamin, "On the Concept of History," # VI, trans. Dennis Redmond. Available online at http://www.efn.org/~dredmond/ThesesonHistory.html.

retelling"[63] of chattel slavery from modernity's insistence that its abolition denotes progress. Rather, such a view overlooks the neoslavery that followed emancipation and sealed black bodies in *un*freedom for nearly nine decades. Moreover, the plantation is not a relic of the past; the prison-industrial complex reinscribes the agony of slavery—surveillance, violence, discipline, control of the black body. In protecting the remembering and retelling of the stories of chattel slavery, we must prepare to face dismissal of that memory or indifference toward it: "That's in the past"; "We are beyond that"; "I was not born here"; "I am not related to that past." In order to contest such indifference, distress, and fear, theology can help us by integrating the memory of chattel slavery with the memory of the suffering and death of the Jewish Jesus and his solidarity with the poor, dispossessed, and abject. Further, we members of the church must attend to practices of Eucharistic remembering, contemplation, and solidarity.

Theology must protect the memory of chattel slavery from *voyeurism*. To make visible the black body battered in chattel slavery incriminates "the precariousness of empathy and the uncertain line between witness and spectator."[64] Feminist scholars in particular have come to question artistic representations of the battered body of the crucified Jewish Jesus insofar as those representations direct believers to a masochism that caricature the virtues of patience, long-suffering, and forbearance. Similarly, in remembering chattel slavery, we question any careless or exploitative or spectacular materialization of the black body. Indeed, the historic degradation of that body has been prolonged, even by black men and women, through representations that feed off of and feed the base preferences of the dominant culture— money over people, expediency over long-term solutions, imme-

---

63. Johann Baptist Metz, "Unity and Diversity," in Johann Baptist Metz and Jürgen Moltmann, *Faith and the Future: Essays on Theology, Solidarity, and Modernity* (Maryknoll, NY: Orbis Books, 1995), 63.

64. Saidiya Hartman, *Scenes of Subjection: Terror, Slavery, and Self-Making in Nineteenth Century America* (Oxford: Oxford University Press, 1997), 4.

diate gratification over postponement, duplicity over the truth. In this cultural and social context, violence permeates every sector of life, and women, in particular, endure its intensification. To borrow a phrase from Johann Baptist Metz, theology can help us find "new eyes" with which to see one another and to find new ways through which we honor *all* bodies.

Finally, we who member the church must begin to lament or mourn our complicity in the dehumanizing suffering caused by chattel slavery.[65] Such lament and mourning may acknowledge and confess failure, but such acknowledgment and confession ought not to allow us as church to "fall into a neurotically arrogant cult of self-accusation." We must learn to "honor our eschatological hope and venture conversion and new ways" of behavior in light of that promise.[66] Lament or mourning, then, may be considered a manifestation of hope—a hope that neither forgets nor fails to remember. When we appropriate such hope, we face up to and integrate our failures and obstacles and breakdowns through prayer and in the work of justice. Lament or mourning names and grieves publicly and announces what is unjust publicly and creates "spaces of recognition and catharsis" that form us for the reparations of justice.[67] And as the work of justice, lament resists that calculus of power by which the weak and the vulnerable suffer oppression and abuse. Bradford Hinze writes:

> Laments serve as a furnace that releases base ingredients of pity and anger, retribution and remorse. This cauldron need not produce deadly toxins, but can provide a crucible for compassion, where baser forms of pain yield purer forms of

---

65. Bradford E. Hinze, "Ecclesial Images: What Can We Learn from Our Laments," *Theological Studies* 72, no. 3 (September 2011): 470–95; see Bryan N. Massingale, *Racial Justice and the Catholic Church* (Maryknoll, NY: Orbis Books, 2009).

66. Johann Baptist Metz, "1492—through the Eyes of a European Theologian," in Metz and Moltmann, *Faith and the Future*, 71.

67. Kathleen O'Connor, *Lamentations and the Tears of the World* (Maryknoll, NY: Orbis Books, 2002), 128.

love-in-action and a truer, more purified understanding of the identities of self, others, and God.[68]

Conclusion

Chattel slavery as the memory of the suffering of an oppressed people constitutes a dangerous memory for the church—and for theology. In no deep and thoroughgoing way has the Catholic Church as an institution or as a body of members in the United States or theology responded to the memory of chattel slavery in the way in which they have with such loving and fierce generosity to the sadistic crucifixion of the poor of Latin America and the violent destruction of the Jewish people. This is a statement of poignant fact; it does not rank or compare. These ignominious events require, *even demand* our solidarity; so too does the memory of chattel slavery.

The black children, women, and men who lived and died in chattel slavery oblige us to remember, and to mourn. Their lives in chattel slavery come to us as dangerous memory. This memory cannot be erased, for the very bodies of the descendants of those who remained and survived continue to provoke the memory of an unapproached and unresolved past that reaches into the present and must be engaged. In risking memory, overcoming forgetfulness, collectively taking responsibility, commemorating, we lovingly embody ethical responsibility for the past in the present for the future. The love of an unreservedly loving God will hold us in our risk, will not allow us to forget, will hold us in hope.

---

68. Hinze, "Ecclesial Images," 479.

PART THREE

Following Jesus Crucified and Risen

CHAPTER FIVE

To Live at the Disposal of the Cross

Mystical-Political Discipleship
as Christological Locus

Out of his very self, that is, out of his body, [Jesus
Christ] has made a stairway, so as to raise us up from
the way of suffering and set us at rest!
—Catherine of Siena

O, the old sheep know the road
The old sheep know the road
The young lambs must find the way?
—Negro Spiritual

We are climbing Jacob's ladder,
Every round goes higher higher/ Soldier of the Cross.
—Negro Spiritual

Standing in the laundry room of her apartment building, the theologian fidgets as the rinse cycle of the washing machine slows to
an end. She bends to clear away a thick wad of lint from the dryer;
absently, she looks out of the window. In the parking lot below, a
black woman picks through the building's refuse dumpster. Mes-
merized, the black woman doing laundry cannot but watch. The
woman below works systematically, opening and inspecting small
white bags, setting some aside and discarding others. It is difficult from the eighth floor to see precisely what the black woman

below selects, but the black woman looking from above wonders if the woman below has found the remains of her half-eaten roasted chicken or salad or bread or cheese.

Uncomfortable, angry, and sad, I turn away and put my things in the dryer. I take the elevator to my apartment. I sit down at the computer where I am struggling to write about discipleship and the cross of Christ. I am unnerved. Writing on such a theme, after such looking, provokes recognition and dis-ease. The woman in the parking lot below is no one other than Christ. Such glimpses of him beg for a theology of the cross, a theology of discipleship that makes both his presence and a praxis of concrete solidarity and compassion more visible in our time. What sort of christological reflection is needed in our situation? What can it mean to tell the woman who searches my garbage that God in Jesus is also alienated, a stranger, a despised "other"? Can memory of his passion and death unmask our pretense to personal and communal innocence, to social and religious neutrality before structural evil and suffering? What sort of christological reflection can do justice to Jesus of Nazareth, to his radical freedom and profound consciousness of God and neighbor, to his desire for life, to his acceptance of the cross? What sort of christological reflection can address adequately the meaning of the cross to children, women, and men brutalized by social suffering?

Here I explore these questions by sketching discipleship as a *locus* or starting point from which to understand Jesus of Nazareth as the absolute meaning of life for the world. This topic, discipleship as a christological locus, can make no claim to novelty; it forms a conspicuous strand in Christian tradition. Scholars suggest that the word disciple (*talmîd*) appears rarely in the Hebrew scriptures, but its usage was part of the fabric of the ancient world. However, in the Gospel narratives, Jesus of Nazareth invests the relationship of teacher (*rabbi*) and disciple (*mathetes*) with new and remarkable meaning. For, rather than appeal solely to the conventional prerogatives of the rabbi, acquired knowledge and presumptive authority, Jesus invites and nurtures in his disciples faith in *who* he is and in the "good news" he is sent to proclaim. Yet, Jesus tests their faith. To follow the "way" he teaches requires that his disciples take up a new and different "way" of being *in* and *for* the world. Thus, these followers of rabbi Jesus confront a commanding and paradoxical challenge: "If any want to become my followers, let them deny themselves and take up their cross and follow me.... For those who want to save their life will lose it, and those who lose their life for my sake, and for the sake of the gospel, will save it. For what does it profit them to gain the whole world and forfeit their life?" (Mark 8:34–36; Luke 9:23, 24a, 25; cf. John 6:35–51).

For our purposes, the Lukan account of the story of the life, death, and resurrection of Jesus of Nazareth will provide the basic performative meaning of discipleship. Biblical exegetes have identified the theme of discipleship almost exclusively with the Markan Gospel. To borrow a term from Ched Myers, scholars have read this Gospel as a kind of "catechism" on discipleship.[1] But, since the whole of the New Testament stands as an invitation to radical discipleship, the Lukan account need not be excluded from reflection on this theme. Further, Luke's account of the story of Jesus strategically adverts to and incorporates Torah texts that foreground the tradition and customs of "jubilee," that is, the complex of cyclical practices concerned with restorative justice, reparation and release, healing and re-creation (Leviticus 25). These references coupled with parables in which Jesus describes the reign of God underscore the importance of justice in the Lukan narrative.

At the same time, feminist scholars have called into question the treatment of women in Luke-Acts, for while the writer shows

---

1. Ched Myers, "Mark's Gospel: Invitation to Discipleship," in *The New Testament: Introducing the Way of Discipleship,* ed. Wes Howard-Brook and Sharon H. Ringe (Maryknoll, NY: Orbis Books, 2002), 49. For some examples of such scholarly interpretation, see Ched Myers et al., *"Say to This Mountain:" Mark's Story of Discipleship* (Maryknoll, NY: Orbis Books, 1996); and Brian Blount, *Go Preach! Mark's Kingdom Message and the Black Church* (Maryknoll, NY: Orbis Books, 1998).

an interest in women, it is an ambiguous interest.[2] Clarice Martin writes that the Lukan writer demonstrates "redactional and apologetic tendencies [that] actually restrict women's prophetic ministry in some instances, reinforcing women's conformity to conventional, culturally prescribed roles of passivity, submission, silence, and marginality."[3] Turid Karlsen Seim concurs, yet alerts us to the possibility that the Lukan Gospel may carry a "double message . . . [with] an ironic twist." While the very structure of the narrative may enable male domination and co-optation of women, nonetheless, it

> preserves extraordinary traditions about the women from Galilee . . . [who] were indeed capable and qualified, but the men suspected and rejected them. The male consolidation of power occurs against a story in which the men have shown weakness and failure rather than strength.[4]

For, in order to tell the story of Jesus, Luke must tell the story of the women from Galilee. Silenced by male power, they "continue to speak." Moreover, the women and their roles in the story of the life, death, and resurrection of Jesus of Nazareth constitute a "dangerous remembrance."[5] Through faith, commitment, and service, these women teach us what it means to be a disciple of Jesus.

Scholars date the writing of Luke-Acts in the final decades of the first century, and Sharon Ringe argues that Luke wrote for a community of mixed economic and social standing. Textual evidence suggests that Luke sought to address strained relations between the poor and the nonpoor. But, as Ringe states, he "pulled

---

2. For some examples, see Barbara E. Reid, *Choosing the Better Part? Women in the Gospel of Luke* (Collegeville, MN: Liturgical Press, 1996); Turid Karlsen Seim, *The Double Message: Patterns of Gender in Luke-Acts* (Nashville: Abingdon, 1994).

3. Clarice J. Martin, "The Acts of the Apostles," in *Searching the Scriptures: A Feminist Commentary*, vol. 2, ed. Elisabeth Schüssler Fiorenza (New York: Crossroad, 1994), 770.

4. Turid Karlsen Seim, "The Gospel of Luke," in *Searching the Scriptures*, 761.

5. Ibid.

his punches": Luke speaks *about* the poor, but speaks *to* the rich; he emphasizes charity, but not change in repressive political and economic arrangements.[6] Certainly, for us Christians living in nations of wealth and power, for we who are the privileged of "first worlds," Luke's Gospel presents a challenge: How can we live as disciples of Jesus? Will we speak truth to power or pull our punches?

To live as Jesus's disciple means to live at the disposal of the cross—exposed, vulnerable, open to the wisdom and power and love of God. Lived response to his call requires a praxis of solidarity and compassion as well as surrender to the startling embrace of Divine Love. Christian discipleship as a lived mystical-political way forms the locus for the fundamental grasp of who Jesus of Nazareth is and what following and believing in him means. This thesis will be elaborated in four sections. The first section, "The Way of Jesus," sketches his ministry and the demands he places on those who would follow him. The second section, "The Cross," draws on the work of Martin Hengel to retrieve the horror and disgust felt by the men and women of the ancient world toward crucifixion. I want to suggest some of the shock they would have experienced at Jesus's summons to "take up your cross and follow me." This discussion prepares the background for the next section, "The Cross as a Condition of Discipleship." For the women and men drawn to his prophetic praxis, Jesus offered a new and compelling "way" of being for God and God's people and that way included, even demanded, the cross. The fourth section, "The Way Jesus Is," offers a meditation on the crucified Jesus as the way through the Spirit to union with the Father. This section draws on insights gleaned from reflection on the mystical experiences of Catherine of Siena and of enslaved Africans in the United States. There is, I suggest, a resonance in these experiences that discloses what being caught up in the love of God means. They capture what it means to understand that the power of God in the cross is the power to live and to love—even in the teeth of violence and death.

---

6. Sharon H. Ringe, "Luke's Gospel: 'Good News to the Poor' for the Non-Poor," in Howard-Brook and Ringe, eds., *The New Testament*, 65.

The Way of Jesus

In the Lukan account, the ministry, that is, the teaching, preaching, and healing, through which Jesus of Nazareth met a death on the cross, began in a small synagogue in his hometown. Jesus takes the scroll from the attendant and reads: "The Spirit of the Lord is upon me, because he has anointed me to preach good news to the poor. He has sent me to proclaim release to the captives and recovering of sight to the blind, to set at liberty those who are oppressed, to proclaim the acceptable year of the Lord.... Today this scripture is fulfilled in your hearing" (Luke 4:18–19, 21; Isaiah 61:1, 2; 58:6). The narrator portrays the congregation as reacting with pleasure and pride: "And all spoke well of him and wondered at the gracious words which proceeded out of his mouth; and they said, 'Is not this Joseph's son?'" (Luke 4:22). But Jesus's evocation of Isaiah stings the conscience, and neither the cautious nor the cynical can tolerate the concluding coda—an irruption of messianic time that hints at the meaning of who Jesus is. Appreciative amazement pitches into anger and attempted violence: "They rose up to put him out of the city, and led him to the brow of the hill ... that they might throw him down headlong" (Luke 4:24–29).

Almost from the outset of the Lukan narrative, Jesus is identified with the prophecy. His ministry signals the in-breaking of the reign of God: he is sent to those who are wounded and impaired; who are possessed by demons; who are poor, broken-hearted, and despised; who are imprisoned by occupation or disfigurement and, thereby, rendered incapable of ritual purity. These children, women, and men are without choice, without hope, and without a future. Jesus announces to these "least" the comfort and judgment of the reign of God. He pledges that God is *for* them and *with* them.

Jesus eats and drinks with women and men of questionable character—tax collectors, prostitutes, outcasts, and public sinners. When questioned about his associates, he replies, "Those who are well have no need of a physician, but those who are sick; I have not come to call the righteous, but sinners to repentance" (Luke 5:31–32). Women—Mary Magdalene, Joanna, the wife of Herod's steward, Susanna, Mary the mother of James (Luke 8:1–3)—form part of the band of disciples who travel with Jesus to various cities and villages and share in his ministry. Jesus does not shy away from talk and debate with women; he heals them, forgives them, and takes them and their experiences seriously. When a woman named Mary sits at his feet as a disciple, Jesus affirms her agency over against narrow and constricting roles set for women by culture and society (Luke 10:38–42). Finally, the proclamation of the resurrection itself is entrusted to women; their remembrance of the very words of Jesus grounds their witness (Luke 24:9).

Through his audacious proclamation of the reign of God and his astonishing healing power, Jesus attracts crowds and, eventually, disciples. The men and women who would follow him (Luke 8:2–3) are challenged to sever all ties with the past (Luke 5:11), to address God intimately in prayer, to fast without ostentation, to practice self-examen (Luke 11:1–4; 6:42), and to allow no familial obligation, no cultural custom, no ritual observance to turn them to another way (Luke 14:26; 9:57–62; 12:22–23).

Through word and deed, Jesus taught his disciples to center themselves *in* and *on* the God whom he knew and loved with all his heart, all his soul, all his strength, and all his mind (Luke 10:25–27; 11:1–13). He enjoined them to love others—particularly, poor, outcast, and despised children, women, and men—concretely and without reservation, to act on behalf of these "little ones" for restoration to God and to community (Luke 10:29–37).

The proclamation of the reign of a God "slow to anger, rich in mercy" (Jonah 4:2) formed the core of Jesus's preaching. In parables and sermons, he drew a vivid portrait of life lived under the reign of this God. What would this new life be like? Like the watchfulness of a farmer at harvest, like the consolation of acceptance, like a lavish and festive feast for those who neither can return the honor nor provide a comparable meal, like the joy at rescuing a stray lamb in the parched wilderness, like the relief at recovering lost funds, like the unshakable love of a broken-hearted parent for a wayward child, like the fruitfulness of the mustard seed and the capaciousness of its tree, like the force of leaven (Luke 8:4–18,

44–48; 14:12–14; 15:4–10, 11–16; 13:18–21). Jesus envisioned life lived under the reign of this God as a realization of truth and love, holiness and grace, justice and peace. Moreover, this God staked the gift of that reign *in us* and *in* present existential reality (Luke 17:21). Finally, Jesus taught his followers to pray that the reign of God might come—and to pray for its coming in the way in which God wills it. The disciples are to pray for that reign of justice and peace which, while not yet realized, is seeded in the here and now, the point of change where the old order yields to God's dream (Luke 11:2–4).

Jesus cultivated in his disciples a desire, a yearning, an expectation for the coming of God's reign. He led them through the "narrow gate" to glimpse the secrets of living for God (Luke 13:24), to discern just what was required of those who would enter the way (Luke 12:22–48), to grasp the purity of heart and action its realization needed (Luke 12:49–53; 16:13; 14:26). Jesus granted his disciples a share in his healing power; the miracles they worked were a sign for him that the reign of God was breaking through.

But, the ministry of Jesus is a dangerous ministry. Discipleship costs. The praxis of compassionate solidarity that he inaugurated on behalf of the reign of God disrupted social customs, religious practices, and conventions of authority and power. Without hesitation, Jesus made the cross an undeniable condition for discipleship (Luke 9:23; 14:27). By his own death on the cross, Jesus incarnated the solidarity of God with abject and despised human persons. The disciples who heard and responded to his word and the deed of his life came, even if haltingly, gradually, fitfully, to dedicate their lives and their living to the concerns, commitments, and compassion of the God of Jesus. In this way, they placed their lives at the disposal of the cross.

The Cross

From the beginning of his ministry, Jesus taught a "way" of life that not only offered a distinctive "understanding [of] the fulfillment of Israel's hope," but substantively "radicalized [his religious] tradition."[7] In his prophetic "performance" of parable, sign, and deed, Jesus broke open "the prevailing worldview and replace[d] it with one that was closely related, but significantly adjusted at every point."[8] But, it is his crucifixion, his brutal death on the cross (Luke 23:33, John 19:18), that set "the way" apart from other religious movements in the ancient world.

The cross was the mark of shame, the sign of the criminal and the slave. Martin Hengel delineates this point in *Crucifixion in the Ancient World and the Folly of the Message of the Cross.*[9] To accept the message of the cross, first-century Jews would have had to overcome deep-seated religious, cultural, and political sensibilities toward the very act of crucifixion, while, at the same time, they would have had to grapple with a new notion of the meaning of messiah. Recall the injunction in the Torah: "a hanged man is accursed by God . . ." (Deuteronomy 21:23).

In the Hebrew scriptures, the promise of a messiah is bound up with the covenant established by God with the chosen people. Yet, as N. T. Wright argues, during the Judaism of Jesus's day, there was no single or uniform conception of the messiah. The various messianic movements shared no common notion of the messiah and exhibited "considerable freedom and flexibility" toward the "idea of Israel's coming king."[10] However, these movements shared the expectation that with the arrival of the messiah, Israel's divinely ordained destiny would be realized: the Roman occupation, colonization, and defilement of sacred land would end and a new age would begin.

The conflicting aspirations of long-subjugated women and men were projected onto the notion of messiah. He would lead the final victorious battle against the enemies of Israel. Not only would he

---

7. N. T. Wright, *Christian Origins and the Question of God: Jesus and the Victory of God*, vol. 2 (Minneapolis: Fortress Press, 1996), 176.

8. Ibid., 175.

9. Martin Hengel, *Crucifixion in the Ancient World and the Folly of the Message of the Cross*, trans. John Bowden (Philadelphia: Fortress Press, 1977).

10. Wright, *Christian Origins and the Question of God,* vol. 2, *Jesus and the Victory of God*, 482.

bring about the political liberation of the people and the transformation of their historical situation, the messiah would transform history itself. The messianic age would bring an end to suffering, alienation, and exile. God's chosen people would be gathered in to their ancestral home. A crucified messiah, a messiah who would die dishonored as a criminal, was unthinkable. A crucified messiah was not, could not be, the true messiah at all. Paul's message of the cross was offensive, monstrous; it could not be tolerated. A crucified messiah would have to be rejected on the grounds of fidelity to religious orthodoxy.

Gentile groups also would have been scandalized by the notion of a crucified God. For these women and men, religious revulsion at the cross was joined to intellectual objections. Potential converts, particularly sophisticated Romans and Greeks, held the notion of a crucified God and of any who would follow him in contempt.[11] In the *City of God*, Augustine preserves an oracle of the Greek god Apollo, as recorded by the philosopher Porphyry nearly two hundred years earlier. A man petitions the oracle about how to dissuade his wife from Christian belief. The god replies: "Let her go [continue] as she pleases, persisting in her vain delusions, singing in lamentation for a god who died in delusions, who was condemned by right-thinking judges, and killed in hideous fashion by the worst of deaths, a death bound with iron."[12] Belief in a crucified God was deemed madness, mania.[13]

Given the disgust that both Jews and Gentiles felt toward crucifixion, Paul's proclamation of the cross, as Hengel explains, "ran counter not only to Roman political thinking, but to the whole

---

11. Hengel (*Crucifixion in the Ancient World*, 2) cites Pliny the Younger, who insisted that belief in a crucified god was a "pernicious and extravagant superstition" (*Epistulae* 10.96.4–8).

12. Augustine, *City of God*, trans. Henry Bettenson; ed. David Knowles (New York: Penguin Books, 1972), 19.23.884–85.

13. Justin writes, "They charge us with madness, saying that we give the second place after the unchanging and ever-existing God and begetter of all things to a crucified man" (13.4), "First Apology," in *Early Christian Fathers*, ed. and trans. Cyril C. Richardson (New York: Macmillan, 1970), 249.

ethos of religion in ancient times."[14] The contemporary Christian remains equally as perplexed. There is little in modern or post-modern life to assist us in comprehending the shame that crucifixion denoted in the ancient world. The supreme Roman penalty, crucifixion was a military and political punishment primarily used against insurrectionists, murderers, robbers, and reserved in nearly all instances for men and women of the lower classes, slaves, and subjugated peoples.

Crucifixion was intended to intimidate by example and subdue by spectacle; it was high state theatrical violence. Crucifixion called for the public display of a naked victim in some prominent place—at a crossroads, in an amphitheater, on high ground. Often the condemned was flogged, then made to carry a crossbeam through the streets to the place of execution. The victim's hands and feet were bound or nailed to the wood. If, after this torment, the victim were still alive, he could expect to die by suffocation: unable to support the weight of the body with torn hands, the upper body pressed down and slowly crushed the diaphragm. Further dishonor and insult accompanied death: crucified bodies were left to wild beasts and to rot, or, sometimes, as Tacitus reports, "when daylight faded, [they] were burned to serve as lamps by night."[15] Jesus was spared this last indignity, although the very manner of his death confounded the claim of divinity. By his death on the cross, Jesus demonstrated the cost of discipleship, even as the cross hallowed in him the capacity for radical resurrection life.

Whatever resurrection means, the disciples "saw" the risen Jesus. If the sight of him left them dazed, they remain gripped by an unshakable certainty that the Jesus of Nazareth who had been crucified was, by the power of the God of Israel, raised from the dead. The body in which Jesus is raised does not belong to this world; his resurrected body is a new and different reality and signals a new and different mode of living. Not to be confused with resuscitation, resurrection breaks radically with material reality as we

---

14. Hengel, *Crucifixion*, 1.
15. Tacitus, *Annals* 15.44.4, cited in Hengel, *Crucifixion*, 26.

experience it. Yet, the appearances on the road to Emmaus (Luke 24:13–32) and in Jerusalem (Luke 24:33–43) are characterized by an insistent corporeality: Jesus eats with the disciples, invites them to examine his hands and feet, to touch him, to feel flesh and bone. "Handle me, and see!" (Luke 24:39). The recognition of the heart is grasped by the senses and confirmed by the mind.

Resurrection is an event for Jesus; something radical has happened to him. Resurrection is also an event for the disciples. Jesus's postresurrection appearances awaken in them the embers of a bold witness that the gift of the Spirit will fan into flame. Even as resurrection characterizes the destiny of Jesus, it is not a private destiny intended for him alone. It is the beginning of the absolute transformation of all creation. Resurrection breaks through, formally and materially, the cosmic, psychic, and moral disorder brought about by the reign of sin. Resurrection signals eschatological healing and binds back to the heart of God a marred and broken creation.

The appearances of the risen Lord to the disciples are gratuitous and, as such, remind us that the resurrection is not primarily about the sight of Jesus, but rather about *insight* into his mission. Real, transformative encounters with the risen Lord, these appearances refine for the disciples (and for us) just what it costs to live the way of Jesus, to confess him as the absolute meaning of life for the world. At the same time, the death of Jesus discloses God's own struggle against the powers and principalities of this world and manifests God's desire to emancipate those ensnared in psychic or religious or cultural or social bondage. The crucified Jesus is the sign of the cost of identification with poor, outcast, abject, and despised women and men in the struggle for life. He incarnates the freedom and destiny of discipleship.

The Cross as a Condition of Discipleship

With this background, perhaps, we now may be able to grasp the astonishment of the disciples and the people gathered around Jesus when he said, "If any want to become my followers, let them deny themselves and take up their cross and follow me" (Mark 8:34). Given the humiliation associated with crucifixion, these words could scarcely have been inviting. Surely, more than once, these ordinary women and men of the ancient world had witnessed the barbaric rite of crucifixion: the brutalized man dragging the cross-beam through the streets, the staggering arrival at the place of execution, the torture and mutilation, and, finally impalement.[16] The summons to such imitation ("take up your cross") surely provoked incredulity and bewilderment; they wanted no part of it. Perhaps, more than once, these ordinary women and men had joined a mob watching the spectacle—feeding on the terror, amazed by their own relief: it is finished. Now, listening to the rabbi from Nazareth ("take up your cross and follow me"), these ordinary people are, at once, attracted and repulsed.

In the third Gospel, the Lukan Jesus puts the cross as a condition for discipleship quite starkly:

> Whoever does not carry the cross and follow me cannot be my disciple. For which of you, intending to build a tower, does not first sit down and estimate the cost, to see whether he has enough to complete it? Otherwise, when he has laid a foundation and is not able to finish, all who see it will begin to ridicule him, saying, "This fellow began to build and was not able to finish." Or what king, going out to wage war against another king, will not sit down first and consider whether he is able with ten thousand to oppose the one who comes against him with twenty thousand? If he cannot, then, while the other is still far away, he sends a delegation and asks for the terms of peace. So therefore, none of you can become my disciple if you do not give up all that you possess. (Luke 14:27–33)

Jesus demands that his disciples go the distance, walk the entire "way." His illustrations here are simple but striking nonetheless. He teaches a lesson designed to drive home the necessity of self-examen, sacrifice, personal resolve, and love. The prosperous builder and the successful military strategist meet their goals

---

16. Hengel, *Crucifixion*, 22–32.

through painstaking attention to detail, thorough planning, and meticulous assessment. The outcomes of such exacting preparation earn admiration. The lesson the disciples are to absorb is sharpened by contrast: "the children of this world are far more shrewd in dealing with their own generation than the children of light" (Luke 16:8). Jesus entrusts to them (and to us) a venture of absolute importance—his own mission, that is, announcing and preparing a context for the coming reign of God. If a builder or military strategist can succeed, certainly his disciples can muster similar dedication, sacrifice, and personal resolve. But, the reign of God is no utopian project; it is a very different kind of reality. Over time and in time, the disciples (we as well) learn that they (and we) can and must prepare a context for its advent, but it is, most fundamentally, God's gratuitous gift. Moreover, this absolute endeavor calls not merely for planning, self-examen, sacrifice, and personal resolve but for love unmeasured, unstinting, overflowing, fearless, passionate. Thus, his mission on behalf of the reign of God required of Jesus something bold: that he stake his whole life and very personhood on their being absolutely directed toward God in love without measure.

The Way Jesus Is

The foremost lesson of Christian discipleship is that Jesus is the way, and the way Jesus is *is* the way of the cross. While walking that way is, at once, the same yet distinctive for each woman and man who would follow him, it will include the same privation, intense longing, an acute awareness of emptiness and failure, confusion and loss. On the way that Jesus is, the disciple is exposed, humbled, and opened to the wisdom and power of the Spirit. Just as the cross hallowed in Jesus a capacity for resurrection life, so too it hallows in the disciple a kind of infinite desire and capacity for life in and with God.[17]

---

17. In a vision, God tells Catherine of Siena, "I am infinite Good and I therefore require of you infinite desire" (104:197), in *Catherine of Siena: The Dialogue*, trans. Suzanne Noffke (New York: Paulist Press, 1980). This is a familiar image

Catherine of Siena knew more than a little about the way Jesus is. In the *Dialogue*, she tells us that in order to draw us into God's extravagant love, Christ makes a bridge and a staircase of his very crucified body.[18] So eager is God for our love, for union with us, that the Son is sent to demonstrate that love through the sacrifice of his own life on the cross for love of us.[19] Catherine writes,

> The first stair is the feet, which symbolize the affections. For just as the feet carry the body, the affections carry the soul. My Son's nailed feet are a stair by which you can climb to his side, where you will see revealed his innermost heart. . . . Then the soul, seeing how tremendously she is loved, is herself filled to overflowing with love. So having climbed the second stair, she reaches the third. This is his mouth, where she finds peace. . . .[20]

The disciple scales the tree of life, moving upward in love and virtue, seeking the fruit of union. At each phase of the ascent, the disciple is drawn on by great desire to know and love as Jesus knew and loved. Just as a mother nurses her child, so too Christ nourishes the disciple. "Through the flesh of Christ crucified, we suck the milk of divine sweetness."[21]

Like the roots of the tree, the nailed feet secure the disciple in the initial stage of the climb. Here, at the first stair, the disciple confronts and comes to know self in order to know and love Christ. In a letter to cloistered women religious, Catherine

---

for Catherine and appears in her correspondence; see Letter T74/G119, to Fratre Niccolò da Montalcino of the Order of Preachers in Montepulciano, February to April 1376, in *The Letters of Catherine of Siena*, vol. 1, trans. with introduction and notes by Suzanne Noffke (Tempe, AZ: Arizona Center of Medieval and Renaissance Studies, 2000), 313–14.

18. For another discussion of this metaphor, see Catherine M. Meade, *My Nature Is Fire: Saint Catherine of Siena* (New York: Alba House, 1991), esp. 107–28.

19. *Catherine of Siena: The Dialogue*, 26:65.

20. Ibid., 26:64.

21. *The Letters of Catherine of Siena*, vol. 1, Letter T109/G41/DT51, to Bérenger, Abbot of Lézat, Apostolic Nuncio to Tuscany, January to February 1376, 266.

comments on the significance of reaching the heart of the crucified Jesus in the second stage of the climb. His great heart, she
writes, is "open and utterly spent for us."[22] Immersed in the heart
of Christ, the disciple is nourished for a praxis of solidarity and
compassion. At the final stage of the climb, the disciple reaches
the mouth of Christ and "learns to savour souls . . . [to] become
a true shepherd ready to lay down [her or his] life" for [the little
ones].[23] The disciple is *for* others. Yet, the disciple flames with
desire for the very God who with unimaginable love has looked
upon us and fallen in love with us.[24]

The familiar spiritual "Jacob's Ladder" provides a metaphori-
cal resonance with Catherine's image of the body of the crucified
Christ as a staircase. The spiritual conflates and fuses the story of
Jacob's vision (Gen 28:10–17) with the cross of Jesus.

> We are climbing Jacob's ladder, / We are climbing
>   Jacob's ladder,
> We are climbing Jacob's ladder, / Soldier of the cross.
>
> Every round goes higher, higher, / Every round goes
>   higher, higher,
> Every round goes higher, higher, / Soldier of the cross.
>
> Sinner do you love my Jesus? / Sinner do you love my
>   Jesus?
> Sinner do you love my Jesus? / Soldier of the cross.
>
> If you love Him, why not serve him? / If you love Him,
>   why not serve him?
> If you love Him, why not serve him? / Soldier of the
>   cross.

As simple as the spiritual is, it is more than simplistic repetition,
call and response; it engages singer, listener, and disciple in a medi-

---

22. *I, Catherine of Siena: Selected Writings of St. Catherine of Siena,* trans.
Kenelm Foster and Mary John Ronayne (London: Collins, 1980), Letter 31, 146.
23. Ibid.
24. *Catherine of Siena: The Dialogue,* 13:49.

tative dialogue about growth in the life of the spirit, knowledge of God, and discipleship.

In Genesis, Jacob, fearful and yearning, dreams of a ladder that reaches upward from earth into the heavens and up which angels ascend and descend. Jacob is gifted with both a disclosure of God's identity ("I am the Lord, the God of Abraham your father and the God of Isaac," Gen 28:18) and a *promise* ("I am with you and will keep you wherever you go. . . . I will not leave you until I have done that of which I have spoken," Gen 28:15). The first and second stanzas of the spiritual offer a thematic statement of the ladder's direction toward and its end in God. But, unlike Jacob, those of us who would be disciples are awake; we sin even as we seek. We climb toward the God who is our destination, but the weight of sin slows our ascent. The makers of the spiritual invoke soldierly virtues of courage and fortitude, but these are not enough. Love must be added to the list. The first stanza discloses our true end, union with God; the final stanza calls those who profess to love God to love neighbor, to take up a praxis of solidarity and compassion.

The spirituals give us access to the "experience[s], expression[s], motivations, intentions, behaviors, styles, and rhythms" of African American religio-cultural life.[25] They open a window onto the lives of the enslaved peoples and shed light on their religious, social, aesthetic, and psychological worldview. They emerge from the people's wrestling with and surrender to the power of the Spirit which set them on the "way."

A former enslaved man who became a minister of the gospel, Josiah Henson exemplifies similarly committed discipleship. In his autobiographical narrative, first published in Boston in 1849, Henson vividly recalls his conversion to Christ. Urged by his mother to go to hear preacher John McKenny, young Henson obtained permission to do so from the slaveholder, Isaac Riley. Henson reports that he walked three or four miles to the place of the meeting, but upon arrival was barred because of his race from

---

25. Charles H. Long, *Significations: Signs, Symbols, and Images in the Interpretation of Religion* (Philadelphia: Fortress Press, 1986), 7.

entering the building. After some effort, Henson positioned himself near the open front door to hear and see McKenny. Henson recalls:

> I saw [Mr. McKenny] with his hands raised . . . and he said: "Jesus Christ, the Son of God, tasted death for every man; for the high, for the low, for the rich, for the poor, for the bond, the free, the [N]egro in his chains, the man in gold and diamonds. . . . I stood and heard [the sermon]. It touched my heart, and I cried out: "I wonder if Jesus Christ died for me."[26]

McKenny preached Jesus's "tender love for mankind, his forgiving spirit, his compassion for the outcast and despised, his cruel crucifixion" and reminded the congregation that the message of salvation was universal. Jesus Christ died not for a select few but for all. Henson writes, these, indeed, were "glad tidings." The message of Jesus was intended for

> the slave as well as the master, the poor as well as the rich, for the persecuted, the distressed, the heavy-laden, the captive; even for me among the rest, a poor, despised, abused creature, deemed by others fit for nothing but unrequited toil—but mental and bodily degradation. Oh, the blessedness and sweetness of feeling that I was loved! . . . I kept repeating to myself, "The compassionate Savior about whom I have heard, 'loves me.' 'He looks down in compassion from heaven on me. . . .'" I thought . . . "[Jesus will] be my dear refuge—He'll wipe away all tears from my eyes." "Now I can bear all things; nothing will seem hard after this." . . . Swallowed up in the beauty of the divine love, I "loved my enemies and prayed for them that did despitefully use and [mistreat] me."[27]

---

26. Josiah Henson, *An Autobiography of the Reverend Josiah Henson* in *Four Fugitive Slave Narratives*, ed. Robin W. Winks et al. (Reading, MA: Addison-Wesley, 1968), 24.

27. Ibid., 25.

Meditating on this message as he returned to the plantation, Henson tells us he grew so excited that he turned into the woods nearby, knelt down, and prayed for guidance and aid. From that day forward, Henson set himself the task of climbing Jacob's ladder and leading others in that ascent. He soon began to gather other enslaved women and men, to speak with them about the love of the crucified Jesus, to pray with them, to exhort them, and to comfort them.

Separated by centuries, Catherine of Siena and Josiah Henson are united in committed discipleship. Both understood that Jesus of Nazareth is the absolute meaning of life for the world. He offered them a love that drew them to himself, and their love of him flowed over into a praxis of compassionate solidarity on behalf of women and men in need. Loving as Jesus loved, Catherine challenged a warring society and a fragmented church with a message of peace and reconciliation. Loving as Jesus loved, Henson confronted a slaveholding society and church with a demand for justice and transformation. Catherine and Henson took up the time-shaped challenge to love Jesus, to follow him, to live his command, to share the good news of his love, to stand in solidarity and compassion with others.

Conclusion

I have attempted to tease out what it means to follow Jesus of Nazareth, to be his disciple, to stand as he stood at the disposal of the cross. I began with the sad spectacle of a black woman combing through the refuse bins of my apartment building. Here is a woman whose back is against the wall; her situation imposes on Christian discipleship. What can it mean to tell her that God in Jesus is also alienated, a stranger, a despised "other"? What word, what compassionate act of solidarity do we Christian disciples have for her? Moved by the sight of her, I went on to examine the terrifying spectacle of the crucifixion of Jesus of Nazareth and to interrogate the cross as an indispensable condition of Christian discipleship. The experiences of Catherine of Siena and of Josiah Henson testify both to the unity of the mystical-political for the Christian disciple and to discipleship as the locus, the site, in which Christ makes himself present.

This exploration took the performative meaning of discipleship from the Lukan narrative of the story of the life, death, and resurrection of Jesus of Nazareth. Even with its ambivalent attitudes toward women, Luke's Gospel affords those of us who belong to privileged groups (for example, whites or black theologians) an occasion for critical self-examination: How do we understand the relation of our own social locations to the coming reign of God? How often do those of us who belong to privileged groups conveniently overlook the incriminating criticisms of the privileged that the narrator of Luke's Gospel places in the mouth of Jesus? How often do we excuse ourselves from human communion with poor, despised, hungry women and men? These are questions that any of us who would be disciples must follow in order to find the Christ of God, questions to be answered by living in search of the One whose great love for us gives absolute meaning to life.

Throughout, I have kept the cross at the forefront, but in concluding I want to shift a bit. My starting point for working out the meaning of discipleship as christological locus was the sad spectacle of a black woman searching garbage. I choose the word *spectacle* deliberately, since the image of the woman leaning into stench and filth seized me, suffused my senses, entered into my theologizing, and remains vivid and authoritative in my memory. I know nothing about her: she may have fallen through the gaping cracks of the so-called safety net established by the State of Wisconsin in its haste to eliminate welfare. Or she may have been homeless and simply, terribly hungry. Or perhaps she was poor and refrained from eating in order to feed her children. How hungry and desperate she must have been to stand in the morning sun opening bags of garbage. How hungry she must have been to endure the stares of disgust and condescension from passers-by. But to this woman scraping the dregs for life, the Lukan Jesus offers reassurance: "Blessed are you who are poor, for yours is the kingdom of God. Blessed are you who are hungry now, for you will be filled" (Luke 6:20–21).

The spectacle of a woman searching through rot for food cannot but point the Christian disciple toward the Bread of Life. This phrase, "bread of life," belongs in a special way to the Johannine Jesus, but the Lukan Jesus (like the Jesus of the Synoptics) blesses, breaks, and identifies bread with himself before he completes his way to the cross. In this Gospel, the breaking of bread is the gesture that clears the tear-filled eyes of those forlorn disciples who met a stranger on their way to Emmaus (Luke 24:30–31). In *Seeing the Lord*, Marianne Sawicki comments on Luke's association of hunger with the possibility of understanding resurrection life and of recognizing the resurrected Lord.[28] This recognition, I would add, is crucial for mystical-political discipleship and for an authentic praxis of compassion and solidarity.

In Luke 14, we find Jesus on a Sabbath at table, a dinner guest of a Pharisee. Jesus bluntly tells his host: "When you give a dinner or a banquet, invite the poor, the maimed, the lame, the blind, and you will be blessed, because they cannot repay you. You will be repaid at the resurrection of the just" (1–14). Jesus is insisting that we make space in our hearts, at our tables, in our communities for the little ones. Perhaps to drive home the point, Jesus reiterates this lesson in the parable of the great banquet. Someone invites guests to a wonderful meal, then sends a servant to summon them when all is ready. But the guests retort with excuses and rebuff his hospitality. Angry, the householder tells the servant, "Go out quickly to the streets and lanes of the city, and bring in the poor, the crippled, the blind, and the lame." The servant does so and returns to report that there is still room at table. Again the host sends the servant "out into the roads and lanes, and compel people to come in, so that my house may be filled. For I tell you, none of those who were invited will taste my dinner" (15–24).

Hunger constitutes a possibility for mystical-political discipleship and an authentic praxis of compassion and solidarity. If we would be disciples of Jesus, we must be willing to recognize and

---

28. Marianne Sawicki, *Seeing the Lord: Resurrection and Early Christian Practices* (Minneapolis: Fortress Press, 1994), 90.

alleviate hungers—whether for food or truth or justice, whether our own or those of others.[29] A praxis of compassionate solidarity, justice-love, and care for the poor and oppressed is a sign that we are on the "way" Jesus is. The resurrected Lord himself sends us into streets and alleys, shelters and schools, homes and hospices to find and feed those who are despised, abused, and marginalized. These children, women, and men are the only sure sign of his presence among us in our efforts to prepare a context for the coming reign of his God.

At the same time, the parable of the great banquet reiterates a warning thrown down earlier by the Lukan Jesus: "Woe to you who are full now, for you will be hungry" (Luke 6:25). All who would be his disciples, especially those of us who have the luxury to stand and watch hungry women and men, are called to critical self-examen and a praxis of compassionate solidarity. In Luke's narrative arrangement, this parable precedes those forceful words about the fundamental condition of discipleship: "Whoever does not carry the cross and follow me cannot be my disciple" (Luke 14:27).

The cross rises between the meal that Jesus shares with his disciples before he dies and the bit of grilled fish that he eats with them in Jerusalem (Luke 24:41–43). At the Passover meal, Jesus declares to his friends that he shall not eat or drink again until the kingdom of God comes (Luke 22:16–18). He promises them that when the kingdom does come, they shall sit with him at his table in places set specially for them, eating and drinking with joy (Luke 22:28–30). If we would sit at his table we too must live in solidarity with the little ones and live at the disposal of the cross.

---

29. Ibid., 90–91.

CHAPTER SIX

Following the Tears of a Crucified World

A Theological Meditation on Social Suffering, Solidarity, and the Cross

For I decided to know nothing among you except Jesus Christ, and him crucified.
—1 Corinthians 2:2

I regard everything as loss because of the surpassing value of knowing Christ Jesus my Lord.
—Philippians 3:8

In order for Christian theology to be theology—credible, humble, if the probable and authentic mediation of God's word in history, culture, and society—it must stand at the foot of the cross of the Jewish Jesus of Nazareth, the Christ of God. To authenticate its fidelity to Jesus and his ignominious death on the cross, Christian theology must know, love, and serve the crucified Lord. That theology cannot and must not remain silent before the tears of a crucified world, the tears of crucified peoples. Indeed, when that theology comes face to face with the historical reality of the social oppression and immense suffering that oppression inflicts on God's human creatures, theology must name the social, physical, and existential damage done by structural or social as well as personal or individual sin. Moreover, that theology must work out the relation between the murderous crucifixion of the Jewish Jesus of Nazareth and the murderous crucifixion of countless children, women, and men whom we have impoverished, marginalized, and excluded through our power, privilege, and position. For to follow Christ crucified is to know and love and serve these least (Matt 25:45).

To take as a point of departure for doing theology the historical reality of social oppression and the suffering of such oppression is to risk an encounter and engagement with the purifying powers of the Incarnate Word of God in history. For the incarnation, that concrete, particular, powerful, paradoxical, and unnerving point of entry and engagement of God in human history changes forever our perception and reception of one another. Jesus of Nazareth, the Incarnate Word, forever changes our perception and reception of human others. For the human person is and remains the concern of the Incarnate Word—neither merely nor incidentally, but rather fully, comprehensively. For the Incarnate Word gave his life for the full flourishing and realization of the destiny of humanity.

Four sections comprise this theological reflection on what it might mean to know Christ crucified, to know the tears of a crucified world, to know the suffering and tears of a crucified people. A first section places emphasis on the massive, public, social suffering that social oppression produces. A second section considers the social suffering and tears of children, women, and men in our crucified world. The third section follows their tears to the ground beneath the cross of the crucified Jewish Jesus, and there we confront the paradox and power of his cross and death. Finally, we consider the call to discipleship as solidaristic compassionate action alongside, with, and for those whom we have impoverished, excluded, and despised through oppression in our societal context.

Suffering

"There is no way not to suffer," James Baldwin observed in an essay entitled "The Uses of the Blues."[1] Like death, suffering is inevitable;

---

1. James Baldwin, "The Uses of the Blues," in *The Cross of Redemption: Uncollected Writings*, ed. with intro. Randall Kenan (New York: Pantheon Books, 2010), 59.

like death, it neither favors status nor acknowledges privilege, but levels the human condition. There is no way not to suffer. Always, suffering evokes pain, disruption, and incompleteness. Raw and brutal, suffering may render us powerless and mute, may drive us to the borders of hopelessness and despair. Insistent and prolonged, suffering can maim and wither the heart. And yet, in other cases, as theologian and spiritual writer Howard Thurman insists, suffering coaxes freedom and growth so authentic that the change is literally evident: "Into their faces come a subtle radiance and a settled serenity; into their relationships a vital generosity that opens the sealed doors of the heart in all who are encountered along the way."[2] From still others, it squeezes a delicious ironic, spirit, expressed in tough laughter and tough action. Consider Bessie Smith's "Backwater Blues":

> When it thunders and lightnin,' and the wind begins
> to blow
> When it thunders and lightnin,' and the wind begins
> to blow
> There's thousands of people ain't got no place to go
> Backwater blues done caused me to pack my things
> and go
> Backwater blues done caused me to pack my things
> and go
> 'Cause my house fell down, and I can't live there no
> mo'
> [But] picked up my bag, baby, and I tried it again.[3]

Smith accepts the disaster and does so with, what Baldwin calls, "passionate detachment . . . inwardness coupled with outwardness, [an] ability to know that it's a mess, and you can't do anything about it . . . so . . . you *have to do* something about it."[4]

---

2. Howard Thurman, *Disciplines of the Spirit* (Richmond, IN: Friends United Press, 1963, 1977), 76.

3. Angela Y. Davis, *Blues Legacies and Black Feminism: Gertrude "Ma" Rainey, Bessie Smith, and Billie Holiday* (New York: Pantheon Books, 1998), 109.

4. Baldwin, *The Cross of Redemption*, 59, emphasis mine.

As a working definition, consider suffering as the disturbance of one's inner tranquility caused by physical, mental, emotional, and spiritual forces that are apprehended as jeopardizing one's very existence. Suffering, although not identical with evil, the negation and deprivation of some good, presses close to it. The human suffering brought about by some natural or physical evil,[5] for example, a flood or hurricane, may bring out a person's courage and fortitude as well as cowardice and venality; such evil may also elicit generous and open acts of compassion and hospitality.

The enslaved Africans and their descendants in the United States have encountered the monstrous evil of chattel slavery and its legacy of virulent institutionalized racism and have been subjected to unspeakable protracted physical, psychological, social (i.e., political, economic, technological), moral, and religious suffering. In the June 2014 issue of *The Atlantic*, Ta-Nehisi Coates figured that suffering in years: "250 years of slavery, 90 years of Jim Crow, 60 years of separate but equal, 35 years of state-sanctioned redlining," and an ongoing, intentional disruption of human flourishing.[6]

The residual effects of these historical conditions congeal in structural or social oppression and result in maldistributed, negative, enormous, and transgenerational ethnic and social oppression and social suffering.[7] To say that such conditions congeal in structural or social oppression and result in social suffering refers to the massive and cumulative moral failure of human intelligence

---

5. By natural or physical evil, I mean, with Bernard Lonergan, the "shortcomings of a world order that consists in a generalized emergent probability. For in such an order the unordered manifold is prior to the formal good of higher unities and higher orders . . . there are false starts, break-downs, failures." See *Insight: A Study of Human Understanding*, 5th ed., rev. and aug. Collected Works of Bernard Lonergan, vol. 3 (Toronto: University of Toronto Press, 1988), 689.

6. Ta-Nehisi Coates, "The Case for Reparations," *The Atlantic* 313, no. 5 (June 2014): 54–71.

7. William R. Jones, *Is God a White Racist: A Preamble to Black Theology* (Garden City, NY: Anchor Press/Doubleday, 1973), 21–22; see also Richard Rubenstein, *After Auschwitz: Radical Theology and Contemporary Judaism* (New York: Bobbs-Merrill, 1966); and Beverly Eileen Mitchell, *Plantations and Death Camps: Religion, Ideology, and Human Dignity* (Minneapolis: Fortress Press, 2009).

and human responsibility. *This is sinful*: a society in which structural oppression holds sway equals a society structured by and in social sin. Even if I advert to black historical, religious, cultural, social, and existential suffering to explicate social sin, this sin impugns us all, marks us all, deforms us all. The particularizing of suffering requires neither qualification nor apology; yet, there can never be any ranking of oppression or suffering. No children, no women, no men may be excluded from the canon of human anguish. Social sin is bred from the cumulative and massive effect of acting from bias (i.e., perverse and self-serving individual—and group—interest), of distorting and upending crucial social values, of refusing to ask further questions or pursue additional information and insights in order to make knowing authentically relevant to right doing, and of deliberate preference for short-term rather than long-term solutions. Such cognitive and moral behavior has become so habitual that the ability "to choose and do what is genuinely worthwhile [has become] a virtual if not real impossibility."[8] When we willfully block practical intelligence, moral impotence can only but follow, and the oppressive and oppressing society that is generated coalesces as a "social surd," a "false fact," "*the actual existence of what should not be*."[9] In other words, the societal order within which we live has become so riddled with strategies and tactics, decisions and actions for the political, economic, and technological survival of a few by any means necessary that the societal order has become alienated from social good and intentional human flourishing. Intellect, reason, and morality (including humanistic values) have little, if any, place, while religion has bartered its soul for a seat at the dealer's table.[10]

Social suffering mutates in a societal order in the forms of exploi-

---

8. Tatha Wiley, *Original Sin: Origins, Developments, Contemporary Meanings* (Mahwah, NJ: Paulist Press, 2002), 195.

9. Bernard Lonergan, *Understanding and Being*, rev. and aug. Collected Works of Bernard Lonergan, vol. 5 (Toronto: University of Toronto Press, 1990), 236.

10. Lonergan, *Insight*, 689, 691; Bernard Lonergan, *Method in Theology*, 2nd ed. (New York: Herder and Herder, 1973), 27–55.

tation, marginalization, powerlessness, cultural imperialism, and violence. In explicit theological terms, these oppressive mutations of social good stem from and are reinforced through individual or personal sins of omission and commission that enable, encourage, facilitate, and breed evil and oppression. Sin can never be merely an interior or private state of alienation between individuals and God; sin disrupts personal and group relations, as well as ecological probabilities. Sin presents real consequences for real children, women, and men, for a real ecological order in a real world. The notion of social sin recognizes these consequences and the concatenation of sin in social structures and institutions in the public square. Our failures or refusals to oppose evil through personal laziness or fear, silence or indifference, collude in replicating and sustaining the long reign of sin.

The notion of social suffering points to intentional disruption of human flourishing as a theo-social problem. What happens to human persons happens in a social (i.e., political, economic, and technological) set-up that expresses concretely cultural, religious, personal, and societal values or disvalues. Such intentional disruption of human flourishing manifests itself as "events of massive public suffering" such as cultural decimation, "disappearance," enslavement, "ethnic cleansing," extermination, feminicide, genocide, systemic racism, torture, trafficking, starvation, structural indifference. Such suffering possesses what Rebecca Chopp called a "nonidentity character." That is to say that the events of massive public or social suffering

> have no identity or completed meaning in history; they cannot be fully explained, understood, or represented. The nonidentity character of suffering means that suffering cannot be forgotten or ignored in history's interpretation or construction; once progress has shoved the masses of humanity onto life's margins, history is broken, its end forever in question, and its purpose lost in suspension.[11]

---

11. Rebecca Chopp, *The Praxis of Suffering: An Interpretation of Liberation and Political Theologies* (Maryknoll, NY: Orbis Books, 1986), 2.

A People Crucified, a Crucified World

If we would follow the moans and tears of children, women, and men brutalized and burned, raped and mutilated, enslaved and trafficked across the centuries, we cannot but find ourselves standing in a crucified world and standing before a crucified people. The notion of "crucified people" comes from the thought of Ignacio Ellacuría:

> What is meant by the "crucified people" is that collective body, which as the majority of humankind owes its situation of crucifixion to the way society is organized and maintained by a minority that exercises its dominion through a series of factors, which taken together and given their concrete impact within history, must be regarded as sin.[12]

For Ellacuría, Kevin Burke writes, "the crucified people is not merely a colorful metaphor for human suffering in general, nor does it simply represent the sum total of all individual injuries and griefs. It refers to a historical theological reality that embraces a communion of victims."[13] My use of this theological category does not intend metaphor; rather it signifies and anticipates ontological compassion and solidarity for those who have been and are mauled and sinned against in history with intentionality and intensity. To know and to follow Christ crucified is to know and love those children, women, and men who are poor, excluded, and despised, made different and unwelcome, lynched and crucified in our world. To know and follow Christ crucified is to know and love these women and men.

If we would follow Christ crucified, we would hear the echoes of ululation and bitter weeping in Gaza and in Rafah, in Baghdad and in Beirut, in Cairo and in Kigali . . .

---

12. Kevin Burke, *The Ground Beneath the Cross: The Theology of Ignacio Ella-curía* (Washington, DC: Georgetown University Press, 2000), 181. The words are those of Ignacio Ellacuría, "El pueblo crucificado" (1978), cited in *The Ground Beneath the Cross*, 201.

13. Ibid., 181.

If we would follow Christ crucified, we would hold in memory the tears and blood that dripped from the eyes and maimed bodies of Aztecs forced to mine for gold . . .

If we would follow Christ crucified, we would hold in memory the tears that fell on the rude and bloodied floors of the holding forts of Cape Coast, Elmina, and Christiansborg; that fell in the holds of the Wanderer, the Diligent, the Esperança, the Zong, the Bom Jesu Triunfo . . .

If we would follow Christ crucified, we would press to our hearts the tears that flowed from the eyes of Cherokee, Seminole, and Choctaw children and women and men who limped through the cold and hunger from Oklahoma to Arkansas and Alabama and Mississippi . . .

If we would follow Christ crucified, we would recover the tears that fell from the eyes of frightened Armenian children, women, and men forced, beaten, sexually abused, and murdered in the desert . . .

If we would follow Christ crucified, we would recover the tears that fell on the floors of the camps at Auschwitz, Treblinka, and Sobibór . . .

If we would follow Christ crucified, we would retrieve the tears that streamed from the eyes of terrified girls and women, boys and men abducted, raped, and murdered in the United States and Kosovo, in India and Nigeria . . .

If we would follow Christ crucified, we would retrieve the tears that flowed from the eyes of children and women and men who crowded into flimsy boats and old trucks and shipping containers to suffocate and die in front of fences strung across the desert, at abandoned check points on the outer edge of rural towns, and at heavily guarded borders near rivers and waterways . . .

If we would follow Christ crucified, we would gather the tears that fell from the eyes of terrified young girls and women trafficked and raped, battered and abused, murdered and mutilated in Ciudad Juárez and Cape Town, in New York and Milwaukee . . .

If we would follow Christ crucified with attention, reverence, and devotion, we would recognize that the tears and blood and moans of the innocent have been absorbed into the air we breathe, have seeped into our streams and rivers and swamps and seas and oceans, into the earth in which we plant and from which we harvest and eat.

If we follow with attention, reverence, and devotion the moans and tears of the brutalized and burned, raped and mutilated, enslaved and captive across the centuries, we are lead to the ground beneath the cross of the crucified Jewish Jesus of Nazareth.

The ground beneath his cross figures as an ambiguous, even contested, place. The cross of the crucified Jesus has been misused to blasphemous ends. In the name of the cross, peoples and cultures have been derided, colonized, and destroyed. In the name of the cross, women and men have been tortured and abused, raped and lynched. In the name of the cross, women and men have been made to surrender their souls to an ersatz salvation. The cross as advanced by Christendom—old and new—in its collusion with powers of domination, exploitation, and oppression taints the story of the crucified Jewish Jesus. To situate theological meditation on the social suffering of the countless poor, excluded, and despised human beings who ever have lived, are living, and will live is to understand not only the crucified Jesus "in the light and context of his resurrection and, therefore, of freedom and hope,"[14] but the ineluctable relation between these children, women, and men and the constitution and self-realization of the community of the resurrected Lord, the Mystical Body of Christ. The crucified Jewish Jesus stands as "the prototype"[15] of God's new creation, triumphing over the horrific and failed attempt to defeat the reign of God. Who is this crucified and defiled Jew? He is

---

14. Jürgen Moltmann, *The Crucified God: The Cross of Christ as the Foundation and Criticism of Christian Theology*, trans. R. A. Wilson and John Bowden (New York: Harper & Row, 1974), 4.

15. Jean-Marc Éla, "The Memory of the African People and the Cross of Christ," in *The Scandal of a Crucified World: Perspectives on the Cross and Suffering*, ed. Yacob Tesfai (Maryknoll, NY: Orbis Books, 1994), 28.

the first-born of all creation . . . the head of the body . . . the beginning, the first-born of the dead. . . . In him all the fullness of God was pleased to dwell, and through him to reconcile to himself all things, whether on earth or in heaven, making peace by the blood of his cross. (Col 1:15–19)

The Crucified Jewish Jesus

The crucified Jewish Jesus is no stranger to colonization and exploitation and domination, to torture and abuse and lynching, to terror and fear and anxiety. Before he was covered in luminous dark glory, before he reigned from the subversive tree of life, Jesus of Nazareth submitted to John the Baptizer, who plunged him into the waters of the Jordan where he experienced in his very being the vivid power of the Spirit and love and union with the God whom he knew as Father. Jesus of Nazareth was an itinerant and iconoclastic teacher who appropriated and reflected on his religious and cultural traditions and strenuously taught his disciples not only to revere Torah but also to "practice and internalize the right way of life."[16] Jesus of Nazareth was a healer who touched and allowed himself to be touched by children, women, and men afflicted by deadly diseases, suffering bodily abuse and battered hearts. He was a prophet and social critic who looked deep into human hearts to name sin and to challenge individuals and communities to turn again to the way of the covenant and to repair the injustices they had committed against their brothers and sisters. Jesus of Nazareth was a rabbi who not only dared to forgive sin but recognized faith in the broken and lonely places of the human psyche, and invited women and men to new life and love. Jesus of Nazareth was the living, enfleshed parable of God's passionately compassionate and solidaristic love for the whole of humanity, for the whole of creation.

---

16. Gerhard Lohfink, *Jesus of Nazareth: What He Wanted, Who He Was,* trans. Linda M. Maloney (Collegeville, MN: Liturgical Press, 2012), 74.

If we, who would be his disciples, recall the night before he died, we are led to a table, from a table to a garden, from a garden to a courtyard, from a courtyard to a hill, from a hill to a grave, from a grave to life. The table holds the self-gift of his very flesh and blood; the garden is watered by his tears and blood; and the cross holds him, even as the One whom he knows and loves lifts him up from the grave to release him into the surprise of hope and life.

The last table at which Jesus of Nazareth sat down to eat was the *Pesach* Table, the ritual meal that commemorates the great feast of thanksgiving for the mighty acts of God, for freedom, for the covenant, for life. Jesus and his disciples and friends well may have begun their meal with eggs, then, goat meat (lamb would have been a rich man's dish), unleavened barley bread, arugula or mustard greens, wine, and, perhaps, for dessert, fruit. During this period of Jewish history, the *Pesach* meal ended with the singing of the little *Hallel*, Psalms 114 (115)–118.[17] These prayers proclaimed the mighty acts of God's powerful and saving arm, took joy in the steadfast faithful love of a God not made of metal or stone, and confessed complete confidence in the power of the divine to answer supplication, to vindicate and to rescue the beloved one:

> The LORD is my strength and my might;
> he has become my salvation.
>
> I shall not die, but I shall live,
> and recount the deeds of the LORD.
> The LORD has punished me severely,
> but he did not give me over to death.
>
> Open to me the gates of righteousness,
> that I may enter through them
> and give thanks to the LORD.
>
> This is the gate of the LORD;
> the righteous shall enter through it.

---

17. Ibid., 270.

> I thank you that you have answered me
> and have become my salvation.
> The stone that the builders rejected
> has become the chief cornerstone.
> This is the LORD's doing;
> it is marvelous in our eyes. (Psalm 118:14–23)

Jesus rises from the table and asks his closest disciples and friends, Peter, James, and John, to accompany him to the garden of Gethsemane at the foot of the Mount of Olives. There he falls to his knees, "distressed and agitated" (Mark 14:33). Jesus is afraid; he senses—knows—that death looms. He asks these friends for support and comfort (Mark 14:34). The weight of the knowledge of death forces him to his knees, and he wrestles with God in prayer: "Abba, Father, for you all things are possible; remove this cup from me; yet, not what I want, but what you want" (Mark 14:35–36). Jesus pleads that "the cup of wrath and of desolation . . . the cup of death" be taken away. In agonizing mental and spiritual distress, Jesus begs not to die. He turns to his friends, but they are asleep, weak and unable to support him in this time of crisis; he is utterly alone. Even the God whom he knows and loves as Father seems distant, hidden; yet Jesus entrusts his life and future completely to God.

Then, "Judas, one of the twelve, arrived; and with him there was a crowd with swords and clubs, from the chief priests, the scribes, and the elders" (Mark 14:43). This crowd, Gerhard Lohfink tells us, was an "improvised posse with nightsticks."[18] Stunned, bewildered, scared out of their wits by the police action and Jesus's arrest, the disciples run away; they abandon him (Mark 14:50). Peter makes some effort to stay close to the events, following at a distance, lingering for a while in the courtyard of the high priest's house, sitting with the guards, engaging in conversation, warming himself at the fire. Then, the servant girl exposes him: "This man is one of them" (Mark 14:69). The distinctive Galilean accent

---

18. Ibid., 271.

has given him away.[19] Peter protests: He has no affiliation with this man; he even curses and swears an oath that he does not know him. The second crow of a cock pierces Peter's consciousness; he breaks down and weeps at his betrayal, then vanishes from Mark's account (Mark 14:54, 66–71; 16:1–8). When the interrogation and trumped-up accusations by the Sanhedrin come to naught, Caiaphas charges Jesus with blasphemy. The whole court joins in to "condemn [Jesus] as deserving death" (Mark 14:64). He is transferred to Pilate's jurisdiction for judgment and execution under the aegis of the Roman Empire (Mark 15:1).

The entire cohort of soldiers assembles in the courtyard of Pilate's headquarters. They toy with Jesus—draping a purple cloak around his shoulders and crowning him with a wreath of thorns, taunting, humiliating, beating, and spitting on him (Mark 15:16–20).[20] Then a squad of soldiers leads him away from the city to Golgotha, the place of execution. Perhaps the beating and torture have so weakened Jesus that he can barely stand or walk; he staggers and falls along the road. The soldiers coerce a passer-by, Simon of Cyrene, to carry the crossbeam for Jesus (Mark 15:22–24). At the hill site, the execution squad crucifies Jesus, then sits down to watch him die, gambling over his clothes. Jesus twists and gasps for air as passers-by, townspeople and pilgrims, gawk and jeer:

---

19. Obery M. Hendricks, *The Politics of Jesus: Rediscovering the True Revolutionary Nature of Jesus' Teaching and How They Have Been Corrupted* (New York: Doubleday, 2006), 70. In his discussion of the intense stigmatization and marginalization of the country folk and peasants from Galilee, Hendricks calls attention to their "distinctively accented pronunciation of Hebrew" (70). The Markan writer does not comment on Peter's speech pattern or accent, but the Matthean writer does: "After a little while the bystanders came up and said to Peter, 'Certainly you are also one of them, for your accent betrays you" (Matt 26:73).

20. David Tombs, "Crucifixion, State Terror, and Sexual Abuse," *Union Seminary Quarterly Review* 53, nos. 1–2 (1999): 89–109. Tombs raises the disturbing possibility that perhaps Jesus may have been sexually humiliated or abused in the privacy of the praetorium. Tombs comes to this conclusion from his comparative analysis of accounts of first-century Roman and twentieth-century Latin American intimidation and torture (106). He raises this possibility on the pastoral grounds that confronting this possibility could "provide practical help to contemporary victims of torture and sexual abuse" (109).

"'Let the Messiah, the King of Israel, come down from the cross now, so that we may see and believe.' [Even] those who were crucified with him also taunted him" (Mark 15:32). The spectators shout that the true messiah never would endure such derision and abuse, such a death. The true messiah would destroy his opponents and vindicate the oppression of Israel.

Finally, according to Mark's account, at about three o'clock Jesus cries out in a loud voice the initial lines of Psalm 22:

> My God, my God, why have you forsaken me?
> Why are you so far from helping me, from the words
>   of my groaning?
> O my God, I cry by day, but you do not answer;
> and by night, but find no rest. (vv. 1–2)

The Psalm continues:

> Yet you are holy,
> enthroned on the praises of Israel.
> In you our ancestors trusted;
> they trusted, and you delivered them.
> To you they cried, and were saved;
> in you they trusted, and were not put to shame.
>   (vv. 3–5)

And the psalm concludes:

> From the horns of the wild oxen you have rescued me.
> I will tell of your name to my brothers and sisters;
> in the midst of the congregation I will praise you.
> You who fear the LORD, praise him!
> All you offspring of Jacob, glorify him;
> stand in awe of him, all you offspring of Israel!
>
> For he did not despise or abhor
> the affliction of the afflicted;
> he did not hide his face from me,
> but heard when I cried to him.

From you comes my praise in the great congregation;
my vows I will pay before those who fear him.
The poor shall eat and be satisfied;
those who seek him shall praise the LORD.
May your hearts live forever!

All the ends of the earth shall remember
and turn to the LORD;
and all the families of the nations
shall worship before him.
For dominion belongs to the LORD,
and he rules over the nations.

To him, indeed, shall all who sleep in the earth bow
        down;
before him shall bow all who go down to the dust,
and I shall live for him.

Posterity will serve him;
future generations will be told about the LORD,
and proclaim his deliverance to a people yet unborn,
saying that he has done it. (vv. 22–31)

Praying this psalm releases, at once, a cry of despair and a cry of lament. The one praying this psalm admits that God is silent, yet is confident that God will reply; the one praying endures the horrible absence or hiddenness of God, yet believes that God will show the divine face (v. 24); the one praying experiences terrifying loneliness, yet anticipates the gift of consolation and community.[21] Praying this psalm brings together protest and witness against injustice, pushes against that calculus of power by which the vulnerable suffer oppression and abuse. The one praying boxes, wrestles with God, takes seriously God's compassionate love and care in the thick of social oppression and the suffering it causes. This is why we may say that even if the God whom Jesus knows and loves as

---

21. Lohfink, *Jesus of Nazareth*, 284.

Father seems silent, absent, or hidden, Jesus completely entrusts his life and future to the compassion and love of the Holy One.

Beginning with that original Sabbath eve and down through the ages, the cross and death of Jesus have constituted, for many, an obstacle and a stumbling block (1 Cor 1:18, 22–25); for others, they simply signified madness (Justin Martyr, *Apology* 1.13.4). And yet for others still they betokened a mystery, the paradox of the wondrous love of God. These various responses implicate the disciples, the earliest followers of "the way," and those of us today. Yet, the cross and death of Jesus constitute an awakening: "an enlargement of the present and a new promise for the future."[22] The crucified Jesus enfleshes for all and for us the very meaning of being human, of being a person who embraces and lives out God's gracious gift of love and freedom.

"If any want to become my followers, let them deny themselves and take up their cross and follow me" (Mark 8:35–36). Jesus of Nazareth "chose and decided to live a life of poverty and suffering, [experiencing and dying] in abandonment, unjustly and cruelly [because of us], thinking of us and thinking of what we need to attain [our own graced life]."[23] We who would be his disciples discover our humanity, our personhood in imitation of him—in taking up our cross in order to transform evil into good, for the cross belongs not only to Christ but to all humanity. "He chose it because of us, and we choose it because of him."[24] We who would be his disciples incarnate the meaning of our own lives by following the moans and tears of the brutalized and burned, raped and mutilated, enslaved and captive across the centuries—into a crucified world, taking up an active, compassionate, solidaristic mission to crucified peoples.

---

22. Sebastian Moore, *The Crucified Jesus Is No Stranger* (New York/ Mahwah, NJ: Paulist Press, 1977), 75.

23. Bernard Lonergan, "The Mediation of Christ in Prayer," in *Philosophical and Theological Papers, 1958–1964*, Collected Works of Bernard Lonergan, vol. 6 (Toronto: University of Toronto Press, 1986), 181.

24. Ibid.

Solidarity as Discipleship in Compassionate Action

There is no more concrete example of the cost of self-transcending love than the cross of the crucified Jewish Jesus, and it is from the ground beneath his cross that Christian discipleship as solidaristic praxis or compassionate action arise and is always judged.

What is solidarity? A commonsense understanding of the notion of solidarity adverts to some relation or connection, but such commonsense understanding often overlooks the conditions of the possibility of solidarity. On the one hand, commonsense understanding and use of the rhetoric of solidarity may provoke expectations of a certain person or group in relation to certain other persons' or groups' ability (or inability), willingness (or unwillingness) to fulfill those expectations. On the other hand, merely sharing in common with others some characteristic or attribute (e.g., history or nationality, religion or belief, gender or sexual orientation, race or ethnicity, culture or social class) ensures neither genuine responsibility, nor authentic solidarity. In such instances, solidarity dissolves into a cliché, an empty sign signifying nothing authentic or essential. Moreover, such commonsense understanding may result in a type of moral idealism that lacks any practically intelligent and effective basis for transformative social praxis.

A theological understanding of solidarity realizes itself in intelligent and effective compassionate action, in doing, in discipleship. To express the notion of compassion, the New Testament uses the Greek word *splagchnizomai*, which refers to "innards" or "entrails." When the authors of the Gospel depict Jesus as stirred to pity, to mercy, to compassionate action, they use this word because it emphasizes the deep, visceral manner in which the condition of those whom Jesus encounters affects him. His very bowels churn and revolt against what he sees and hears. The image of Jesus responding in compassion, mercy, and love to crowds gathered to hear him, by feeding and healing them, shows us just who he is: the very compassion of God among us.[25] The Jewish Jesus of Nazareth

---

25. For some instances, see Matt 9:36; 14:14; 15:32; 18:27; 20:34; Mark 1:41; 6:34; 8:2; 9:22; Luke 7:13; 10:33; 15:20.

incarnates "the tender mercy [compassion] of our God, the dawn from on high [who has broken] upon us" (Luke 1:77–79). The Holy One discloses divine *chesed* (mercy and compassion) and *rehem* (womb love) in the flesh of Jesus of Nazareth.

What does solidarity require? Compassionate action. The English word *compassion* derives from the Latin *compassio,* from *com-pati,* meaning to sympathize, to bear, to suffer. Compassionate action entails attentive consciousness of others, informed and critical awareness and understanding of others and their condition, and acts with them to resist unjust suffering, to liberate and heal the human spirit, and to repair breakdowns in the natural, religious, cultural, social, and interpersonal realms. Solidarity as discipleship in compassionate action requires a woman's and a man's "whole self"—as an attentive and feeling and questioning, understanding and interpreting, judging and valuing, deciding and acting other-directed human person.[26] Solidarity as discipleship in lived compassionate action calls for, in the words of womanist ethicist Katie Geneva Cannon, "a justice-praxis for members of our species and the wider environment in which we are situated in order to resist conditions that thwart life, arriving at new understandings of our doing, knowing, and being."[27]

Jesus enfleshes for us what discipleship requires: feeding the hungry; giving drink to the thirsty; welcoming the stranger, the immigrant, the refugee; clothing the naked, homeless, and poor; caring for the man with Ebola or AIDS; consoling the prisoner and protesting mass incarceration: "Truly I tell you, just as you did it to one of the least of these who are members of my family, you did it to me" (Matt 25:35–40). The crucified and resurrected Lord sends us into streets and alleys, shelters and schools, homes and hospices to find and embrace poor, excluded, and despised children, women, and men. "Creation," Ellacuría maintained, "has turned

---

26. Wendy Farley, *Tragic Vision and Divine Compassion: A Contemporary Theodicy* (Louisville, KY: Westminster/John Knox Press, 1990), 69, 74.

27. Katie Geneva Cannon, *Katie's Canon: Womanism and the Soul of the Black Community* (New York: Continuum, 2002), 141.

out badly for God":[28] vicious and crippling poverty, malnutri-
tion, disease, and misery stalk the continents of Africa and Latin
America; anti-Semitism has become globally habitual; we accept
the normalization of the incarceration and the criminalization of
youth, women, and men who are impoverished—white and black
and brown alike. Certainly, in Latin America and in Africa—and
in so many other parts of our crucified world—the political, economic, and technological conditions of ordinary people represent
grievous sin and evil. We have crucified these poor, excluded, and
despised children, women, and men through corrupt consciences
and crooked systems. Yet, these crucified people are the only sure
sign of God's presence in our world. For these children, women,
and men offer us a graced and saving encounter with God's mercy,
compassion, and love. These are our brothers and sisters, members
of Jesus's own family. They are our partners and companions in the
work of justice; together, side by side, we struggle to find out what
it means to live "the way" of Jesus. Only together, side by side, we
glimpse the promised parousia.

What does solidarity cost? "If any want to become my followers, let them deny themselves and take up their cross and follow
me" (Mark 8:34). In a word: self-dispossession is the price solidarity exacts. We cannot hold back our lives, ourselves. We are
called to give our very selves away, to give our lives away. Be sure:
This is no easy slogan, no simplistic appeal, no romantic aspira-
tion: In *Torture and Eucharist,* William Cavanaugh underscores
that in the face of rampant and random violence, some individuals may be quite averse to protest oppression or to act on behalf of
others.[29] And, as Katie Cannon reminds us, we as church may be
too easily "shaped by obeisance" to a social system and its interests
and, thus, "legitimate exploitation."[30] Solidarity as compassionate
action always must resist reduction to selfish self-regard or self-

---

28. Jon Sobrino, *The Principle of Mercy: Taking the Crucified People from the Cross* (Maryknoll, NY: Orbis Books, 1992, 1994), 49.

29. William Cavanaugh, *Torture and Eucharist: Theology, Politics, and the Body of Christ* (Oxford: Blackwell, 1998).

30. Cannon, *Katie's Canon*, 160.

protection, always must resist every tendency to overlook or evade the scope and depth of the cruelty and conflict that domination causes.

Self-dispossession (*kenosis*) calls for critique of autonomy as will-to-power, of obscurant individualism, of irresponsibility; but, we must go further, deeper, beyond the boundaries of our lives/ourselves to a new way of being in the universe, in God's future. Dispossession of self implies the absolute surrender to God of all our cultural and social and religious and personal securities, the purification of our hearts and memories, the reorientation of ego, forgiveness. Dispossession of self is the costliest fruit of passion for God; it fructifies only in losing one's self and receiving the self that is returned from the loving hand of God.

Conclusion

"If any want to become my followers, let them deny themselves and take up their cross and follow me." Then Jesus adds, "For those who want to save their life will lose it, and those who lose their life for my sake, and for the sake of the gospel, will save it. For what does it profit them to gain the whole world and forfeit their life?" (Mark 8:35–36).

Solidarity forms the heart and substance of Christian discipleship, for our compassionate, practical, and intelligent action makes the very presence of the Holy One vivid among us. This action revises relationships, heals wounds, and binds us together again as God's new creation. This demands our active and sustained engagement: We cannot hope to think about "God in depth," that is, in the concrete; we cannot draw close to God in "understanding," unless we "re-enact within ourselves the conditions of [divine] being, which is to say dispossession of the self for the sake of the other."[31] The cross teaches us this lesson, and it is the only lesson worthy of the God who made us, the Incarnate Word who

---

31. Oliver Davies, *A Theology of Compassion: Metaphysics of Difference and the Renewal of Tradition* (Grand Rapids, MI: William B. Eerdmans Publishing Company, 2001), 252.

redeemed us, the Spirit who sanctifies and holds us. The cross—strange and mysterious paradox of power and self-emptying—reveals all the fruitful possibility and costliness of love. To follow the tears of a crucified world, the tears and weeping of a crucified people, is to arrive at the foot of the cross—the place where a disciple must stand, must take a stand rooted in knowing and loving Christ crucified.

CHAPTER SEVEN

Resurrection Hope

> I want to know Christ and the power of his resurrection and the sharing of his sufferings by becoming like him in his death, [that] I may somehow attain the resurrection from the dead. —Philippians 3:10

> I tell you, unless a grain of wheat falls into the earth and dies, it remains just a single grain; but if it dies, it bears much fruit.
> —John 12:26

In the witness of African American religious experience, Jesus of Nazareth is the clearest example of what it means to identify with abandoned, tortured, oppressed children, women and men—to take their side in the struggle for life no matter the cost. The itinerant Jewish rabbi, preacher, and miracle worker acted in solidarity with and alongside children, women, and men who were marginalized and despised by privileged elites and powerful political, economic, and religious authorities. Jesus committed his very life to the cause of those who endured relentless violence, economic exploitation, powerlessness, cultural imperialism, physical and sexual abuse. He became one with them and challenged whatever and whoever caused their needless misery and pain. His cross was "God's act of self-identification with all people in that extremity of the human condition and that heart of all suffering that is the absence of God. It is the furthest point to which God's self-giving love in incarnation goes."[1]

---

1. Richard Bauckham, *Jesus and the God of Israel: God Crucified and Other*

The enslaved people knew that this crucified Jesus was one with them, that he challenged whatever and whoever inflicted their misery and pain. In the witness of African American religious experience, Jesus of Nazareth *is* Lord and Christ, he *is* freedom enfleshed. He *is* the one who in "wondrous love . . . lays aside his crown" and chooses to share "the dreadful curse of enslavement."[2] Theo Witvliet recognizes this: "In the context of racism and slavery, [Jesus'] self-emptying is his blackness."[3] In the witness of African American religious experience, the Jewish Jesus of Nazareth *is* black as they are black; he is one with them. The Jewish Jesus of Nazareth *is* the black messiah.

Three sections comprise this chapter. The first, "Cross and Liberation," briefly sets out the relation between the suffering of the enslaved people and the suffering of the crucified Jesus. In a world shaped by privilege and power, poverty and enslavement, crucifixion and lynching reek of defeat. But African American religious experience witnesses to the "power of the cross to create a new situation," to resist destruction, to evoke a new and liberating response.[4] The second section, "Singing Resurrection," before sketching a resurrection theology rooted in three spirituals, explores critical issues relevant to that sketch—New Testament meanings of resurrection and challenges in interpretation of the spirituals. The third section, "Resurrection Hope," draws out the

Studies on the New Testament's Christology of Divine Identity (Grand Rapids, MI/ Cambridge, UK, 2008), loc. 3307 of 4302, Kindle.

2. "When I Was Sinkin' Down," liner notes. The Fisk Jubilee Singers, *The Gold and Blue Album* (FA 2372; Folkways Records, 1955). "When I Was Sinkin' Down" is a variant of the hymn "What Wondrous Love Is This." According to LindaJo H. McKim, "The words to this American folk hymn were published in 1811 in a camp meeting songbook, *A General Selection of the Newest and Most Admired Hymns and Spiritual Songs Now in Use* (Lynchburg, Virginia). It also appeared in a Baptist hymnal published in Frankfort, Kentucky"; see *The Presbyterian Hymnal Companion* (Louisville, KY: Westminster John Knox Press, 1993), 78.

3. Theo Witvliet, *The Way of the Black Messiah: The Hermeneutical Challenge of Black Theology as a Theology of Liberation* (Oak Park, IL: Meyer-Stone Books, 1987), 265.

4. Paul S. Fiddes, *The Creative Suffering of God* (Oxford: Oxford University Press, 1992),164.

connection between the community of the crucified Jesus and the community of the resurrected Lord.

Cross and Liberation

The story of the crucifixion of Jesus of Nazareth substantively shaped the horizon or worldview of the enslaved African people in the United States. Led by their bards and poets, these women and men crafted and sang of the man Jesus and that bloody, awe-filling event with aching solemnity and feeling. They knew the torment and abuse Jesus endured in their very own flesh. If the spirituals seem to linger upon, to caress that terrible event, surely it is because the circumscribed life situation of the enslaved people permitted them no share in attitudes and postures of conquest or victory as commonsense understandings of the resurrection too often convey. Matthew Johnson rightly observes, "There is a deep, even euphoric, triumphalism radiating heavily from the common understanding of the Resurrection as the most significant event of the Christian faith."[5] The men and women who crafted and sang the spirituals were confident in their relationship with Jesus of Nazareth. They knew in their hearts, in their minds, in their flesh that

> Christ [was] a god of compassion and suffering, a promul-gator of freedom and peace and opportunity, a son of an omnipotent Father. Christ and his Father had proved them-selves. They had brought justice out of many impossible situ-ations and could and would bring it boldly out of slavery, when the time came. They were already bringing it out, to some extent, since they were guiding so many black people (runaways) to the realms of freedom.[6]

The spirituals disclose a people's profound spiritual sensibility achieved through "aural" appropriation of biblical literature and

---

5. Matthew V. Johnson, *The Tragic Vision of African American Religion* (New York: Palgrave Macmillan, 2010), 126.

6. John Lovell Jr., *Black Song: The Forge and the Flame—The Story of How the Afro-American Spiritual Was Hammered Out* (New York: Macmillan, 1986), 189.

careful scrutiny of white Christian preaching. Theirs is a finely tuned interior life: yearning for and open to the presence and action of the Divine, steeped in prayer, critically conscious of the disciplines and meanings of right doing and right living, committed to active struggle for freedom and justice, courageous in resistance to oppression. The spirituals propose a liberating theology that, James Cone asserts, "is based on the biblical contention that God's righteousness is revealed in deliverance of the oppressed from shackles of human bondage. . . . The slave firmly believed that 'God would make a way out of no way,' meaning that God's providential care of God's children cannot be thwarted by white masters."[7] The spirituals witness to the living, vibrant hope of a people determined "to realize their human potentialities grounded in the faith that God's liberation is at work in the world; and that God's will to liberate black slaves will become a reality in this land."[8] Thus, in strenuous effort to appropriate and recast communal experience, to recover communal meanings, values, and critical solidarities, and "to overcome and transcend their painful, restrictive, oppressive environment, to begin to experience liberation and the privilege of emancipation,"[9] the enslaved people composed and sang a daring dream and their deepest hope.

Singing Resurrection

The spirituals sing resurrection because it symbolized and expressed the enslaved people's radical hope for freedom in this world and in the hereafter. The resurrection confirmed their expectation of freedom as the end of enslavement and of otherworldly fulfillment of the relationship with Jesus that had begun in this world. The spirituals sing escape and map the way to the

---

7. James H. Cone, *The Spirituals and the Blues* (Maryknoll, NY: Orbis Books, 1972, 1992), 33–34.

8. Ibid.

9. Cheryl Kirk-Duggan, *Exorcizing Evil: A Womanist Perspective on the Spirituals* (Maryknoll, NY: Orbis Books, 1997), 14. This work is remarkable for its comprehensive character, for its cultural and theo-ethical insight into the spirituals, and for its sophisticated musicology.

"promised land," to freedom; and they paint a picture of "heab'n" and "the welcome table," where despised and excluded women and men will meet, sit, talk with, and enjoy the company of King Jesus. They will "shoulder up" their crosses and exchange them for a crown and, like the angels, they too will have a harp, a robe, and slippers. The makers of the spirituals sang the enslaved community's dream and hope: "Before I'd be a slave, I'd be buried in my grave and go home to my Lord, and be free"; "I want to go heaven when I die / To shout salvation as I fly."

Preliminary Considerations: Reading Resurrection Appearances

The meanings and the surplus meanings of resurrection depend upon the particular Gospel or testimony that bears witness to it. Thus, New Testament scholars caution against the temptation to disregard the diversity and particularity of the Gospel traditions and the communities that invigorated those narratives. Perhaps, for the Johannine writer, resurrection takes some of its meaning and power from notions of exaltation—but as these are expressed contrapuntally; the Lukan writer joins the ambiguity of the empty tomb to the stubborn faith of the disciples—female and male—that clings to the reality of the appearances of Jesus.

All four of the Gospel narratives include (1) the empty tomb and (2) the importance of the women as the first to learn of the resurrection, with Mary Magdalene assuming a preeminent role; indeed, according to Mark 16:9 and John 20:14, Jesus appeared first to her. Mark and Luke affirm that the announcement of the resurrection is made first to women. In Matthew's Gospel, Mary Magdalene is accompanied by the "other Mary"; leaving the empty tomb behind, they rush to tell the news, when they both meet the risen Jesus (28:1, 5, 8-9).

In writing of the resurrection, Luke refers back to the company of women who had been with Jesus very early on, traveling with him and the Twelve through cities and villages: "Mary called Magdalene . . . Joanna, the wife of Herod's steward Chuza, Susanna, and many others, who provided for them out of their resources"

(8:2–3). These same women followed those who carried Jesus's body from the Place of the Skull to Joseph of Arimathea's tomb; they took note of the location. As soon as it was ritually possible, they went to the tomb carrying spices they had prepared in order to anoint Jesus's body (Luke 23:55–56). The empty tomb awaits them; two men in dazzling clothes greet them and nudge them to remember all that Jesus had told them in Galilee. Mary Magdalene, Joanna, Mary the mother of James, and the other women with them, tell all that they had seen and heard to the apostles. But, the men do not believe the women; their "words seemed to them an idle tale" (Luke 24:1–11).

The Johannine narrative brings Mary Magdalene to the fore. Grieving and alone in the twilight hours of the morning, Mary finds the tomb open and empty. She runs to tell "Simon Peter and the other disciple, the one whom Jesus loved" (John 20:2). The two men rush to the tomb, find only burial linens; they return to their homes. Mary remains weeping by the tomb. In this Gospel, "the tears of a single, kneeling anguished woman summon the presence of the risen Lord. A woman's tears command that Jesus deal with the crisis of mortality in the garden as he had dealt with that of Lazarus—in person."[10]

Seeing the risen Jesus left the disciples—female and male— unsettled and amazed. Their reactions ought not to be dismissed lightly. Contemporary life admits no parallel through which to understand the horror, the shame, the repulsion associated with crucifixion in the ancient world. Primarily a military and political punishment, crucifixion was the supreme Roman penalty. In nearly all instances, it was reserved for the lower classes, for slaves, for subjugated peoples. Crucifixion called for the public display of a naked victim in some prominent place—a crossroads, an amphitheater, high ground. Crucifixion was sadistic and cruel; it was the violent and visceral expression of dishonor, dehumanization,

---

10. Allen Dwight Callahan, "The Gospel of John," in *True to Our Native Land: An African American New Testament Commentary*, ed. Brian K. Blount (Minneapolis: Fortress Press, 2007), 208.

desecration. It was within this cultural and social milieu that Jesus of Nazareth, a Jewish rabbi and prophet, powerful in action before God and the people, was crucified. The very one whom so many had hoped was the messiah, the one who would set Israel free, died the death of one accursed by God (Deut 21:23). Now wrapped in the radiant glory of God's lovingkindness (*chesed*), this same Jesus stands in their midst. The Crucified One must be embraced if the Resurrected One is to be recognized.

The disciples—female and male—"saw" the risen Jesus. They were gripped by an unshakable certainty that the Jesus who had been crucified, by the power of the God of Israel, somehow was raised from the dead. The crucified Jesus *is* the risen Christ. These appearances are characterized by an insistent corporeality: Jesus eats with the disciples, invites them to examine the imprint of the nails in his hands and feet, to touch him, to feel flesh and bone. The recognition of the heart is to be confirmed by the senses and the mind. Yet, the risen body of Jesus transcends the world of scientific logic. This body is of a new and different reality; it betokens a new and different mode of living. Not to be confused with resuscitation, it is a radical break with material reality as we experience it. Resurrection is an event for Jesus; something radical has happened to him.

At the same time, something happened to the disciples. The appearances are neither the psychological effects of mere enthusiasm nor the by-products of frenzied despair. An explanation grounded in psychological origins can account neither for the complete change in the behavior of the disciples nor for their willingness and courage in embracing sacrifice and death in the name of Jesus. But neither are the appearances simply solitary singular inner experiences. Indeed, they possess the character of public event and involve groups as well as individuals.

Finally, the appearances are gratuitous and, as such, serve to remind us that the resurrection is not primarily about the sight of Jesus but rather about insight into who he was. The appearances are real, transformative encounters with the risen Lord; moreover, these encounters critically re-form the disciples' grasp of just who

Jesus is. Not only their eyes but also their minds are opened to understand the scriptures so that they might take their place as witnesses to all that they have seen and heard, so that they might receive the Spirit.

Resurrection characterizes the destiny of Jesus, but it is not a private destiny intended for him alone. The resurrection is the beginning of the absolute transfiguration of all creation. That is to say, the resurrection binds back to the heart of God all creation, which has been scattered by sin. The resurrection breaks through, formally and materially, the cosmic, psychic, and moral alienations that promote unintelligibility and chaos. The resurrection proclaims that "God's salvation is involved in Jesus in such a way that after Easter Jesus becomes the norm for the relationship between humanity and God."[11] What was required of Jesus was something quite extremely bold: that he stake his whole life on its being absolutely directed toward God, that he trust his life had a definite meaning in God, that he believe that God would save him and deliver him absolutely.

Preliminary Considerations: Reading Resurrection Spirituals

In the witness of the New Testament, whatever resurrection was and is, belief and affirmation of it was/is constitutive of Christian identity. Yet, Christian identity or self-understanding and Christian belief, while intending what is true and normative, may be expressed in diverse or plural ways. Christian tradition allows for, must thrive on, such diversity. Marianne Sawicki argues the issue in a manner that affirms this work: "Christian origin happens continually, and always with the contrapuntal structure of enframing and frame-breaking. . . . The Gospels impose definition upon the character of Jesus and closure upon his career [and] those narratives have seams designed to split."[12]

---

11. Pheme Perkins, *Resurrection: New Testament Witness and Contemporary Reflection* (Garden City, NY: Doubleday, 1984), 29.

12. Marianne Sawicki, *Seeing the Lord: Resurrection and Early Christian Practices* (Minneapolis: Fortress Press, 1994), 301.

If the "seams" of the Gospel narratives seem designed to split and if "faith comes by hearing" (Rom 10:17), the religious witness of the enslaved people exemplifies Christian origination. We know that their religious instruction was often haphazard, indifferent, or limited to depredations of the injunction "Slaves be submissive to your masters" (Col 3:22–25; Eph 6:5–8; 1 Pet 2:18–25). Yet they intuited and insisted that "that the true message of the Christian gospel . . . was a message of inspiriting and empowering freedom under God."[13] Jesus breaks out of the frame of slaveholding Christianity and takes his place in "the slave quarter," among and beside the dispossessed. One freed woman, Nancy Williams, insisted: "Ol' white preacher used to talk with their tongues without saying nothin', but Jesus told us slaves to talk with our hearts."[14] Talking "with [their] hearts" suggests an encounter with Jesus, who breaks out of the frame to offer an ongoing, dynamic relationship they can trust: "O a little talk with Jesus makes it right, all right" or "When every star refuses to shine . . . I know King Jesus will be mine."

On the strength and grace of relationship with Jesus, the enslaved people reframed their experience of the Christian Bible, culling from it sayings, events, characters, stories, images, metaphors, symbols, and so on. They searched for what resonated with the root paradigms or cognitive and moral orientations, religio-cultural memories, spiritual sensibilities and aspirations that survived the Middle Passage. In this way, the enslaved people developed and utilized an "aural" text. Through the spirituals, they and their poets transposed much of the material from that "aural" text into song, deploying vivid and immediate images, some of which biblical scholars and theologians understand today as associated with the apocalyptic and anamnesis (or memory). The people allowed the truth ("the truly true") of the biblical mes-

---

13. Clarice J. Martin, "The Haustafeln (Household Codes) in African American Biblical Interpretation: 'Free Slaves' and 'Subordinate Women,'" in *Stony the Road We Trod: African American Biblical Interpretation*, ed. Cain Hope Felder (Minneapolis: Fortress Press, 1999), 213.

14. Julius Lester, *To Be a Slave*, 30th anniversary edition (New York: Penguin Books, 1998, orig. 1968), 79.

sage to absorb them and their condition even as they absorbed that truth. They sang their sorrow and their joy, reaching, with authenticity, an experience and a glimpse of the eschatological.[15]

Intertextual reading and excavation of "compressed meanings" in spirituals enables the theologian to identify phrases or words that "compress several biblical reference into one image."[16] Such a method may facilitate a sketch of an implicit resurrection theology. For this purpose, three spirituals receive detailed attention: "He Arose"; "De Angel Rolled the Stone Away"; and "De Angels Done Bowed Down." But before turning to this task, some preliminary observations are in order.

First, these songs complexly collate disparate settings or places, protagonists or characters, events or actions, or sounds and images. Thus, the spirituals mediate their message by appealing to the affective, the kinesthetic, the auditory, and the visual.[17] The songs allow us to see key places or sites of action and encounter: Golgotha, the garden in which Joseph of Arimathea's tomb is located; the garden of Eden; the garden on the other side of the Kidron Valley; a cluster of willow trees, mountains, and Galilee. Jesus, angels, Joseph of Arimathea, Mary Magdalene, Roman soldiers, Pontius Pilate and his councilors, the Lord, and God comprise the main characters or protagonists in these spirituals. Further, the makers and singers of the spirituals insert themselves and us in the action; they take up the position of first-person witnesses and narrators of

---

15. Harold Courlander commented, "[I]f these songs are arranged in a somewhat chronological order, they are equivalent to an oral version of the Bible. Each song presents in a capsulized or dramatic form a significant Biblical moment. . . . [Thus] it would be possible to put a large body of Negro religious songs together in a certain sequence to produce an oral counterpart to the Bible, if printed they would make a volume fully as thick as the Bible itself" (*Negro Folk Music, U.S.A.* [New York: Columbia University Press, 1963], 43). Lovell states that the known corpus of the spirituals is approximately six thousand songs, five hundred of which he consults in *Black Song*.

16. Will Coleman, *Tribal Talk: Black Theology, Hermeneutics, and African/American Ways of "Telling the Story"* (University Park, PA: Pennsylvania State University Press, 2000), 128.

17. Kirk-Duggan, *Exorcizing Evil*, 14.

key actions or events. They allow us to hear Joseph beg, Mary weep, the sound of the trumpet, the heavy silence of the angels, and the voice of Jesus/God. They permit us to watch Mary run, the angels at work on various tasks, Jesus rising upon the pillar of cloud, the soldiers helpless, Pilate and his councilors stunned.

Second, the spirituals conflate different time frames: the time of the flood, morning, New Testament time, messianic time, plantation time, linear chronological time (past, present future), the singer's (changing) present, *kairotic* time, and apocalyptic time.[18] In order to grasp some of the implications of time in the spirituals, let us consider briefly the traditional African concept of time. That concept of time differs markedly from the linear and progressive concept of time reflected by Western cultures and societies. Philosopher John Mbiti explains that for Africans,

> time is a composition of events which have occurred, those which are taking place now and those which are inevitably or immediately to occur. What has not yet taken place or what has no likelihood of an immediate occurrence falls in the category of "No-time." What is certain to occur, or what falls within the rhythm of natural phenomena, is in the category of *potential time*.[19]

Given this traditional understanding, "time is a two-dimensional phenomenon, with a long *past*, a *present*, and virtually *no future*."[20] In fact, in many African languages there are no words or verb tenses that can be deployed to express the future "beyond a few months from now. This means the future is virtually non-existent as actual time, apart from the relatively short projection of the present up to two years hence."[21]

When Africans "reckon time, it is for a concrete and specific

---

18. Lauri Ramey, *Slave Songs and the Birth of African American Poetry* (New York: Palgrave Macmillan, 2008), 74.

19. John S. Mbiti, *African Religions and Philosophy,* 2nd ed. (Oxford: Heinemann, 1989), 16.

20. Ibid.

21. Ibid., 17.

purpose, in connection with events."[22] The day and the month are reckoned in accord with essential or unusual events, such as the time to draw water or the month of rains or planting; the year is reckoned in terms of the completion of seasons, for example, two rainy seasons, two dry seasons. "Outside the reckoning of the year, African time concept is silent and indifferent."[23]

Space and time are closely conjoined in an African worldview. On this point, Mbiti makes an important comment: "[W]hat matters most to the people," he states, "is what is geographically near. . . . Africans are tied to the land. To remove Africans by force from their land is an act of such great injustice that no foreigner can fathom."[24] If we consider the absence of a linear temporal future in an African worldview, if we take into account the consequences of slavery's forced separation of people from their land, and if we consider the centuries-long trajectory of enslavement, perhaps we may begin to glimpse the ontological courage, creativity, and humility required of the enslaved people to reorient their worldview. Perhaps, we may begin to admire truly the testimony of formerly enslaved Alice Sewell: "We prayed for dis day of freedom. We come four and five miles to pray together to God dat if we don't live to see it, to please let our chillen live to see a better day and be free, so dat dey can give honest and fair service to de Lord and all mankind [*sic*] everywhere."[25]

Formed by and within African notions of time, the enslaved people may well have thought that slavery would be enforced day after day after day; they were "a-rolling thro' an unfriendly world." Through the performance of recurring tasks, or witnessing unusual, even, dreadful events, the people reckoned the rhythms of the plantation; but in spirituals, at an ontological level, the people reoriented space and time. Marked as commodities, objects for purchase and sale, the enslaved people sang themselves a new

22. Ibid.
23. Ibid., 21.
24. Ibid., 26.
25. Norman R. Yetman, ed., *Voices from Slavery* (New York: Holt, Rinehart and Winston, 1970), 263.

identity: "Born of God I know I am"; "Ah tol' Jesus it would be all right, if He changed mah name." Homeless, they sang themselves a lasting abode: "I got a home in that rock"; "Deep river, my home is over Jordan." Caught in the futile future of slavery, they felt time anew: "I been in de storm so long"; "Soon-a will be done with the troubles of the world . . . Goin' home to live with God." Freedom was a both a spiritual and political destination, both a social and cultural event. If they could grasp a future at all, it was conceived and concretized as freedom. So the enslaved people sang:

> Oh let us all from bondage flee . . .
> And let us all in Christ be free . . .
>
> We need not always weep and moan . . .
> And wear these slavery chains forlorn. . . .

Interpretation: "He Arose" and "De Angel Rolled the Stone Away"

Both *"He Arose"* and *"De Angel Rolled the Stone Away"* disclose an eagerness to tell the story of Jesus raised from the dead and to shout confident joy at their relationship to and with him.

> He arose, He arose
> He arose, He arose, from the dead, and the Lord shall
>   bear my spirit home.
>
> Joseph begged His body and laid it in the tomb
> Joseph begged His body and laid it in the tomb
> And the Lord shall bear my spirit home.
> He arose, He arose, from the dead, and the Lord shall
>   bear my spirit home.
>
> Down came an angel and rolled the stone away,
> and the Lord shall bear my spirit home.
> He arose, He arose, from the dead, and the Lord shall
>   bear my spirit home.
>
> O Mary came a-weeping her Savior for to see
> But the Lord had gone to Galilee

> He arose, He arose, from the dead, and the Lord shall
>   bear my spirit home.

In a quite straightforward way, "He Arose" tells the Easter story and testifies to the bodily resurrection of Jesus of Nazareth. The song relies on the narrative of the resurrection in the Synoptic Gospels, in particular, Matthew and Mark. Joseph of Arimathea, a wealthy man, possibly a disciple of Jesus but a member of the Sanhedrin, asks Pilate for the body of Jesus (Matt 27:57–59; Mark 15:42–47; Luke 23:44–49). In Matthew's telling, Pilate cooperates without further probing, but in Mark's narrative, the governor requires verification of the death. He summons the centurion in charge of the execution and questions him about the condition of the condemned man. Assured that he is dead, Pilate releases Jesus's body.

The spiritual then reports miraculous action: "Down came an angel and rolled the stone away." In many spirituals, angels work actively and effectively to carry out the commands of Jesus, the Lord, and God. And, "Rarely," writes Lovell, "does the angel of the spiritual work alone." But this particular angel is "celebrated . . . because he rolled the stone away at some time between Good Friday evening and Easter sunrise."[26]

Mary (Magdalene) enters the scene. The singular witnesses to the resurrection are not named in the Lukan account, but Matthew and Mark name the women. Mary Magdalene is mentioned by name in their accounts, and Mark specifies the identity of the other Mary, the mother of Joses (Mark 15:47). Mary enters the scene weeping; she worries (in Mark's Gospel) about the weight and size of the stone at the grave.

Instead of repeating the line "O Mary came a-weeping her Savior for to see," the poet introduces another idea: "The Lord had gone to Galilee." Here while the spiritual concurs with the Synoptic Gospels on the "new" spatial location of the body of the risen Jesus (Matt 28:10, 16; Mark 16:7; Luke 24:6), it differs from them

---

26. Lovell, *Black Song*, 238.

as to who announces this news. In Mark's Gospel, a "young man, dressed in a white robe, sitting on the right side" of the tomb, greets Mary Magdalene and the other Mary. He instructs them: "Go, tell his disciples and Peter that he is going ahead of you to Galilee; there you will see him, just as he told you" (Mark 16:5–7). In Luke's rendition, two young men in dazzling clothes appear to the women: "Why do you look for the living among the dead?" they ask. "He is not here, but has risen" (Luke 24:4–6).

In Matthew's gospel, following the burial of Jesus, the religious authorities (the chief priests and the Pharisees) petition Pilate to secure the tomb against Jesus's declaration of resurrection or theft of his body. Pilate tells them to take a guard of soldiers and seal the tomb (Matt 27:62–66). At dawn, the next day, as the women approach the tomb, there is an earthquake as an angel of the Lord descends from heaven and rolls back the stone from the tomb. "His appearance was like lightning, and his clothes were white as snow." Fear paralyzes the guards. The angel soothes the women: "Do not be afraid; I know you are looking for Jesus who was crucified. He is not here . . . indeed, he is going ahead of you to Galilee, there you will see him." The women leave the tomb quickly in fear and great joy, only to meet Jesus himself who says, "Do not be afraid; go and tell my brothers to go to Galilee; there they will see me" (Matt 28:2–10).

In the geography of the spirituals, Galilee most often refers to the "home" country of Jesus, his disciples, his followers, and believers. Perhaps, the song's line "The Lord had gone to Galilee" suggests a space or place of new life and freedom, a refuge from the "necropower"[27] of the plantation. Whose voice introduces the site of Galilee in the spiritual: the angel, the believer, the singer? Is the line intended to comfort Mary or believers? Or might it intend to prompt or to signal escape, or is it a warning? Still, the enslaved singer repeats: "The Lord shall bear my spirit home." The singer is a believer, certain of salvation, of freedom;

---

27. Achille Mbembé, "Necropolitics," *Public Culture* 15, no. 1 (Winter 2003): 11–40, at 27.

she trusts Jesus to bring her through the troubles of the world. She has a home in that rock.

Interpretation: *"De Angel Roll de Stone Away"*

> De angel roll de stone away;
> De angel roll de stone away;
> 'Twas on a bright an' shiny morn,
> When de trumpet begin to soun';

Sister Mary came a runnin'
at de break o' day,
Brought de news f'om heaben,
De stone done roll away.

> De angel roll de stone away;
> De angel roll de stone away;
> 'Twas on a bright an' shiny morn,
> When de trumpet begin to soun';

I'm a lookin' for my Saviour,
tell me where he lay,
High up on de mountain,
De stone done roll away.

> De angel roll de stone away;
> De angel roll de stone away;
> 'Twas on a bright an' shiny morn,
> When de trumpet begin to soun';

De soljahs dere a plenty,
standin' by de do',
But dey could not hinder,
De stone done roll away.

> De angel roll de stone away;
> De angel roll de stone away;
> 'Twas on a bright an' shiny morn,
> When de trumpet begin to soun';

> Pilate and his wise men,
> didn't know what to say,
> De miracle was on dem,
> De stone done roll away.

>> De angel roll de stone away;
>> De angel roll de stone away;
>> 'Twas on a bright an' shiny morn,
>> When de trumpet begin to soun'.

As Lauri Ramey clarifies, this spiritual brings together several disparate time frames; she identifies some of these as:

> the past time frame of Jesus at the time of the resurrection; the future time frame of the apocalypse; the present time of the poetic persona; the mysterious time frame or frames when the speaker encounters the angel; the equally mysterious time frame or frames in which the speaker encounters Mary Magdalene, who has come running at the break of day after returning from heaven. . . ."[28]

This spiritual seems to assume that Mary is/has been in heaven, literally and metaphorically. "Sister Mary" comes running from heaven with the good news that the angel has rolled the stone away. Taking the song metaphorically, Ramey proposes two readings of this verse: that Mary may have felt as if she "were in a heavenly place when she discovered that Jesus had risen." Alternatively, Mary "actually might have gone to heaven, either in the body, 'or out of the body,' or in a dream state."[29] Certainly these interpretations find support from biblical narratives and the religious experiences of enslaved people. Biblical examples include Jacob, who in a dream state climbs a ladder to heaven (Gen 28:12), or Paul's confession of being "caught up to the third heaven, whether in the body or out of the body" (2 Cor 12:2).

---

28. Ramey, *Slave Songs*, 74.
29. Ibid.

Or consider the resonant metaphorical language of African American conversion narratives: "God struck me dead with his power";[30] or the language of spiritual travel of the soul to heaven or to hell. "Dream consciousness was believed by the slave community to be a metaphysical gift from God that had placed the one experiencing conversion outside of the temporal self for the purpose of turning the universe of oneself and one's fellow human beings into objects of contemplation."[31] These various possible interpretations of Mary's dream or vision or visitation along with her announcement from heaven that Jesus is risen cohere in the joy and trust the enslaved people felt toward Jesus.

Like the Matthean account of the resurrection, the third and fourth verses of the spiritual mention the presence of soldiers posted to guard Jesus's tomb and Pilate's interest in this aspect. This Gospel records that after the resurrection, as soon as the women leave the tomb, some of the guards went into the city and reported to the chief priests what had happened. The priests meet with the elders and together they devise a cover-up. The authorities pay off the soldiers, then instruct them to lie: "Tell the governor and any others who inquire that his disciples came during the night and stole him away while we were asleep." This shabby alibi is to protect the soldiers from the governor's anger, so they comply (Matt 28:11–14).

The New Testament writers are silent on Pilate's reaction to the soldiers' report of resurrection. But the fourth verse of the spiritual muses on it and rings with wit:

> Pilate and his wise men,
> didn't know what to say,
> De miracle was on dem,
> De stone done roll away.

---

30. Clifton H. Johnson, ed., *God Struck Me Dead: Voices of Ex-Slaves* (Cleveland, OH: Pilgrim Press, 1993; orig. 1969), 59–60.

31. Riggins Earl, *Dark Symbols, Obscure Signs: God, Self, and Community in the Slave Mind* (Maryknoll, NY: Orbis Books, 1993), 53.

God's power confounds Roman power. Pilate and his councilors can say nothing; the manifestation of God's power leaves
them speechless. Pilate and his councilors are unable to mount a
response; they can do nothing. Pilate knew the tomb was sealed
(Matt 27:62–66); likely, he gave no further thought to Jesus. So,
surely, the poet relishes singing: "De miracle was on them / De
stone done roll away."

Roman power had come down hard on Jesus and "inflicted
upon him punishment worthy of a rebel king."[32] But the miracle of
resurrection came down even harder on the power of the Roman
imperium. Another spiritual makes the political critique directly:

> He is King of Kings, He is Lord of lords,
> Jesus Christ the first and the last, no man works like
>   him.
> He built his throne up in the air . . .
> And called his saints from everywhere . . .
> He pitched his tents on Canaan's ground.
> And broke the Roman kingdom down.

The crowd may have shouted "We have no king but Caesar" (John
19:15), but the spiritual shouts in reply: "He is King of Kings, He
is Lord of Lord / Jesus Christ is the first and last." In the world of
the spirituals, King Jesus overturns the power of Rome. Theirs is
a shout of freedom in the teeth of oppression, a shout of hope in
assurance of divine vindication.

Interpretation: "The Angels Done Bowed Down"

In the song "The Angels Done Bowed Down," the enslaved poets
strike a somber and meditative mood, singing a sorrowful joy:

> O the angels done bowed down
> O the angels done bowed down
> O the angels done bowed down

---

32. Allen Dwight Callahan, *A Love Supreme: A History of the Johannine Tradition* (Minneapolis: Fortress Press, 2005), 90.

> While Jesus was a-hanging upon the cross,
> The angels kept quiet till God went off,
> And the angels hung their harps on the willow
>   trees
> To give satisfaction till God was pleased.

O the angels done bowed down
O the angels done bowed down
O the angels done bowed down

> His soul went upon the pillar of cloud,
> O God he moved and the heavens did bow,
> Jehovah's sword was at his side,
> On the empty air He began to ride.

O the angels done bowed down
O the angels done bowed down
O the angels done bowed down

> "Go down angels to the flood
> Blow out the sun, turn the moon into blood!
> Come back angels bolt the door
> The time that's been will be no more."

O the angels done bowed down
O the angels done bowed down
O the angels done bowed down

At least five time frames are activated in this spiritual: (1) eternity, in which the angels dwell even as they are capable of entering other space-time continuums; for instance, they keep silent watch at the crucifixion of Jesus and are ordered to participate in future apocalyptic time, as the third verse implies. Eternal existence is an attribute of God. Eternity is timeless—without past, present, or future; God chooses to enter into time or history; (2) the time of Noah or the time of the flood or time before the patriarchs of Israel; (3) New Testament past time in which Jesus is crucified and rises, the rupture of time the resurrection represents; (4) future apocalyptic time when the angels are ordered to carry out various tasks in the third verse; and (5) the enigmatic present time frame when the singers observe the activities of the angels, God's departure, the death of Jesus, the soul of Jesus rise, the sun go dark, the moon turn to blood or "cast themselves into the future, as if already in the afterlife or a post-apocalyptic state."[33]

In the first verse of the spiritual, angels are found at or near the site of the crucifixion keeping silent watch, bowing down low in awe at the sight of the Son of God being crucified. God departs this woeful scene, and the angels hang their harps on willow trees; their silence is an effort to please God. The silence of these heavenly messengers brings to mind the scene of Jesus fearful and weeping in the garden of Gethsemane (Matt 26:36–45, Mark 14:32–41). Luke's Gospel names the place where Jesus goes with friends and disciples as the "Mount of Olives." There, he is bowed down in sorrow, his "sweat like great drops of blood," and "an angel from heaven appeared to him and strengthened him" (Luke 22:39–44). Both the Gospel account and the spiritual suggest Rembrandt's pen drawing "The Agony in the Garden," which depicts an angel with arms wrapped around Jesus.

The second verse witnesses to the death of Jesus: The whole of the heavens bow low as his "soul" mounts the pillar of cloud and rides the air with Jehovah's sword at his side. The pillar of cloud recalls the care and protection God lavishes on the Israelites as they move through the wilderness (Exod 13:21). Additionally, Exodus also celebrates the Lord God as "a man of war" (Exod 15:3). This verse resonates with Joshua's vision: as he draws near Jericho, Joshua sees a man standing before him. When he inquires of his identity, the man who holds a sword replies that he is the captain of the army of the Lord (Josh 5:13–15).

The verse also evokes other passages: the words of Hebrews: "the word of God is living and active, sharper than any two-edged sword, piercing until it divides soul from spirit, joints from marrow; it is able to judge the thoughts and intentions of the heart" (4:12); the passage in the book of Revelation in which the author

---

33. Ramey, *Slave Songs*, 76.

records a vision of the Son of Man from whose "mouth came a sharp, two-edged sword" (Rev 1:16).

A voice breaks into the scene of the third verse—perhaps the voice of Jesus or the voice of God—and instructs the angels to go to the (area of the) flood, blow out the sun, turn the moon into blood, and bolt the door. This third verse cannot but summon memory of the "flood of waters upon the earth [that] destroy[ed] all flesh, wherein is the breath of life" (Gen 6:17). On God's orders, Noah builds an ark and in it shelters his family and a mating pair of every creature that God created. When the waters recede and the land dries, God makes a covenant with Noah and through him with "every living creature . . . for all future generations"; the token of that covenant is the "bow in the clouds," the rainbow. The rainbow also signals God's regret; God mercifully pledges to remember the covenant, to never again destroy creation through flood (Gen 9:11–17).

Abruptly, the angels are ordered to "Come back [and] bolt the door." This imperative conjures the expulsion of Adam and Eve from the garden of Eden and the placing of the cherubim at the eastern quarter, and a sword flaming and turning to guard the way to the tree of life (Gen 3:24). The door is bolted: Who or what has been excluded? Why? Who or what is being protected? Why? A declarative pronouncement follows the command to action: "The time that's been will be no more." What might this mean? The Markan Gospel poses an answer: "Now after John was arrested, Jesus came to Galilee, proclaiming the good news of God, and saying: 'The time is fulfilled, and the kingdom of God has come near; repent, and believe in the good news'" (Mark 1:14–15).

Chronological or sequential time—time as we have known it now has ceased. God's *kairos*, God's time, has begun. Kairotic time is beyond measure; it opens out into something quite unimaginable, something quite new. Indeed, in Mark's Gospel Jesus begins to demonstrate, to act out those actions that signal the arrival of the messiah's time: the itinerant rabbi calls disciples, drives unclean spirits and demons, heals people suffering from paralysis, leprosy, blindness, and various diseases, and preaches to the poor and dispossessed, and raises the dead (Isa 61:1–2; Luke 4:16–19). Kairos mediates irruption of critical opportunity; something quite new is now possible; yet its effectuation requires decision.

"The Angels Done Bowed Down" mediates a complex, profound, even subversive message. It begins at the cross. The angels tremble at the brutal death of the Righteous One of God, Jesus of Nazareth; in awe and fear, they bow down, avert their gaze, and are silent. Their harps hang on willow trees; they do not disturb God. Then, Jesus dies. The Gospels tell us that darkness covered the land, the earth shook, rocks split, graves opened, and the curtain of the Temple was torn in two (Matt 27:51; Mark 15:38; Luke 23:45). The spiritual tells us that Jesus's soul mounts the pillar of cloud, the whole of the heavens bow down. Jehovah's sword is at his side, judgment is coming.

"The Angels Done Bowed Down" is saturated with apocalyptic imagery: water, darkness, and blood; cloud, the sword of wrath. These images are multivalent, simultaneously suggestive of death and life, of destruction and birth, of decay and growth. Wes Howard-Brook reminds us to eschew meanings of apocalyptic as put forward in "popular culture, both religious and secular, to refer to the 'end of the world.'" He urges us to appreciate the notion of apocalyptic in light of its etymological meaning: "'to lift the veil,' to reveal something otherwise hidden from human view."[34] As an apocalyptic parable, the spiritual creates a force field in which re-creation (the flood) and resurrection (Jesus's death and his soul upon the pillar of cloud) affirm and reinforce that God's time is *now*, the new has arrived.

The enslaved people believed that God did not (and does not) sanction slavery and oppression: "Let anyone with ears to hear listen!" (Mark 4:9). God's time is now; God's time means that freedom is coming—somehow! These poets of sorrowful joy sang the story of God's fidelity to Jesus; they sang believing that as God was faithful to him, God is/was/would be faithful to them and to their posterity.

---

34. Wes Howard-Brook, *"Come Out, My People!" God's Call out of Empire in the Bible and Beyond* (Maryknoll, NY: Orbis Books, 2010), 300.

Resurrection Hope

On the evening of June 17, 2015, members of Emanuel African Methodist Episcopal Church in Charleston, South Carolina, gathered to study the Bible and to pray. During the course of that evening they welcomed a visitor—twenty-one-year-old Dylann Roof. After about forty minutes, the young white man took out a handgun, shooting and killing nine black Christian women and men: Cynthia Marie Graham Hurd, Susie Jackson, Ethel Lee Lance, Depayne Middleton-Doctor, Clementa C. Pinckney, Tywanza Sanders, Daniel Simmons, Sharonda Coleman-Singleton, Myra Thompson. These followers of the crucified and risen Jesus were martyred—slain only because of their existence as God's image in black. These women and men are descendants of enslaved poets, singers, and seekers—women and men who sustained resurrection hope in the agony of slavery and gifted the world with the spirituals.

Their murder legally was a hate crime, that is, a crime motivated by racial, religious, gender, sexual orientation, or other prejudice. Their murder was carried out within a cultural and social horizon that continues to honor and to feed the putative legitimacy of white racist supremacy. That their murder was a political act was made by the perpetrator's explicit adherence to the insolent ensign of sedition, the Confederate flag. Dylann Roof sought out white supremacists, who, either virtually or actually, advertised, packaged, and sold hatred and its symbols as the heritage, tradition, and common memory of white supremacy. In defense of that heritage, tradition, and memory, Roof aimed to ignite a race war between blacks and whites, to purge his community of so-called impure and corrupting elements.[35] The slaughter of those nine black Christian women

---

35. In an alleged manifesto, Dylann Roof wrote: "I have no choice. I am not in the position to, alone, go into the ghetto and fight. I chose Charleston because it is [the] most historic city in my state, and at one time had the highest ratio of blacks to Whites in the country"; see Frances Robles, "Dylan Roof Photos and a Manifesto Are Posted on Website," *New York Times*, June 20, 2015, https://www.nytimes.com/2015/06/21/us/dylann-storm-roof-photos-website-charleston-church-shooting.html.

and men reverberated with America's original sin of white racist supremacy.[36]

That Dylann Roof's plan failed to accomplish its evil purpose surely may be attributed to the Black Christian Principle: that is, the unwavering belief treasured, taught, and reiterated by *all* black Christian churches—that *all* human beings are made in the image and likeness of God, that *all* human beings are creatures of inestimable dignity and worth, and that life is precious and sacred. Family members of the murdered women and men almost immediately offered the murderer forgiveness. Their gratuitous response attests to the cultivation and manifestation of faith, hope, and love in their lived Christian lives.

As a nation, we were quick to embrace this gracious act of forgiveness as our own! What ambiguous relief we felt! But we Christians ought not to allow the nation to confuse forgiveness with forgetting, pushing the uncomfortable and despicable aside. We ought not to allow this horrific event to be swallowed up and lost to common memory in the mind-numbing surfeit of information delivered almost hourly by various forms of media.

We Christians ought not to allow the nation to confuse forgiveness with justice. Forgiveness ought to neither disregard, nor preempt justice, neither exempt wrongdoing from punishment, nor sacrifice "justice in a foreshortened effort to move on."[37] The (human) capacity to forgive comes from the gift of grace, from the very gratuity of the Divine Self. The act of offering forgiveness to another discloses what is, in fact, a conclusion of a profound existential spiritual undertaking. For some, this process may be years in the making as individuals or groups intentionally seek to come

---

36. Jim Wallis may have been the first to have used this term ("America's Original Sin," *Sojourners* [November 1987]; and "Racism: America's Original Sin," *Sojourners* [July 29, 2013]); see https://sojo.net/articles/remembering-trayvon/racism-americas-original-sin. Theologian James Cone gave it wide and pertinent currency; see his "Theology's Great Sin: Silence in the Face of White Supremacy," *Union Seminary Quarterly Review* 55, nos. 3–4 (2001): 1–14.

37. Martha Minow, *Between Vengeance and Forgiveness* (Boston: Beacon Press, 1998), 15.

to terms with and freely respond in love and hope to those who perpetrate grave wrongs against them. For Christians, the New Testament enjoins us to reject revenge: "Do not resist evil. . . . Love your enemies and do good to those who hate you" (Matthew 5:38–48). The ground of forgiveness is the cross of the crucified Jewish Jesus; there, in weakness and suffering, we may discern with the eyes of love the wisdom and power of God.[38]

The crucifixion and resurrection of Jesus of Nazareth constitute an awakening: "an enlargement of the present and a new promise for the future."[39] The crucified Jesus enfleshes for all of us the very meaning of being human, of being a person who embraces and lives out God's gracious gift of freedom in love and hope. His death finds resolution in the love of the loving God who in the resurrection restores and vivifies his flesh and opens all flesh in freedom to resurrection hope. The resurrection of Jesus signifies and anticipates our own and, thus, that of the nine black Christian women and men at prayer in Mother Emanuel Church. They now are "crowned with glory and honor because of the suffering of death" (Heb 2:9). Following the crucified and risen Jesus, they have stepped into the absolute future who is God.

---

38. Theologically, such discernment denotes a basic law in the economy of salvation: God does not do away with evil through power, but transforms evil into good. Bernard Lonergan names this the "Law of the Cross" and explains this in Thesis 17 at *Collected Works of Bernard Lonergan*, vol. 9, *Redemption*, trans. Michael G. Shields, ed. Robert M. Doran, H. Daniel Monsour, Jeremy D. Wilkins (Toronto: University of Toronto Press, 2018), 196/7-205 (Latin even pages, ET facing).

39. Sebastian Moore, *The Crucified Jesus Is No Stranger* (New York/ Mahwah, NJ: Paulist Press, 1977), 75.

Epilogue

They are crucifying again the Son of God and are holding him up to contempt.   —Hebrews 6:6

You want to know what they did in slavery times. They
were doing just what they do now. The white folks was
beating the [slaves], burnin' 'em and boilin' 'em, wor-
kin' 'em and doin' any other thing they wanted to do
with them.   —Alice Johnson, freedwoman

Knowing Christ Crucified begins in the heart of the slave quarter in
the eighteenth century and stretches to the bowels of brutality in
the United States in the twenty-first century. The deepest desire of
this work is to make clear the brilliance and power, inspiration and
relevance of the witness of African American religious experience.

This witness of the "old slaves" is sorely needed: The nation,
indeed, the geo-political world in which we live, has become a site
of social irrationality. Protracted and virulent political, economic,
social, racial, ethnic, and cultural violence has pushed humanity to the edge. Through ethnic cleansings, religious persecu-
tions, plundering land, dirtying the planet, piracy, kidnappings,
hate crimes, acts of terrorism, assassinations, and mass murders;
through exploitation of the poor, crude and violent misogyny,
mass shootings, trafficking and abuse of human persons, children,
in particular—we despoil and degrade, violate and desecrate the
very meaning of human being, of being human. Here in the United
States that violation and desecration have been made most clearly
and concretely in the deaths of black youth, men, and women either

directly at the hands of police or under suspicious circumstances while in police custody or police tactical responses.

The witness and spirit of our enslaved ancestors has taken root in the BlackLivesMatter movement. Like the Civil Rights movement of the 1950s and 1960s, like the Black Power movement of the 1960s and 1970s, the BlackLivesMatter movement rises as a demand for recognition from a condition of invisibility, a demand for justice in a situation of injustice, a demand for solidarity in broken community. BlackLivesMatter demands the end of "what was done [to black people] in slavery times" and "what is being done [to black people] now."

The BlackLivesMatter movement emerged from the radical love, hope, and collaboration of Alicia Garza, Patrisse Cullors, and Opal Tometi. This strategically innovative movement urges us all to make an option for dispossessed, despised, and excluded black children, women, and men. And true to the black heritage of struggle for human dignity—the dignity of all—the movement agitates for every child, woman, and man who has been marginalized by the relentless drive for progress and prosperity.

BlackLivesMatter is a fierce political and spiritual cry: a cry of presence from a position of invisibility, a cry of justice from within a site of injustice, a cry for freedom in a condition of absurdity. Garza, Cullors, and Tometi clarify BlackLivesMatter as an "ideological and political intervention in a world where Black lives are systematically and intentionally targeted for demise. It is an affirmation of Black folks' contributions to this society, our humanity, and our resilience in the face of deadly oppression."[1]

The women and men and children who are the faces and bodies of BlackLivesMatter teach us all what authentic human being means—to love self, to stand up for ourselves and with and for others, to throw off stifling and negating images, to take joyful possession of our subjectivity, to love, to work, to hope. These women and men and children of all races urge us to reject the crumbs from the

---

1. BlackLivesMatter, "The Creation of a Movement"; http://blacklivesmatter .com/herstory/.

table of neoliberalism, to work out in our bodies a new agenda of critical attentiveness and analysis, of risky solidarity and efforts to bring about a just and renewed future for us all.

The "old slaves" knew the crucified and risen Jesus. They moaned at his suffering and torture; they shouted with him in his signifying glory and power. The witness of African American religious experience has been made and remade in every generation through concrete struggles for freedom. The wisdom of the "old slaves" teaches us to empty ourselves of all that would subvert or stifle or stop the quest for authentic freedom and liberation; to resist white racist supremacy in all its individual, social, and structural forms; to walk with Jesus ... all along our pilgrim journey ... to walk with Jesus.

Bibliography

Abrahams, Roger D. *Afro-American Folktales: Stories from Black Traditions in the New World.* New York: Pantheon Fairy Tale and Folklore Library, 1985.

———. *Singing the Master: The Emergence of African American Culture in the Plantation South.* New York: Pantheon Books, 1992.

Alexander, Michelle. "The New Jim Crow: How Mass Incarceration Turns People of Color into Permanent Second-Class Citizens." *The American Prospect*, December 6, 2010. http://prospect.org/article/new-jim-crow-0.

Aquino, María Pilar, and María José Rosad-Nunes, eds. *Feminist Intercultural Theology: Latina Explorations for a Just World.* Maryknoll, NY: Orbis Books, 2007.

Augustine. *City of God.* Edited by David Knowles. Translated by Henry Bettenson. New York: Penguin Books, 1972.

Babaus, Floyd B. *The Black Power Revolt.* Boston, MA: Beacon Press, 1968.

Babb, Valerie. *Whiteness Visible: The Meaning of Whiteness in American Literature and Culture.* New York and London: New York University Press, 1998.

Baldwin, James. *The Cross of Redemption: Uncollected Writings.* Edited by Randall Kenan. New York: Pantheon Books, 2010.

Bales, Mary Virginia. "Some Negro Folk Songs of Texas." In *Follow de Drinkin' Gou'd.* Vol. 7. Edited by James Frank Dobie. Austin, TX: University of North Texas Press, 1928. https://digital.library.unt.edu/ark:/67531/metadc38315/.

Blassingame, John W. *The Slave Community: Plantation Life in the Antebellum South.* New York: Oxford University Press, 1979.

———. "Using the Testimony of the Ex-Slaves." In *The Slave's Narrative*, edited by Charles T. Davis and Henry Louis Gates Jr. New York: Oxford University Press, 1985.

———, ed. *Slave Testimony: Two Centuries of Letters, Speeches, Interviews, and Autobiographies*. Baton Rouge, LA: Louisiana State University Press, 1989.

Blount, Brian. *Go Preach! Mark's Kingdom Message and the Black Church*. Maryknoll, NY: Orbis Books, 1998.

Boggs, James, and Grace Lee Boggs. *Revolution and Evolution in the Twentieth Century*. New York and London: Monthly Review Press, 1974.

Burke, Kevin. *The Ground Beneath the Cross: The Theology of Ignacio Ellacuría*. Washington, DC: Georgetown University Press, 2000.

Callahan, Allen D. *The Talking Book: African Americans and the Bible*. New Haven: Yale University Press, 2006.

Cannon, Katie Geneva. *Katie's Canon: Womanism and the Soul of the Black Community*. New York: Continuum Books, 2002.

———. "Slave Ideology and Biblical Interpretation." *Semeia* 49 (1989): 9–24.

Carmichael, Stokely, and Charles V. Hamilton. *Black Power: The Politics of Liberation in America*. New York: Vintage Books, 1967.

Cassidy, Richard J. *Jesus, Politics, and Society: A Study of Luke's Gospel*. Maryknoll, NY: Orbis Books, 1978.

Cavanaugh, William. *Torture and Eucharist: Theology, Politics, and the Body of Christ*. Oxford: Blackwell, 1998.

Chauvet, Louis-Marie. *Symbol and Sacrament: A Sacramental Reinterpretation of Christian Existence*. Translated by Patrick Madigan and Madeleine Beaumont. Collegeville, MN: Liturgical Press, 1995.

Clark, Kenneth B. *Dark Ghetto*. New York: Harper & Row, 1965.

Cleage, Albert B., Jr. *Black Christian Nationalism: New Directions for the Black Church*. New York: William Morrow & Company, 1972.

———. *The Black Messiah*. New York: Sheed and Ward, 1969.

Coates, Ta-Nehisi. "The Case for Reparations." *The Atlantic*, June 2014, 54–71.

Collins, Lisa Gail, and Margo Natalie Crawford, eds. *New Thoughts on the Black Arts Movement*. New Brunswick, NJ: Rutgers University Press, 2006.

Comblin, José. *Called for Freedom: The Changing Context of Liberation Theology*. Maryknoll, NY: Orbis Books, 2001.

Cone, James H. *Black Theology and Black Power*. Maryknoll, NY: Orbis Books, 1969, 1997.

———. *A Black Theology of Liberation*. Maryknoll, NY: Orbis Books, 1970, 1986.

———. *The Cross and the Lynching Tree*. Maryknoll, NY: Orbis Books, 2011.

———. *God of the Oppressed*. Maryknoll, NY: Orbis Books, 1975, 1997.

———. *Martin and Malcolm and America: A Dream or a Nightmare*. Maryknoll, NY: Orbis Books, 1991.

———. *The Spirituals and the Blues*. Maryknoll, NY: Orbis Books, 1991.

Cooey, Paula, et al., eds. *After Patriarchy: Feminist Transformations of the World Religions*. Maryknoll, NY: Orbis Books, 1993.

Cornelius, Janet Duitsman. *When I Can Read My Title Clear: Literacy, Slavery, and Religion in the Antebellum South*. Columbia, SC: University of South Carolina Press, 1991.

Crossan, John Dominic. *God and Empire: Jesus against Rome, Then and Now*. New York: HarperCollins, 2008.

Cruz, Jon. *Culture on the Margins: The Black Spiritual and the Rise of American Cultural Interpretation*. Princeton, NJ: Princeton University Press, 1999.

Cullen, Countee. "Heritage." In *The Prentice Hall Anthology of African American Literature*, edited by Rochelle Smith and Sharon L. Jones. Upper Saddle River, NJ: Prentice-Hall, 2000.

Curtin, Philip D. *The Atlantic Slave Trade: A Census*. Madison, WI: University of Wisconsin Press, 1969.

Davies, Oliver. *A Theology of Compassion: Metaphysics of Difference and the Renewal of Tradition*. Grand Rapids, MI/Cambridge, UK: William B. Eerdmans Publishing, 2001.

Davis, Angela Y. *Blues Legacies and Black Feminism: Gertrude "Ma" Rainey, Bessie Smith, and Billie Holiday*. New York: Pantheon Books, 1988.

Davis, Charles T., and Henry Louis Gates Jr., eds. *The Slave's Narrative*. New York: Oxford University Press, 1985.

Douglas, Kelly Brown. *The Black Christ*. Maryknoll, NY: Orbis Books, 1994.

Douglass, Frederick. *Narrative of the Life of Frederick Douglass an American Slave*. Modern Library Classics. New York: Random House, 1984.

Du Bois, W. E. B. *Darkwater: Voices from within the Veil*. Mineola, NY: Dover Publications, 1999.

180   *Knowing Christ Crucified*

DuBois, Page. *Slaves and Other Objects*. Chicago and London: University of Chicago Press, 2003.

Earl, Riggins R., Jr. *Dark Symbols, Obscure Signs: God, Self, and Community in the Slave Mind*. Maryknoll, NY: Orbis Books, 1993.

Éla, Jean-Marc. "The Memory of the African People and the Cross of Christ." In *The Scandal of a Crucified World: Perspectives on the Cross and Suffering*, edited by Yacob Tesfai. Maryknoll, NY: Orbis Books, 1994, 17–35.

Ellacuría, Ignacio. "El Pueblo Crucificado." In *The Ground Beneath the Cross: The Theology of Ignacio Ellacuría*, by Kevin Burke. Washington, DC: Georgetown University Press, 2000, 49–82.

Elliott, E. N., ed. *Cotton Is King, and Proslavery Arguments*. Augusta, GA: Pritchard Abbot, 1960.

Epstein, Dena. *Sinful Tunes and Spirituals: Black Folk Music to the Civil War*. Urbana, IL: University of Illinois Press, 1977.

Farley, Wendy. *Tragic Vision and Divine Compassion: A Contemporary Theodicy*. Louisville, KY: Westminster John Knox Press, 1990.

Felder, Cain Hope, ed. *Stony the Road We Trod: African American Biblical Interpretation*. Minneapolis: Fortress Press, 1991.

Fiorenza, Elisabeth Schüssler, ed. *Searching the Scriptures: A Feminist Commentary*. Vol. 2. New York: Crossroad Publishing Company, 1994.

Fisher, Mark. *Negro Slave Songs in the United States*. New York: Citadel Press, 1953.

Five Black Lives: The Autobiographies of Venture Smith, James Mars, William Grimes, the Rev. G. W. Offley, and James L. Smith. Middletown, CT: Weslyan University Press, 1971.

Foster, Kenelm, and Mary John Ronayne, trans. *I, Catherine of Siena: Selected Writings of St. Catherine of Siena*. London: Collins, 1980.

Georgakas, Dan, and Marvin Surkin. *Detroit: I Do Mind Dying: A Study in Urban Revolution*. Cambridge, MA: South End Press, 1998.

Gilkes, Cheryl Townsend. "Colonialism and the Biblical Revolution in Africa." *Journal of Religious Thought* 41, no. 2 (Fall-Winter 1984–1985), 59–75.

Glowacka, Dorota. *Disappearing Traces: Holocaust Testimonials, Ethics, and Aesthetics*. Seattle and London: University of Washington Press, 2012.

Goodell, William. *The American Slave Code in Theory and Practice:*

Its Distinctive Features Shown by Its Statutes, Judicial Decisions, and Illustrative Facts. New York: Negro Universities Press, 1968.

Gutiérrez, Gustavo. *A Theology of Liberation: History, Politics, and Salvation.* Translated by Sister Caridad Inda and John Eagleson. Maryknoll, NY: Orbis Books, 1988.

Harding, Rachel Elizabeth. "You Got a Right to the Tree of Life: African American Spirituals and Religions of the Diaspora." *Cross Currents* 57, no. 2 (Summer 2007): 266–80.

Hardy, Edward Rochie, ed. "The First Apology of Justin, the Martyr." In *Early Christian Fathers.* New York: Macmillan, 1970, 242–89.

Haughton, Rosemary. *The Passionate God.* Ramsey, NJ: Paulist Press, 1981.

Hengel, Martin. *Crucifixion in the Ancient World and the Folly of the Message of the Cross.* Translated by John Bowden. Philadelphia, PA: Fortress Press, 1977.

Henson, Josiah. *An Autobiography of the Reverend Josiah Henson in Four Fugitive Slave Narratives.* Edited by Robin W. Winks et al. Reading, MA: Addison-Wesley, 1968.

Hollenweger, Walter. "Intercultural Theology." *Theology Today* 43, no. 1 (April 1986): 28–35.

Holloway, Joseph E., ed. *Africanisms in American Culture.* Bloomington and Indianapolis, IN: Indiana University Press, 1990.

Horsley, Richard A. *Archaeology, History and Society in Galilee: The Social Context of Jesus and the Rabbis.* Valley Forge, PA: Trinity Press International, 1996.

———. *Galilee: History, Politics, People.* Valley Forge, PA: Trinity Press International, 1995.

———. *Jesus and Empire: The Kingdom of God and the New World Disorder.* Minneapolis, MN: Fortress Press, 2002.

Howard-Brook, Wes. *"Come Out, My People!" God's Call out of Empire in the Bible and Beyond.* Maryknoll, NY: Orbis Books, 2010.

Howard-Brook, Wes, and Sharon H. Ringe, eds. *The New Testament: Introducing the Way of Discipleship.* Maryknoll, NY: Orbis Books, 2002.

Hurston, Zora Neale. *The Sanctified Church.* Berkeley, CA: Turtle Island, 1983.

James, Joy, and T. Denean Sharpley-Whiting, eds. *The Black Feminist Reader.* Oxford: Blackwell, 2000.

Jenkins, Esau. *Been in the Storm So Long: A Collection of Spirituals, Folk Tales and Children's Games from Johns Island, SC.* Audio CD. Vol. 14. 2 vols. Smithsonian Folkways Recordings, 1990. 1966–67. https://folkways.si.edu.

Johnson, Clifton H., ed. *God Struck Me Dead: Voices of Ex-Slaves.* Cleveland, OH: Pilgrim Press, 1969.

Johnson, James Weldon, ed. *The Books of American Negro Spirituals.* New York: Viking Press, 1925.

Johnson, Walter. *Soul by Soul: Life Inside the Antebellum Slave Market.* Cambridge, MA, and London: Harvard University Press, 1999.

Jones, Arthur C. *Wade in the Water: The Wisdom of the Spirituals.* Maryknoll, NY: Orbis Books, 1993.

Jones, LeRoi. *Blues People: Negro Music in White America.* New York: William Morrow, 1963.

Jones, William R. *Is God a White Racist: A Preamble to Black Theology.* Garden City, NY: Anchor Press/Doubleday, 1973.

Jubilee Singers, and Fisk University. *Jubilee Songs as Sung by the Jubilee Singers of Fisk University.* New York: Biglow & Main, 1872. http://archive.org/details/jubileesongsassu00jubi.

Käsemann, Ernst. *Jesus Means Freedom.* Philadelphia: Fortress Press, 1977.

Kee, Howard C. *Community for a New Age: Studies in Mark's Gospel.* Philadelphia: Fortress Press, 1977.

Kerber, Linda, Alice Kessler-Harris, and Kathryn Kish Sklar, eds. *U.S. History as Women's History: New Feminist Essays.* Chapel Hill, NC, and London: University of North Carolina Press, 1995.

Kerner, Otto, and United States National Advisory Commision on Civil Disorders. *The Kerner Report: The 1968 Report of the National Advisory Commission on Civil Disorders.* New York: Pantheon Books, 1988.

King, Martin Luther, Jr. *A Testament of Hope: The Essential Writings of Martin Luther King, Jr.* Edited by James Melven Washington. New York: Harper & Row, 1986.

———. *Strength to Love.* New York: Harper & Row, 1968.

Kozol, Jonathan. *Rachel and Her Children: Homeless Families in America.* New York: Fawcett Publications, 1988.

Lamb, Matthew. "The Notion of the Transcultural in Bernard Lonergan's Theology." *Method, Journal of Lonergan Studies* 8 (March 1990), 48–73.

Lead Me, Guide Me: The African American Catholic Hymnal. Chicago, IL: G.I.A. Publications, 1987.

Lohfink, Gerhard. *Jesus of Nazareth: What He Wanted, Who He Was.* Translated by Linda M. Maloney. Collegeville, MN: Liturgical Press, 2012.

Lonergan, Bernard. *Insight: A Study of Human Understanding.* Edited by Frederick E. Crowe and Robert M. Doran. 5th ed. *Collected Works of Bernard Lonergan.* Vol. 3. Toronto: University of Toronto Press, 1988.

———. *Method in Theology.* Edited by Frederick E. Crowe and Robert M. Doran. 5th ed. *Collected Works of Bernard Lonergan.* Vol. 14. Toronto: University of Toronto Press, 1988.

———. *Philosophical and Theological Papers, 1958–1964.* Collected Works of Bernard Lonergan. Vol. 6. Toronto: University of Toronto Press, 1986.

———. *Understanding and Being.* Edited by Frederick E. Crowe and Robert M. Doran. *Collected Works of Bernard Lonergan.* Vol. 5. Toronto: University of Toronto Press, 1990.

Long, Charles H. *Significations: Signs, Symbols, and Images in the Interpretation of Religion.* Philadelphia, PA: Fortress Press, 1986, 9–24.

———. "Structural Similarities and Dissimilarities in Black and African Theologies." *Journal of Religious Thought* 32, no. 2 (Fall/Winter 1975).

Lovell, John, Jr. *Black Song: The Forge and the Flame. How the Afro-American Spiritual Was Hammered Out.* New York: Macmillan, 1972.

Martin, Clarice J. "The Acts of the Apostles." In *Searching the Scriptures: A Feminist Commentary,* edited by Elisabeth Schüssler Fiorenza, Vol. 2. New York: Crossroad Publishing Company, 1994, 763–99.

Mathews, Donald. *Religion in the Old South.* Chicago: University of Chicago Press, 1977.

Maultsby, Portia K. "Africanisms in African-American Music." In *Africanisms in African Culture,* edited by Joseph E. Holloway. Bloomington and Indianapolis, IN: Indiana University Press, 1990, 185–210.

Mbiti, John S. *African Religions and Philosophy.* 2nd ed. Oxford: Heinemann, 1989.

Meade, Catherine M. *My Nature Is Fire: Saint Catherine of Siena*. New York: Alba House, 1991.

Mellon, James, ed. *Bullwhip Days: The Slaves Remember, An Oral History*. New York: Avon Books, 1988.

Meyer, Michael. *Frederick Douglass: The Narrative and Selected Writings*. Modern Library Classics. New York: Random House, 1984.

Mitchell, Beverly Eileen. *Plantations and Death Camps: Religion, Ideology, and Human Dignity*. Minneapolis: Fortress Press, 2009.

Mitchell, Henry. *Black Belief: Folk Beliefs of Blacks in America and West Africa*. San Francisco: Harper & Row, 1975.

Moltmann, Jürgen. *The Crucified God: The Cross of Christ as the Foundation and Criticism of Christian Theology*. Translated by R. A. Wilson and John Bowden. New York: Harper & Row Publishers, 1974.

Mondzain, Marie-José. *Image, Icon, Economy: The Byzantine Origins of the Contemporary Imaginary*. Translated by Rico Franses. Stanford, CA: Stanford University Press, 2005.

Moore, Sebastian. *The Crucified Jesus Is No Stranger*. New York/Mahwah, NJ: Paulist Press, 1977.

Morrison, Toni. *Playing in the Dark: Whiteness and the Literary Imagination*. Cambridge, MA and London: Harvard University Press, 1992.

Muñoz, Ronaldo. *The God of Christians*. Maryknoll, NY: Orbis Books, 1990.

Myers, Ched. "Mark's Gospel: Invitation to Discipleship." In *The New Testament: Introducing the Way of Discipleship*, edited by Wes Howard-Brook and Sharon H. Ringe. Maryknoll, NY: Orbis Books, 2002, 40–61.

———, et al. *"Say to This Mountain": Mark's Story of Discipleship*. Maryknoll, NY: Orbis Books, 1996.

Noffke, Suzanne, trans. *Catherine of Siena: The Dialogue*. New York: Paulist Press, 1980.

———, trans. *The Letters of Catherine of Siena*. Vol. 1. Tempe, AZ: Arizona Center of Medieval and Renaissance Studies, 2000.

Northup, Solomon. *Twelve Years a Slave*. Edited by Sue Eakin and Joseph Logsdon. Baton Rouge, LA: Louisiana State University Press, 1968.

Offley, G. W. *A Narrative of the Life and Labors of Rev. G. W. Offley*. Hartford, CT, 1860.

Olmstead, Frederick Law. *The Cotton Kingdom (1861) American History Landmarks*. Edited by David Freeman Hawke. Indianapolis and New York: Bobbs-Merrill, 1970.

Painter, Neil Irvin. "Soul Murder and Slavery: Toward a Fully Loaded Cost Accounting." In *U.S. History as Women's History: New Feminist Essays*, edited by Linda Kerber, Alice Kessler-Harris, and Kathryn Kish Sklar. Chapel Hill, NC, and London: University of North Carolina Press, 1995, 125–46.

Perkinson, James W. *White Theology: Outing Supremacy in Modernity*. New York: Palgrave Macmillan, 2004.

———. *Messianism Against Christology: Resistance Movements, Folk Arts, and Empire*. New York: Palgrave Macmillan, 2013.

Pinn, Anthony B. *Terror and Triumph: The Nature of Black Religion*. Minneapolis: Fortress Press, 2003.

———. *Why Lord? Suffering and Evil in Black Theology*. New York: Continuum Books, 1995.

Pogge, Thomas W. "The Moral Demands of Global Justice." *Dissent Magazine*, 2000. https://www.dissentmagazine.org/article/the-moral-demands-of-global-justice.

Raboteau, Albert. *Slave Religion: The "Invisible Institution" in the Ante-Bellum South*. Oxford: Oxford University Press, 1975.

Rawick, George P. *The American Slave: A Composite Autobiography*. 19 vols. Westport, CT: Greenwood, 1972.

Reagon, Bernice Johnson. *If You Don't Go, Don't Hinder Me: The African American Sacred Song Tradition*. Lincoln: University of Nebraska Press, 2001.

Rediker, Marcus. *The Slave Ship: A Human History*. New York: Viking Press, 2007.

Reid, Barbara E. *Choosing the Better Part? Women in the Gospel of Luke*. Collegeville, MN: Liturgical Press, 1996.

Richardson, Cyril C., ed. *Early Christian Fathers*. Translated by Cyril C. Richardson. New York: Macmillan, 1970.

Ricoeur, Paul. *Memory, History, Forgetting*. Translated by Kathleen Blamey and David Pellauer. Chicago and London: University of Chicago Press, 2004.

———. *Figuring the Sacred: Religion, Narrative, and Imagination*. Minneapolis: Fortress Press, 1995.

———. "Toward a Hermeneutic of the Idea of Revelation." In *Essays on Biblical Interpretation*, edited by Lewis S. Mudge. Philadelphia: Fortress Press, 1980, 73–118.

Ringe, Sharon H. *Jesus, Liberation, and the Biblical Jubilee.* Philadelphia: Fortress Press, 1985.

———. "Luke's Gospel: 'Good News to the Poor' for the Non-Poor." In *The New Testament: Introducing the Way of Discipleship*, edited by Wes Howard-Brook. Maryknoll, NY: Orbis Books, 2002, 62–79.

Rivers, Clarence Joseph. *The Spirit in Worship.* Cincinnati: Stimuli, 1978.

Rodney, Walter. *A History of the Upper Guinea Coast, 1545–1800.* Oxford: Clarendon Press, 1970.

Roy, Arundhati. *Power Politics.* Boston: South End Press, 2001.

———. *The Cost of Living.* New York: Random House, 1999.

Sawicki, Marianne. *Seeing the Lord: Resurrection and Early Christian Practices.* Minneapolis: Fortress Press, 1994.

Scott, James C. *Domination and the Arts of Resistance.* New York: Yale University Press, 1990.

Seim, Turid Karlsen. *The Double Message: Patterns of Gender in Luke-Acts.* Nashville, TN: Abingdon, 1994.

———. "The Gospel of Luke." In *Searching the Scriptures, A Feminist Commentary*, edited by Elisabeth Schüssler Fiorenza, Vol. 2. New York: Crossroad Publishing Company, 1994, 728–62.

Sen, Amartya. *Development as Freedom.* New York: Anchor Doubleday, 1999.

Smith, Rochelle, and Sharon L. Jones, eds. *The Prentice Hall Anthology of African American Literature.* Upper Saddle River, NJ: Prentice-Hall, 2000.

Smith, Theophus. *Conjuring Culture: Biblical Formations of Black America.* Oxford: Oxford University Press, 1994.

Soares-Prabhu, George. "Anti-Greed and Anti-Pride: Mark 10.17–27 and 10.35–45 in the Light of Tribal Values." In *Voices from the Margin: Interpreting the Bible in the Third World*, edited by R. S. Sugirtharajah. Maryknoll, NY: Orbis Books, 1995, 117–37.

Sobel, Mechal. *Trabelin' On: The Slave Journey to an Afro-Baptist Faith.* Princeton, NJ: Princeton University Press, 1979.

Sobrino, Jon. *The Principle of Mercy: Taking the Crucified People from the Cross.* Maryknoll, NY: Orbis Books, 1994.

Spillers, Hortense. "Mama's Baby, Papa's Maybe: An American Grammar Book." In *The Black Feminist Reader*, edited by Joy James and T. Denean Sharpley-Whiting. Oxford: Blackwell, 2000, 57–87.

Stringfellow, Thorton. "The Bible Argument: Or, Slavery in the Light of Divine Revelation." In *Cotton Is King, and Proslavery Arguments*, edited by E. N. Elliott. Augusta, GA: Pritchard Abbot, 1960, 461–546.

Stroud, George M. *A Sketch of the Laws Relating to Slavery in the Several States of the United States of America*. New York: Negro Universities Press, 1968.

Stuckey, Sterling. *Slave Culture: Nationalist Theory and the Foundations of Black America*. New York: Oxford University Press, 1987.

Sugirtharajah, R. S., ed. *Voices from the Margin: Interpreting the Bible in the Third World*. Maryknoll, NY: Orbis Books, 1995.

Terrell, JoAnne Marie. *Power in the Blood? The Cross in African American Experience*. Maryknoll, NY: Orbis Books, 1998.

Tesfai, Yacob, ed. *The Scandal of a Crucified World: Perspectives on the Cross and Suffering*. Maryknoll, NY: Orbis Books, 1994.

Thurman, Howard. *Deep River and the Negro Spiritual Speaks of Life and Death*. Richmond, IN: Friends United Press, 1975.

———. *Disciplines of the Spirit*. Richmond, IN: Friends United Press, 1977.

———. *Jesus and the Disinherited*. Boston: Beacon Press, 1949, 1996.

Turner, Victor W. *Dramas, Fields, and Metaphors: Symbolic Action in Human Society*. Ithaca, NY: Cornell University Press, 2006.

Washington-Creel, Martha. *"A Peculiar People": Slave Religion and Community-Culture among the Gullahs*. New York: New York University Press, 1988.

Weems, Renita J. "African American Women and the Bible." In *Stony the Road We Trod: African American Biblical Interpretation*, edited by Cain Hope Felder. Minneapolis: Fortress Press, 1991, 57–77.

White, Deborah Gray. *Ar'n't I a Woman?* New York: W. W. Norton, 1985.

Wiley, Tatha. *Original Sin: Origins, Developments, Contemporary Meanings*. Mahwah, NJ: Paulist Press, 2002.

Williams, Delores S. "Black Women's Surrogacy Experience and the Christian Notion of Redemption." In *After Patriarchy: Feminist Transformations of the World Religions*, edited by Paula Cooey et al. Maryknoll, NY: Orbis Books, 1993, 1–14.

———. *Sisters in the Wilderness: The Challenge of Womanist God-Talk*. Maryknoll, NY: Orbis Books, 1993.

Wilmore, Gayraud S. *Black Religion and Black Radicalism*. Maryknoll, NY: Orbis Books, 1972, 1983.

——. *Pragmatic Spirituality: The Christian Faith Through an Africentric Lens*. New York and London: New York University Press, 2004.

——, and James H. Cone, eds. *Black Theology: A Documentary History, 1966–1979*. Maryknoll, NY: Orbis Books, 1979.

Witvliet, Theo. *The Way of the Black Messiah*. Oak Park, IL: Meyer Stone Brooks, 1985.

Wright, Nathan, Jr. *Black Power and Urban Unrest*. New York: Hawthorne Books, 1967.

Wright, N. T. *Christian Origins and the Question of God: Jesus and the Victory of God*. Vol. 2. Minneapolis: Fortress Press, 1996.

Yetman, Norman R., ed. *Voices from Slavery*. New York: Holt, Rinehart, and Winston, 1970.

Young, Iris Marion. *Justice and the Politics of Difference*. Princeton, NJ: Princeton University Press, 1990.

Sources

Part One

"Dark Wisdom from the Slaves" is based on "Knowing Christ Crucified: Dark Wisdom from the Slaves." In *Missing God? Cultural
Amnesia and Political Theology*. Edited by John Downey, Jürgen Manemann, and Steven Ostovich. Berlin: LIT Verlag, 2006,
59–78.

"Meeting and Seeing Jesus in Slaveholding Worlds" is based on "Meeting and Seeing Jesus: The Witness of African American Religious
Experience." In *Jesus of Galilee: Contextual Christology for the
21st Century*. Edited by Robert Lassalle-Klein. Maryknoll, NY:
Orbis Books, 2011, 67–84.

Part Two

"Marking the Body of Jesus, The Body of Christ" is based on "Marking the Body of Jesus, The Body of Christ." In *The Strength of
Her Witness: Jesus Christ in the Global Voices of Women*. Edited
by Elizabeth A. Johnson. Maryknoll, NY: Orbis Books, 2016,
270–83.

"The Dangerous Memory of Chattel Slavery" is based on "Chattel
Slavery as Dangerous Memory." In *Tradition and the Normativ-
ity of History*. Edited by Lieven Boeve and Terrence Merrigan.
Leuven/Paris/Walpole, MA: Peeters, 2013, 155–73.

Part Three

"To Live at the Disposal of the Cross: Mystical-Political Discipleship
as Christological Locus." In *Christology: Memory, Inquiry, and
Practice*. College Theology Society Annual Volume 48. Edited
by Anne M. Clifford and Anthony B. Godzieba. Maryknoll, NY:
Orbis Books, 2002, 177–213.

In Chapters One and Two, Scripture quotations are from the
King James Version of the Bible, 1987 printing, which is in the

public domain in the United States. It is likely that the enslaved people would have heard and been familiar with passages from this version.

Index